EXPLORING THE HIGHLANDS OF SCOTLAND

Stephen Whitehorne
Series Editor Tom Lawton

Photographs by the author
Diagrams in collaboration with Dr William Rouse

WARD LOCK

Delight of Being Alone

I know no greater delight than the sheer delight of being alone.
It makes me realise the delicious pleasure of the moon
that she has in travelling by herself: throughout time,
or the splendid growing of an ash-tree
alone, on a hill-side in the north, humming in the wind.

(D.H. Lawrence)

A WARD LOCK BOOK
First published in the UK 1995
by Ward Lock, Wellington House, 125 Strand, LONDON WC2R 0BB

A Cassell Imprint

Distributed in Australia by Capricorn Link (Australia) Pty Ltd
2/13 Carrington Road, Castle Hill, NSW 2154
A British Library Cataloguing in Publication Data block for this book may be obtained from the British Library

ISBN 0 7063 7371 5
Typeset by Litho Link Ltd, Welshpool, Powys, Wales
Printed and bound in Slovenia by Delo Tiskarna
by arrangement with Korotan Ljubljana.

Page 1: *Looking towards Loch na Sealga from Corrag Bhuidhe, An Teallach.*
This page: *The author on Corrag Bhuidhe, An Teallach.*
Page 4: *The ghostly remains of a Scots pine.*

Contents

Preface

I have just completed the most incredible journey round the Scottish Highlands. I have visited secret places, crossed powder-dry heather moorlands, thrashed my way through saturated bracken, walked within delightful deciduous woodlands, scurried out of dark coniferous forests, waded across watercourses, concealed myself within secluded glens, stood transfixed by the sight of waterfalls cascading through precipitous gorges, watched an eagle soaring overhead, and observed a stag standing proudly on the sanctuary of a protruding rocky ledge, scenting the invigorating mountain air.

High mountains have lured me to explore their summits and I have stood silently on their peaks, gazing down at wondrous and diverse panoramas abounding with shattered rocks, boulders, buttresses and pinnacles of every shape and size, a landscape of connecting ridges, arêtes, gulleys, corries and trapped waters. Streams plunge down steep slopes to spill their ice-cold waters into meandering rivers far below, sometimes drawing my gaze towards a deeply indented coastline and to stacks and islands out to sea.

All of this I have experienced and enjoyed not from trampling across this wilderness but from reading and absorbing Stephen Whitehorne's masterly walking guide, *Exploring the Highlands of Scotland.* It might seem too much to cram between the covers of a single book but Stephen has achieved it in his guide to nature at its wildest. The core of his book is a clear, succinct description of 32 diverse walks that never leaves the walker in the slightest doubt as to the route, accompanied by descriptions of the magnificent scenery along the way. Around this essential nucleus, Stephen has woven geology, wildlife, flora and many more features of interest – and has also found space to chastise the few organizations and individuals who have desecrated this precious heritage that the rest of us respect so much and wish to hold in trust for the benefit of future generations.

Stephen is a professional photographer and his superb landscapes richly embellish the eloquent text. The walking routes are also illustrated by computer-generated diagrams which accurately display the relief of each route and the severity of the slopes. The meticulous processing of the diagrams has been expertly undertaken by my dear friend and walking companion, Bill Rouse.

I commend *Exploring the Highlands of Scotland* to you: it is an outstanding source of accurate reference to all those who venture on foot into these regions. Go into the mountains well prepared; choose routes compatible with your experience, physical capabilities and relish of exposed positions; set off with a clear but flexible route plan in mind; enjoy yourself to the full and always return safely with your appetite only temporarily satisfied and soon wanting more.

Tom Lawton
Series Editor

INTRODUCTION

A move some years ago, which took me away from the main market place for my profession, has since proved to be an immensely satisfying situation. When I began working as Assistant Tutor of photography at Inversnaid Photography Centre, the new landscape came as both a revelation and a shock. That shift, however, from crowded capital to rural seclusion, signified the beginning of my love affair with the Highlands.

Since Inversnaid, my passion for the Highland wilderness has steadily intensified, photographic desires coinciding with a continual need to explore and discover mountains, lochs, burns, forests, beaches and all. From my present home in Edinburgh, I must now venture a little further to find them, but thankfully, the Highlands are never more than a short drive away.

Whilst this book is intended to celebrate and reflect on the scenic splendours that have provided an unending source of inspiration to centuries of poets and artists, a more immediate objective is to guide the walker through a playground of infinite and wonderful possibilities. Perhaps even, it may introduce a few more of you to the uncharted pleasures of far-reaching panoramas from enthralling mountain summits or towards spiritual rejuvenation found in the quiet tranquillity of the intimate corners of glens. Growing demand for a variety of recreational pursuits has imposed new pressures on the Scottish hills. The balance between tourism and conservation is a delicate one, although ultimately it is only by coming into contact with the land that a love and concern for it can be fostered. It is our spiritual and emotional detachment from the landscape, not the bulldozer or the plough, that threatens it most.

I hope you find this book immensely practical in your explorations as well as something to enjoy browsing through at the fireside between walks. *Exploring the Highlands of Scotland* should never find a permanent home on the cushions of your armchair. The pages that follow are in no way intended as a substitute for the real Highlands.

Acknowledgements

In making *Exploring the Highlands of Scotland* happen, I am forever indebted to Virginie. As those closest to you often do, she not only took the brunt of my joys and frustrations but offered endless support in the realization of the book. More directly, with her word-processing skills, she was actually able to transcribe my handwritten scrawls into something far more legible.

As a landscape photographer, I am probably the worst kind of walking partner. Those prepared to entertain my continual lingering diversions with a camera, I can only rate as rare and very special companions on the hills. I thank Dave Leach and Simon Mootz for their friendship as well as their tolerance but also for their suggestions regarding route itineraries.

In my personal discussion with, and in reference to his book *Red Sky at Night*, author and Glen Gyle shepherd John Barrington has been a most enthusiastic and amenable source of knowledge. For accommodating me during my explorations of Torridon, my thanks to Port Henderson crofters Mr and Mrs E. Mackenzie; and for her generosity in loaning a desk-top publishing computer station, I am indebted to Elaine Dunlop.

I would also like to thank Dr William Rouse. His innovations in the field of computer graphics have produced maps and statistical data which complement each of the routes in an especially unique way. In addition, my gratitude goes to the Series Editor Tom Lawton and his wife for their hospitality south of the border, but more especially for his guidance and in providing me with a concept framework for the book.

Last, but not least, I thank the publishers for suggesting and realizing the virtues of *Exploring the Highlands of Scotland*.

1

THE SCOTTISH HIGHLANDS AND THE WALKER

Many of the most challenging high-level walks in England and Wales can be pursued over mostly well-trodden terrain following waymarked footpaths. The Highland landscape is not like that. Scottish hills demand self-reliance from the walker and choosing your own way over rough and pathless ground must, on many routes, be taken for granted. By comparison, many would argue that the upland areas of the National Parks south of the border offer more picturesque and welcoming environs with greater scenic variety. Here too, the climate is generally more agreeable to the fine-weather walker. Yet, despite such attributes, for experience of true wilderness in a vast landscape largely uninhabited by man, for far-reaching summit views and for awe-inspiring mountain scenery, the Scottish Highlands really have no comparison in Britain. And nowhere else on these islands can one experience a quality of light in such continual state of flux. In the Highlands, the same place rarely appears the same twice and one can repeat a walking route without ever feeling too familiar with it.

In land area Scotland is almost equal to England, yet has about ⅛th of its population, most of which is concentrated in cities and towns south of the Highland boundary. For these reasons, there has been little need to create National Parks and Scotland has not faced the problems of access that England has. More recent and specific recreational pressures, however, have heralded calls from some for creating National Parks in the more popular areas such as at Loch Lomond and in the Cairngorms.

The Highland landscape that we see today has been shaped by many factors, both natural and human. Geologically, the great majority of the Scottish mountains belong to the metamorphic group. Metamorphic rocks are those previously igneous (volcanic) or sedimentary in form that have been changed in time by pressure and/or heat within the earth. In most Highland areas, schists or gneisses predominate and some of these rocks are amongst the oldest in the world. Notable exceptions include the igneous granites of the Ben Nevis range and the Cairngorms. Further north a significant band of sedimentary Torridonian sandstone constitutes some of the Highlands' most striking mountains. Relatively recent glacial actions of the last Ice Age (about 10 000 years ago) wrought the final geological changes to the Highland scene, gouging out the corries of the mountains, cutting their narrow crests and broadening the valleys between them.

Following the Ice Age, Scotland became largely a forested land, much of which was covered by the old Scots pine forest of Caledon. Today, less than 1% of this natural forest remains, as human activity in more recent centuries has seen it ravaged to satisfy an insatiable demand for timber and to produce agricultural land. When Dr Johnson made his famous tour of Scotland in 1773, he remarked that 'a tree in Scotland was as rare as a horse in Venice'.

With the breakdown of the clan system after 1745, and the Highland clearances which followed, people made way for sheep and deer estates were established by the new landlords. Forced mass emigration occurred and the Highlands today are far less populated than they once were. The result has been to create a landscape frequently described as a 'wet desert'. Along with the changes (all mostly bad for the land), creatures such as the wolf, elk and brown bear were either exterminated or died out through loss of habitat. The twentieth century has seen reforestation over

13% of the land area of Scotland but these new forests of alien conifer species are ugly commercial plantations by comparison and mostly hostile to wildlife. Plantations aside, a stark beauty today characterizes much of the Highland wilderness.

There are a number of concerns which affect specifically the Scottish Highlands and the walker and these are dealt with below.

Access

Forestry and water privatization schemes, proposals for large quarries and changes in the law through the Criminal Justice Bill all seem likely in the near future to bring about unfavourable conditions with regard to access for the walker in the Highlands. As it stands at present, Scots enjoy a precious and passionately held right of a 'freedom to roam' in wild places. Whilst with this system *de facto* there appears to be no enforceable law of trespass, visitors should nonetheless respect estate needs. This will help prevent conflict and maintain a cordial relationship between walkers and landowners.

DEERSTALKING

Most of the Scottish Highlands is privately owned and, whatever your views on the subject, deerstalking does provide a major source of income for Highland estates. The stag shooting season runs normally from mid-August to mid-October and access is likely to be restricted during these times. Precise times may vary from estate to estate and walkers should consult locally. Alternatively, keep to non-shooting areas such as National Trust for Scotland ground.

GROUSE SHOOTING

Estates may impose access restrictions between 12 August and 10 December for this practice. Again, consult locally.

Few other seasonal practices, except lambing, are likely to affect access for walkers.

The Forest Enterprise initiative by the Forestry Commission, one of the biggest landowners, has allowed easier access into its forests. Scottish Natural Heritage have also created guided and waymarked trails on many of their National Nature Reserves, all part of a positive agenda which seems to go beyond merely public relations exercises.

Climate

Those who peruse only the Tourist Board brochures before visiting the Highlands might be forgiven for thinking the hills are blessed with endless sunny days and a near Mediterranean climate! However, the reality is very different and it would be positively dangerous for walkers not to be prepared for adverse weather conditions.

The Scottish Highlands has higher rainfall levels than most of the United Kingdom. In this respect, it is similar to the Lake District. However, precipitation levels can vary greatly across the region. The western Highlands and those hills just in from the mainland's Atlantic sea-board, for instance, receive over twice the amount of precipitation as the Cairngorms which lie far to the east. This climatic divide is the result of a more 'continental' effect on the east side, with warmer summers than to the west but with colder winters. Thus, the Cairngorms are subjected to more frosts and snow than elsewhere and as such the area is famous for its ski-ing.

Scottish weather is notoriously unpredictable and localized but recent years have seen some kind of weather pattern emerging, with the months of May and September offering a good proportion of dry sunny days. There is another good reason why you might wish to avoid high summer: the Highland Midge!

Highland Midge (*Culicoides impunctus*)

Scottish Tourist Board literature mostly neglects this other curse of the Highlands too. Whilst they are tiny insects, midges are present in large, persistent, man-eating swarms and have been the ruin of many a Highland summer holiday. On the precept that the most effective defence comes from knowing your enemy, here are a few useful facts about her (for it is the female that bites):

- The midge season runs from late May to early September, reaching misery-inducing levels during July and August.
- Midges are most active on still, overcast days and least active in wind or in bright sunshine.
- They are more likely to be encountered at lower levels and under trees.
- They are attracted to dark colours.

There are several effective chemical repellents and sprays available. I have found 'Jungle Formula' to be one of the best. Campers who demand a good night's sleep should purchase a midge net.

Munros

Munro collecting has reached obsessive proportions. For a growing number of walkers in the Highlands, climbing Munros is a main objective of a day spent in the hills.

A **Munro** is simply defined as a separate mountain over 914 m (3000 ft). There continues to be much heated dispute as to what this actually means. Sir Hugh Munro first listed 283 in 1891 though since there has been some tampering. Today the Scottish Mountaineering Club recognizes 277 such summits.

There are 221 **Corbetts**, which are separate mountains over 762 m (2500 ft).

Highland cattle, near Achray Hotel.

Safety

The Scottish Highlands present generally tougher challenges for the walker than do mountains south of the border. Rugged, untamed terrain, remoteness, long distances, steep ascents, navigational problems, unpredictable weather and other factors all conspire to render most high-level routes as serious undertakings, even in summer. In winter, they are mostly the preserve of experienced mountaineers, many routes becoming roped expeditions with an array of additional problems and dangers, not least the problem of fewer daylight hours to complete a route. It is recommended that in winter (October to March), walkers avoid routes graded 5 or 6 and any routes with a time allowance of more than 6 hours. In any season, the Scottish mountains should never be underestimated.

Four-season walking boots should be the norm and in the summer the content of your rucksack should include the following as a minimum:

- Waterproof bag liner (a dustbin liner is ideal)
- Breathable waterproof outershell (cagool and trousers)
- Map
- Compass
- Whistle
- Adequate food and plenty of liquid
- Spare socks
- Basic first-aid kit
- Warm hat and sunhat
- Suncream

At most other times, and certainly in winter, you should add to this list: thermal underwear, emergency food rations, crampons, ice axe, a 'bivvy' bag, head-torch and ski goggles or sunglasses.

For the reasonably fit walker, wading through watercourses in normal summer conditions is unlikely to be more than a minor inconvenience. However, you should never attempt to wade a watercourse that at any point appears to be deeper than the length of your legs or where you do not have a clear view of the river bed. Do not attempt the crossing if you are at all in doubt, and certainly not in winter or when spate conditions prevail after heavy rains.

Apart from the Country Code, which should of course be respected wherever you are in Britain, observe the **Mountain Code** for Scotland (as published on relevant Ordnance Survey Outdoor Leisure Maps):

Before you go

- Learn the use of map and compass
- Know the weather signs and local forecast
- Plan within your capabilities
- Know simple first-aid and the symptoms of exposure
- Know the mountain distress signals (see page 190)
- Know the Country Code (see page 190).

When you go

- If possible, avoid going alone
- Leave written word of your route and report your return
- Take windproofs, waterproofs, woollens and survival bag
- Take map, compass, whistle, torch and food
- Wear climbing boots
- Keep alert all day.

If there is snow on the hills

- Always have an ice axe for each person
- Learn to recognize dangerous snow slopes
- Carry a climbing rope and know the correct use of rope and ice axe.

In case of rescue service being required, dial 999 and ask for the police. Follow the instructions you receive.

2

USING THE BOOK

The walking routes described have each been meticulously researched and carefully tried and tested by the author himself. From the outset, major objectives were to reflect the immense scenic diversity of the Scottish Highlands and to accommodate many levels of ability and types of interest. Consequently, routes range from short, gentle lochside strolls to lengthy and arduous ridge traverses on Britain's highest mountains. The constraints are that a route must:

- Start and finish from the same parking place (a location accessible to all those with motorized transport) and be roughly circular in nature.
- Be able to be completed by walkers of reasonable fitness in a single day, given normal spring, summer or early autumn conditions.
- Require no rock climbing abilities or the use of a rope on any section.
- Offer alternative non-scrambling options on all routes that involve some scrambling.

It is hoped that the reader will find the book user-friendly and will pursue each route with absolute confidence in the text. An eminently practical approach is intended whilst at the same time including features of interest along the way such as summit views, mountain scenery, wildlife, geology, history and legend. A concise summary at the beginning of the route chapters offers an overview of each of the walks; 'Escapes' and 'Extensions' at the end offer alternatives to the main route.

Arrangement

Thirty-two walking routes cover a geographical area from the Trossachs at the southern edge of the Highland boundary fault, just north of Glasgow, to Scotland's most northerly Munro near Cape Wrath which overlooks the North Minch and the remote Sutherland coast. The routes are divided into 16 sections of two walks each; a high-level route and a lower-level route is provided for each. Starting locations from car parks as close to each other as possible are given for both routes. Due to the relatively large geographical area covered, however, this may vary from a few hundred metres to many miles.

In sympathy with most visitors' experience of the Scottish Highlands, the sections begin with the most southerly routes and finish with the most northerly. For walkers unfamiliar with the rigours of Highland terrain, a gradual introduction is thus possible.

Diagrams

Innovative computer-generated diagrams complement each of the route descriptions, giving a plan, a cross-sectional relief and pertinent statistics for the walk.

Camera symbols locate the position and direction of each photograph. These have been allocated a distinctive number identical to that reference beneath each photograph as part of its caption. Photographs taken of the route from locations beyond the immediate vicinity are identified by camera symbols pointing inwards from the edge of the plan.

Munros and other mountain summits are shown in the following way:

▲ Munro
△ Other mountain summit

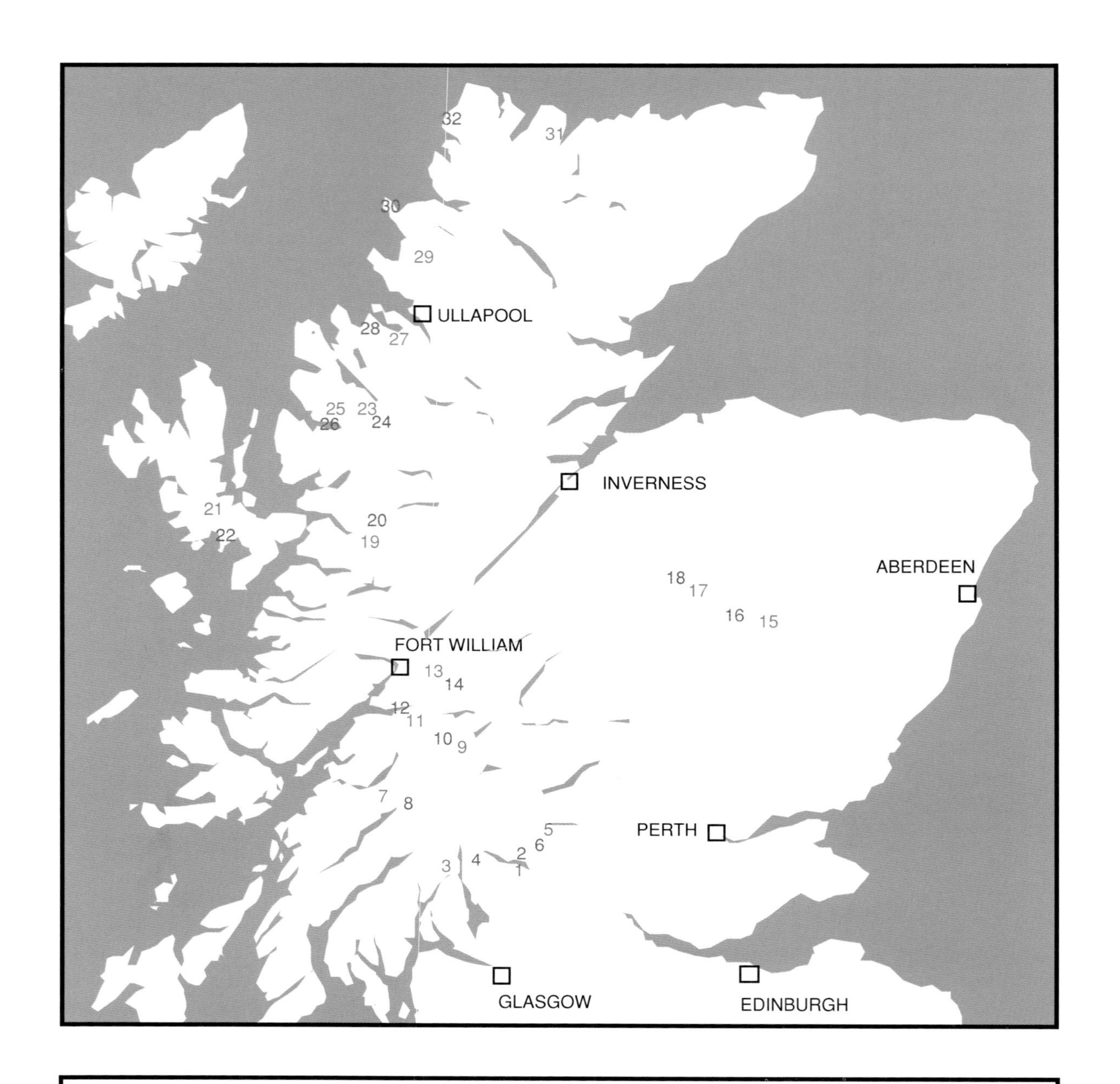

THE WALKS (High Level & Low Level)

1 BEN VENUE
2 BEN A'AN
3 BEN ARTHUR
4 LOCH LOMOND & GLEN GYLE
5 BEN VORLICH
6 GLEN FINGLAS
7 BEN CRUACHAN HORSESHOE
8 STRATH OF ORCHY
9 BUACHAILLE ETIVE MÓR
10 LAIRIG GARTAIN & LAIRIG EILDE
11 PAP OF GLENCOE & SGORR NAM FIANNAIDH
12 LOCH LEVEN
13 BEN NEVIS & CARN MÓR DEARG
14 GLEN NEVIS
15 LOCHNAGAR
16 GLEN QUOICH & GLEN LUI
17 CAIRN GORM
18 LOCH AN EILEIN & ROTHIEMURCHUS
19 THE FIVE SISTERS OF KINTAIL
20 FALLS OF GLOMACH
21 BRUACH NA FRÌTHE
22 LOCH CORUISK
23 BEINN EIGHE
24 LOCH CLAIR & LOCH COULIN
25 BEINN ALLIGIN
26 UPPER LOCH TORRIDON
27 AN TEALLACH
28 GRUINARD RIVER
29 SUILVEN
30 POINT OF STOER
31 BEN HOPE
32 SANDWOOD BAY

Abbreviations

To avoid constant repetition, a limited number of abbreviations have been used in the route descriptions:

L	left	OS	Ordnance Survey
R	right	OSLR	Ordnance Survey Landranger map
N	north	OSOL	Ordnance Survey Outdoor Leisure map
NNE	north north east	OSPF	Ordnance Survey Pathfinder map
NE	north east	K-gate	kissing-gate
ENE	east north east	MR	map reference
E	east	FC	Forestry Commission
ESE	east south east	NTS	National Trust for Scotland
SE	south east	SNH	Scottish Natural Heritage
SSE	south south east	NNR	National Nature Reserve
S	south	VC	Visitor Centre
SSW	south south west	WHW	West Highland Way
SW	south west	RSPB	Royal Society for the Protection of Birds
WSW	west south west		
W	west		
WNW	west north west		
NW	north west		
NNW	north north west		
ft	feet		
m	metre(s)		
km	kilometre(s)		

General glossary

andesite	brown-coloured igneous rock formed by rapid cooling of magma
arête	sharp mountain ridge
bothy	cottage or hut
burn	stream or brook
Corbett	individual mountain over 760 m (2500 ft)
croft	small farmstead
free-ranging	traversing pathless terrain
gabbro	dark igneous rock formed by slow cooling of magma
gneiss	light-coloured coarsely banded metamorphic rock
hag	cutting in a peat bog
kirk	church
misted-out	obscured by mist
Munro	individual mountain over 914 m (3000 ft)
ryolite	light-coloured igneous rock formed by rapid cooling of magma
schist	light-coloured finely banded metamorphic rock
shieling	mountain hut used by shepherds
spate	river or stream in flood condition
white-out	a combination of snow and mist

Glossary of Gaelic names

Most Highland names for features and mountains are Gaelic in origin. As such any OS map of the area covered by this book might easily appear to the newcomer as a confusing spread of unpronounceable mountains, rivers and glens. However, attempts at understanding and pronouncing Gaelic names can be fun and add to the pleasure of walking in Scotland. The words most often encountered and their English meanings are given here.

aber	mouth of loch, river
abhainn	river
allt	stream
aonach	ridge
auch, ach	field
bal, bail	town, homestead
ban	white, fair, pale
bealach	hill pass
beg, beag	small
ben, beinn	hill
bhuidhe	yellow
bidean	pinnacle
blar	plain
both	hut
brae, braigh	upper slope, steepening
breac	speckled
cam	crooked
cairn	pile of stones, often marking a summit
carn	cairn, cairn-shaped hill
caol	strait (kyle)
ceann, kin, ken	head
ciche, cioch	breast, breast-shaped hill
cil, kil	church, cell
clach	stone
cnoc	hill, knoll
coille, killie	wood
corrie, coire, choire	mountain hollow
creag, craig	cliff, crag
dal, dail	field, flat
damh	stag
dearg	red
druim, drum	long ridge
dubh, dhu	black, dark
dun	hill fort
eas	waterfall
eilean	island
eilidh	hind
eun	bird
fada	long
fionn	white
fraoch	heather
gabhar, ghabhar, gobhar	goat
garbh	rough

geal	white
gearr	short
glen, gleann	narrow valley
glias, glas	grey
gorm	blue, green
inch, inis	island, meadow by river
inver, inbhir	confluence
lag, laggan	hollow
larach	old site
lairig	broad pass
leac	slab
liath	grey
loch	lake (diminutive: lochan)
mam	pass, rise
maol	bare or bald (normally refers to mountain top without vegetation)
meall	mound
monadh	upland
mór(e)	big
odhar, odhair	dun-coloured
rhu, rubha	point
riabhach	brindled or striped
ruadh	red, brown
sgor, sgurr	pointed
sneachd	snow
sron	nose
stob	pointed
strath	valley (wider than glen)
tarmachan	ptarmigan
tarsuinn	transverse, across
tom	hillock (rounded)
torr	hillock (more rugged)
tulloch, tulach	knoll
uaine	green, pallid
uisge	water, river

Where known, the most commonly accepted English meaning of a Gaelic name for any mountain ascended is given in brackets in the 'Principal Heights' section of the concise summary for the relevant walk.

Miscellaneous

MAPS AND COMPASS

All the high-level routes, as well as many of the lower-level routes described, demand the accurate use of a map and compass. Even in the best conditions, much of the Highland landscape is bereft of easily recognizable reference features. Remember too that mists and clouds are normal conditions on the highest summits.

COMPASS BEARINGS

All compass bearings have been given to the nearest 22½° point, eg. E, ESE, SE, etc. This is considered sufficiently accurate in most situations but extreme caution is required on a summit in white-out conditions. Note that the gabbro rocks of the Cuillin of Skye are notorious for their compass-deflecting properties.

DYNAMICS

In most areas of the Highlands, footpaths are rarely waymarked or surfaced in any way. Few stiles or other such aids exist and things are not likely to change much in the near future. The exceptions are footpaths on SNH and FC land.

That said, certain other human features are constantly changing and none more so than the erection, dismantling and replacing of deer fencing (being an essential part of estate management). Where reference is made to deer fencing in the route descriptions, you should be prepared for potential anomalies with regard to the location of fence lines and the K-gates between them. Other diversions may be caused by on-going practices such as clear-felling and tree planting.

The number of walkers in the Highlands increases year by year and as a result new paths are being worn in; many of those that are at present little more than sheep tracks are, on the more popular hills, likely to become more established in the years to come. It will be some time after that before they appear on OS maps.

GRADING

In accommodating all levels of ability across a vast range of topographies, each walk has been allocated a grade between 1 and 6. This grading has been included in the concise summary at the start of each route description and can be simply defined as follows:

1 = Easy and undemanding physically, without route-finding problems
2 = Generally straightforward navigation and undemanding physically
3 = Quite demanding physically with route-finding difficulties possible in bad weather
4 = Demanding physically and with likely route-finding problems in bad weather

5 = Very demanding physically, with the probability of route-finding difficulties
6 = Arduous and extremely demanding physically, requiring navigational skill

In grading each route, it is assumed that the walker is reasonably fit. Many factors have been taken into consideration such as steepness, terrain, distance covered, total height gained, seriousness in the event of injury or bad weather and potential navigational problems. The gradings are based on late spring, summer and autumn conditions, without significant snow cover.

All lower-level routes are between grades 1 and 4 and the high-level routes are all between grades 3 and 6. Wherever a route involves a total height gain of more than 1500 m (5000 ft), it has automatically been allocated grade 6.

TIME ALLOWANCE

Also included in the concise summary sections is an estimated time allowance for a reasonably fit walker to complete the route. As a fit walker himself, the time allowances are based on the author's own performance on each route and include rest and food stops.

ORDNANCE SURVEY MAPS

OS maps are essential for all but the very tamest of Highland expeditions and the relevant sheet numbers for each route description have been given. The OSLR maps are adequate for most routes although the greater detail of the larger scale OSOL and OSPF maps can be very useful on mountains bereft of obvious topographical features or in adverse weather situations. Some paths described in the route descriptions are not marked on OS maps; on these occasions, rely on the route descriptions.

Unfortunately, OS maps, despite their general excellence, abound in Gaelic misspellings. In such instances, the spelling that appears on the larger scale OSOL or OSPF maps has been used. Similarly, recorded heights of mountains have been taken from these maps. While the older maps use imperial measurements to quantify heights, more recent reprints use metric. Some minor anomalies between the two sets of measurements have occurred but, wherever possible, the most up-to-date metric measurement has been quoted.

Looking across Hospital Lochan to the mountains at the bottom end of Glen Coe.

Route 1: BEN VENUE

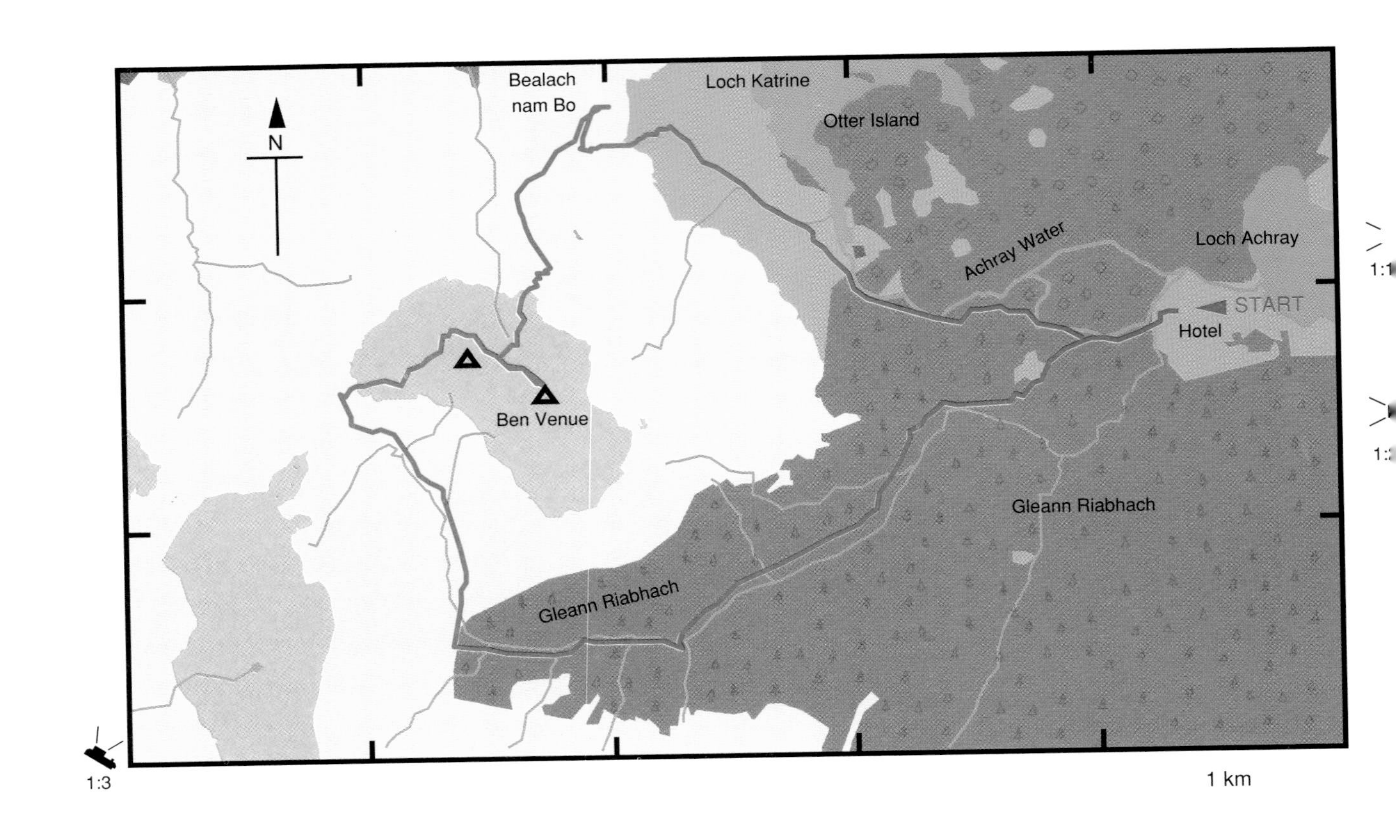

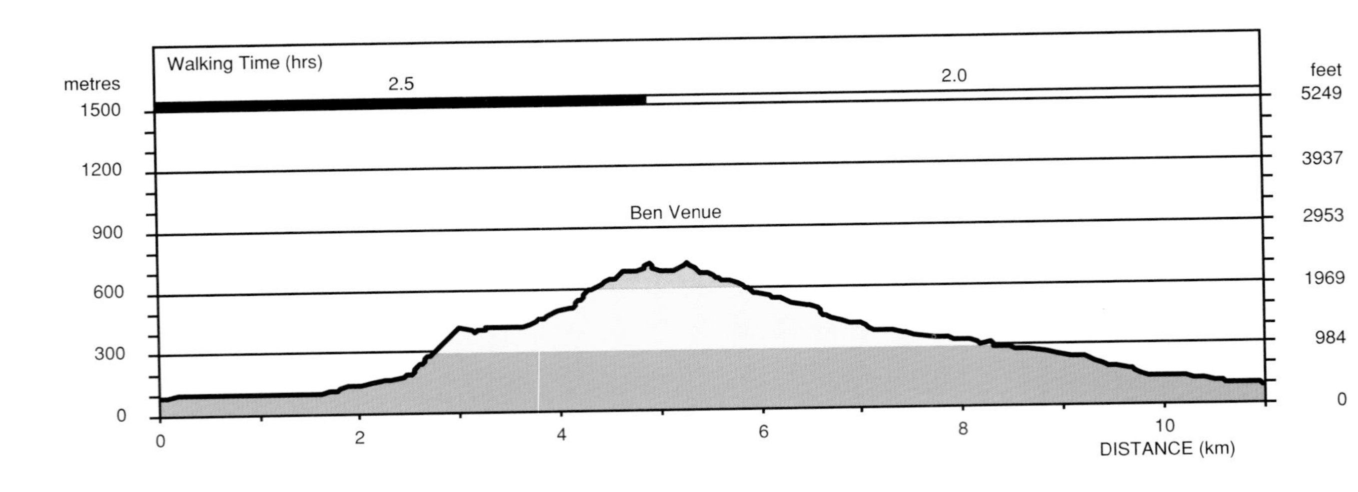

3

THE TROSSACHS

HIGH-LEVEL ROUTE

Route 1 · Ben Venue

STARTING LOCATION
Achray Hotel car park off A821 by S shore of Loch Achray.
OSLR 57 or OSPF 369/MR 503064.
200 m SSW of road bridge over Achray Water.
Accommodates up to 40 cars.

ALTERNATIVE STARTING LOCATION
Parking at FC car park for Ben A'an (see Route 2) and at parking bay by W shore of Loch Achray.

PUBLIC TRANSPORT
Nearest railway station – Stirling.
Regular buses Stirling to Callander.
Postbus, twice daily, Callander to Achray Hotel (except Sunday).

OVERVIEW/INTEREST
Ben Venue: a rugged mountain that falls short of Corbett status but with the character of many a Munro.
Overlooks Loch Katrine, inspiration for Wordsworth's 'Lady of the Lake'.
Fine views to the Southern Highlands from the summit.
Physically quite demanding, especially on ascent.

FOOTPATHS
Indistinct or non-existent from below the Bealach nam Bo to the summit ridge.
Clearly waymarked and colour-coded elsewhere, though muddy in Gleann Riabhach.
Good forestry tracks on the lower reaches in Achray Forest.

GRADING 3

TIME ALLOWANCE
4½ hours.

DISTANCE

Excluding Height	11 km	(7 miles)
TOTAL HEIGHT GAINED	710 m	(2329 ft)

PRINCIPAL HEIGHTS
Ben Venue (Mountain of the Caves)
727 m (2391 ft)

Achray to summit of Ben Venue

Allow 2½ hours

From the car park at the front of the hotel, make your way round to the back of the building and turn R on to the forestry track, signposted 'Forest Walk'.

Cross the bridge over the burn and walk W into Achray forest passing, after 200 m (200 yd), a FC sign indicating route colour-coding. Although the posts marking the official way to the summit are banded blue, this is to be your descent route and so, instead, follow the posts banded white.

Pass through a metal gate and where the track divides take the R-hand fork. Continue W on the L side of Achray Water. At gaps in the trees, looking N, Ben A'an can be seen. The birch-covered NE-facing crags of Ben Venue are seen above and to the L of the track ahead. Adjacent to the weir on the R, and where the forest track ends, cross a line of deer fencing using the ladder stile. Walk NW on the clear, well-worn path, which may be wet in

1.1 *West across Loch Achray to Ben Venue.*

places, to a dam and sluice near where Achray Water enters Loch Katrine. At a sheep fold, cross over more fencing by another ladder stile and proceed beside a little burn on the R. The eastern extremity of Loch Katrine and tiny Otter Island are now in view looking N.

After 400 m (¼ mile), ford the burn and continue NW towards the Bealach nam Bo, the obvious rocky defile ahead and with a solitary tree at its summit on the skyline. Ignore the paths off to the R which lead towards the loch-shore. Instead, walk parallel to fencing on the L and towards a large boulder resembling a monkey's head with a punk hairstyle of heather. In late summer the growth on top conforms to the impression by turning purple! Pass beneath a knarled alder tree and climb over a stile to emerge at the bottom of the Bealach nam Bo.

From here, depart from the FC white-coded walk by turning sharp L and, proceeding SW, walk up steep bracken-covered slopes, keeping to the R of a line of rusty fence posts. Before leaving it behind, the vicinity of the bealach is well worth your while scanning with binoculars for peregrines and ravens.

A rudimentary path climbs steeply between a burn on the L and the line of fence posts. Height is gained quickly and views emerge E towards Loch Achray and Loch Venachar. That NE over Loch Katrine also becomes more extensive. Below Ben A'an's densely wooded slopes, it is likely that distant figures will be promenading the far shores of this popular beauty spot. The famous steamer, the SS *Sir Walter Scott* may be seen plying its waters.

From the last of the fence posts, veer to the R and cross the top of the burn, here merely a trickle. Walk N on a sheep track to gain a small grassy plateau immediately above the Bealach nam Bo on its W side, MR 478073. Turn L and head SW but soon veering S, pursuing further sheep tracks if you can find them. Free-ranging is more likely.

At a broader heathery plateau, bear SE and clamber across peat bogs into the Druim nan Sasunnach immediately below the mountain's rugged summit crags. From here, negotiate your own route up the steep mossy outcrops on your R. Even where the gradient is at its most severe the rocks should provide for a sure footing.

After 200 m (700 ft) of ascent, all the hard work is rewarded on reaching the ridge connecting the two summits. Turn L and walk SE for 300 m (330 yd) on a severely eroded path as far as the triangulation pillar at 727 m (2391 ft). You are forgiven for believing that you have climbed a Munro! Indeed, the vast panorama from the summit is a wonderful surprise for a mountain that fails to reach even Corbett status.

The main mountain features include: WSW, Ben Lomond; W, The Cobbler (Ben Arthur), Beinn Narnain and the Arrochar Alps, Ben Vorlich; WNW, Ben Lui; NW, Cruach Ardrain; NNW, Ben More and Stob Binnien.

Situated as it is on the southern edge of the Highlands, the view S and E (beyond the Queen Elizabeth Forest park) looks out across the flatter lowlands as far as the Campsie Fells.

Summit of Ben Venue to Achray

Allow 2 hours

To leave the summit, walk WNW on the ridge path. Pass across the top of the Bealach Mór na Beinne on your L and after 400 m (¼ mile), bear L from the cairn marking the more northerly summit peak at 729 m (2397 ft). Descend steeply, heading WSW to reach a larger cairn at the junction of footpaths. Turn sharp L and continue SSE into the upper reaches of Gleann Riabhach. A post with a green dot, the first of many, marks the beginning of the official descent route through the Gleann. Blue dots on the other side of the posts are to indicate the ascent route. Follow further green-marked posts and lower down veer S and ford a burn to gain its W side. Thereafter, the burn should be roughly followed to the bottom of Gleann Riabhach.

At the tree line enter the perpetual darkness of the plantation that is the westerly limit of Achray Forest. Bear E, beneath the trees, and follow the orange ribbons that are tied to the trunks of the trees. This is a temporary route-finding measure organized by the FC and after 1995 there should be some permanent and improved passage. As it is, the path can become exceedingly muddy in certain places.

A little way into the forest, ford a tiny burn and walk out into a clearing on the R of the burn. Continue E beside the water and follow further ribbons on re-entering the forest. Ford numerous further tiny burns, flowing from the R, and after a few hundred metres of tree-dodging, emerge at a second more airy clearing. In the light again, the ground is flatter, the stream is broader and the trees less mature. Walk to where the path ends at the FC access track.

Turn L, cross the allt and follow the track ENE through the forest clearing. Ahead, on the skyline, Ben Ledi dominates the view between the trees. After 1 km (⅔ mile), leave the track by the path on the R and walk down to gain another track after 200 m (220 yd).

Simply pursue the maze of forest tracks and paths in whatever direction has been signposted 'Ben Venue path'. The FC is carrying out a massive programme of clear-felling at Achray and for safety reasons walkers are constantly being diverted and re-routed. However, you will not get lost and for this section you will generally be well directed NE.

Return to the junction where you first encountered a diversion in the track. Turn R and retrace your earlier footsteps for the remaining 400 m (¼ mile) to the hotel.

1.2 Opposite: *West across Achray Forest to Ben Venue from the Duke's Pass.*

1.3 Above: *On the south approach to Ben Venue, from above Kinlochard.*

Alternative routes

ESCAPES

The most straightforward route to the summit is through Gleann Riabhach, in other words ascending the descent route. This of course denies you an interesting circuit on the mountain. However, a less steep circular walk can be made via the Bealach nam Bo. For this option proceed a little beyond the limit of the 'white' route, to the top of the bealach, and turn S to walk up the N-facing slopes of Ben Venue.

For short and easy low-level routes in the Trossachs, see 'Escapes' for Ben A'an (Route 2) on page 27.

EXTENSIONS

If you do not have the encumbrance of a vehicle, or can arrange for a driver at Kinlochard, then you can avoid the relative monotony of dense plantation and come down on the S side of the mountain. Stay on the path heading SW from the summit for 2 km (1¼ miles) passing to the L of Beinn Bhreac. Then veer S and descend on the footpath next to the Ledard Burn. Beyond Ledard Farm, emerge at the B829 road by the N shore of Loch Ard. Allow an extra ½ hour.

For those with a car to return to, fill your day by combining the Ben Venue route with that on Ben A'an (see Route 2). Allow an extra 3 hours, including the walk between car parks.

Route 2: BEN A'AN

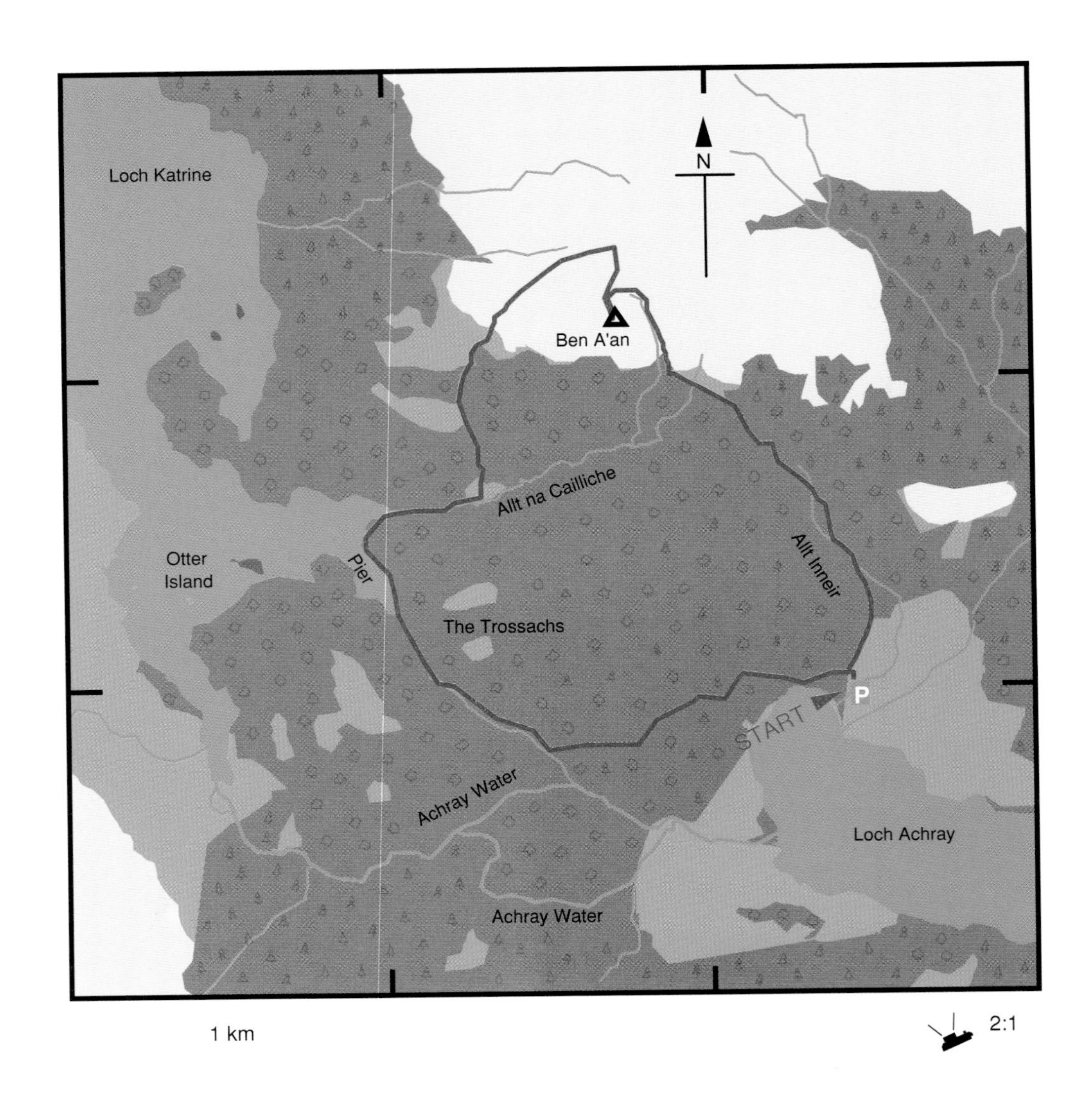

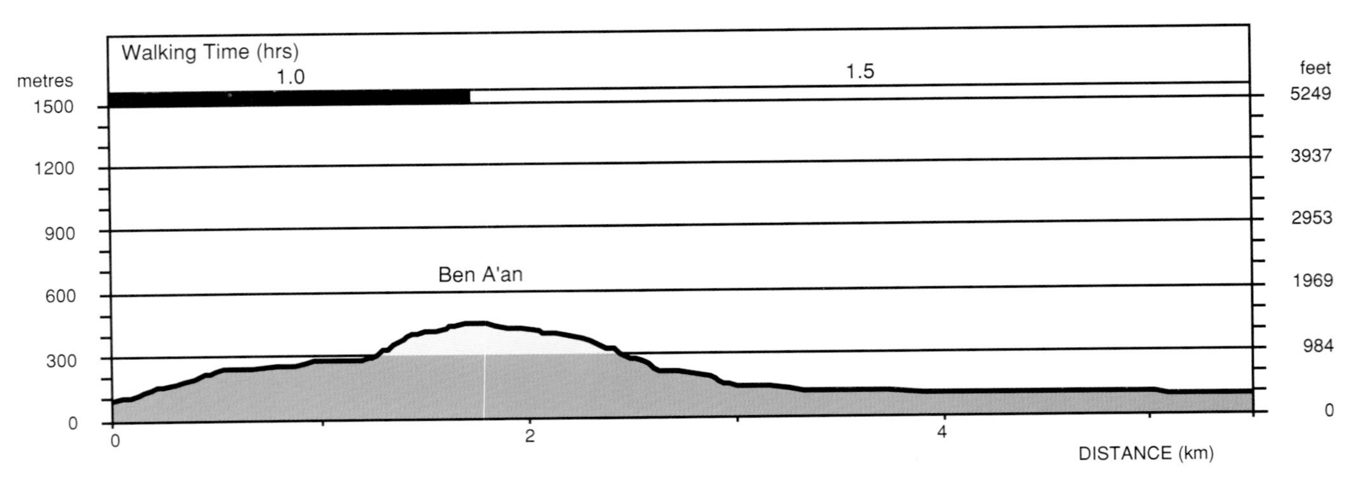

Route 2 · Ben A'an

STARTING LOCATION
FC car park on S side of A821 by N shore of Loch Achray.
OSLR 57 or OSPF 369/MR 509071.
200 m (220 yd) W of Trossachs Hotel.
Accommodates approximately 25 cars.

ALTERNATIVE STARTING LOCATION
Parking bay 600 m (1/3 mile) WSW by W shore of Loch Achray.
Trossachs car park beside Loch Katrine.

PUBLIC TRANSPORT
Nearest railway station – Stirling.
Regular buses Stirling to Callander.
Postbus, twice daily, Callander to Achray Hotel (except Sunday).

OVERVIEW/INTEREST
Superb views across the Trossachs and Loch Katrine out of all proportion to the effort invested.
Attractive ascent on forest path and descent through wild deciduous woods.
Ascent route is one of the Trossachs' most popular walks.
'There and back' option (see 'Escapes') is an excellent introduction for those unfamiliar with the Highlands.
Generally straightforward and undemanding circuit.

FOOTPATHS
Clear if eroded, sometimes wet in places.
Well-maintained on ascent route.
Almost non-existent on descent and steep in places.
Metalled spur road through the Pass of Trossachs.

GRADING 2

TIME ALLOWANCE
2½ hours.

DISTANCE

Excluding Height	5.5 km	(3½ miles)
TOTAL HEIGHT GAINED	370 m	(1214 ft)
PRINCIPAL HEIGHTS		
Ben A'an (The Pinnacle)	454 m	(1490 ft)

Loch Achray to Ben A'an *Allow 1 hour*

Ben A'an lies on the N edge of the Queen Elizabeth Forest Park, a 75 000 acre tract of mountains, forests and lochs managed by the FC. Much of the area that is generally defined as the Trossachs falls within the park's boundaries.

From the car park, cross the A821 and ascend the stone steps beginning on the path signposted by the FC, 'Footpath to Ben A'an'. Walk up the steep path NNE between mixed conifer and deciduous woodland on your L and a fenced field on the R. The Trossachs Hotel can be seen just E, an attractive building, distinctively Scottish in grey stone adorned with Victorian turrets and spires. Alas, a little further up the hill on the R, the builders of a modern house have tried to echo its style.

After 150 m (165 yd), continue uphill on the path winding between more tightly spaced larch trees. Ascend steeply over a rooty section and shift to a generally NNW bearing. Coming close to the Allt Inneir, follow it upstream on its L side for a little way until reaching the wooden footbridge that crosses it. After passing between moss-covered boulders, walk over the bridge to gain the opposite side of the allt, soon bearing L, then continuing NW and now walking upstream on its E side. Pursue the good path on the route through the forest clearing for a further 150 m (165 yd) to where, at a gap in the trees on your L, you can walk out on to the rocky promontory, signposted as a view point. Make this short diversion a convenient resting place to catch your breath and to enjoy a superb view NW towards Ben A'an's summit. Seen from here between the trees as a distinct cone, the prospect of scaling its rugged slopes seems far more distant and daunting than is the reality. For any mountain, there is always something uplifting about viewing your objective

in profile early on. Loch Achray is also visible, looking SE down through the cleared gap in the trees and between forested slopes.

Return to the main path, turn L and continue NW, descending a little way to the Allt Inneir and fording it easily by rock-hopping. Walk up on far less steep slopes along the broad path, a surprisingly pleasant experience for a route through a forestry plantation. It seems the FC has made some effort in recent years to plant the more attractive larch together with a few light-admitting deciduous species, especially along some of its forest access channels and borders. Walk on between lichen-encrusted branches; lichens are primitive plants and reliable indicators of the purity of the air. It seems difficult to believe that you are little over an hour from the traffic-clogged streets of either Glasgow or Edinburgh!

The trees give way to more open ground 1.2 km (3/4 mile) from the car park. Emerging from the northern edge of the forest, walk over a grass and bracken-covered plateau. Follow the path N towards the prominent summit cone which is here suddenly revealed at close range. You realize at once why its steep crags are so popular with climbers. Before approaching them, it is worth a quick 50 m (55 yd) diversion to cross to the L of the main path, in order to enjoy a first good view of Ben Venue.

On the main path again, walk N, descending a little at first but then begin a steep ascent on a severely eroded path. Rock steps mark the route immediately to the R of the summit cone. Begin to ascend these steep slopes after crossing a tiny burn tumbling from the R, walking up on the R side of another burn that flows through this bouldery cleft. On approaching the summit, where the path divides, a rougher route heads off up to the L. This steeper option begins opposite a striking bright white quartzite boulder on the R. It is unmistakable, looking like a giant snow ball protruding above the heather. However, continue along the main path NNW to gain easier ground which becomes flatter, if a little wetter, at the top of the cleft. From here, bear W around to SSE, thus

2.1 *From Achray Forest to Ben A'an.*

skirting outcrops in a near 180° turn to emerge at the summit.

While the summit vista may lack the feeling of remoteness and drama valued in panoramas from summits further N, the view NW to SW through Strath Gartney is one of the most picturesque and serene in all of Scotland – a reward entirely out of proportion to the relatively little effort invested. The view W across Loch Katrine, to the Arrochar Alps beyond Stronachlachar, is especially memorable and is perhaps what makes this walk such a good one to save for sunset. Look out for the SS *Sir Walter Scott* plying the waters of the loch in summer. The view to other summits includes: SW, Ben Venue; W, the Arrochar Alps; NW, Ben Lui, Ben More.

Predominantly deciduous trees cloak the slopes towards the E shores of Loch Katrine, immediately below. The attractively wooded glen seen SSW, between Loch Katrine and Loch Achray, is the area strictly referred to as the Trossachs. However, today the Trossachs is generally considered to be a much larger area extending S to Aberfoyle and E to Callander, straddling the boundary between Highland and Lowland. From the edge of the summit crags, the scene S is to somewhat flatter country with the extensive plantations of Achray forest spreading out on either side of the Duke's Pass.

Summit of Ben A'an to Loch Achray

Allow 1½ hours

Turn and head away from the summit NW, pursuing the less worn path to the L where it divides. The path on the R is for those returning via the ascent route which is also the recommended descent for the inexperienced or anyone else on the summit with less than an hour of good daylight. Other walkers should continue across the heather and, where the path divides again, take the L fork. Maintain a route above Ben A'an's W-facing slopes. Soon the ground falls away a little on the R too. Descend to your L and pursue a grassy gap between outcropping rocks, heading SW towards Ben Venue on the skyline. Walk down making a beeline for the far E end of Loch Katrine. The path from here onwards can be difficult to follow though it is becoming an increasingly popular descent route. It makes little difference whether or not you pursue it exactly as described. The vital point to bear in mind is to maintain progress SW and continually make for the near shore of Loch Katrine directly below the summit of Ben Venue. Despite steepness, thick vegetation here provides a mostly good, non-slip surface for boots. Cross a flat, grassy area and then follow a route down between heathery banks lined by a ribbon of birch trees. Underfoot, the ground becomes wetter and it is advisable to stay close to the R bank. Further below, move across towards the centre of the depression. You will soon pick up the route of a tiny burn. Follow it downstream to a flat and wet grassy plateau. Descend S via an obvious gap between the outcrops surrounding you.

On lower slopes, the woods become quite delightful, augmented by other tree species including rowan, oak and alder. Pick up the route of another burn and walk beside its R bank. If the bracken is high, which is usual at the end of summer, cross to the L side where progress may be easier. The burn takes you to a large grassy clearing in the woods, about 100 m (330 ft) in diameter, surrounded on all sides by trees and heather-covered outcrops. Veer R and cross the wet boggy ground to gain the R bank of the Allt na Cailliche. Continue downstream and W. After crossing an old low fence, ford easily the narrow allt to gain an obvious path up on the L bank. Pass under power lines and emerge at a Water Department road and public cycleway beside Loch Katrine. A few metres to the R, the allt enters the loch beneath the white railings of a bridge. Green metal fencing borders the road on the lochside.

Turn L and proceed by the loch-shore, here overshadowed by Ben Venue. The restricted access road doubles as a cycleway as well as being frequently promenaded by visitors to the Trossachs. Pass on your R a sign 'Loch Katrine – Glasgow's Water Supply' which asks visitors kindly to respect the concerns of Strathclyde Regional Council Water Department in keeping the water pure. After 100 m (110 yd), bear L and pursue the track S to arrive opposite the pier from where the SS *Sir Walter Scott* departs on its summer tours. Pass 'The Trossachs Pier Shop' on your R and, on your L, the castle-like 'Trossachs Tea Room'. Beyond a white metal gate, cross the large car park. A modest Visitors' Centre is on your L before reaching a brown timber ticket kiosk.

Leave the Trossachs car park and walk SE along a metalled road, the Pass of Trossachs, a rarely busy 1½ km (1 mile) spur to the A821. Pass a sewage reed bed on your R. After a junction with a private road beside Achray Water, also on your R, bear E and note the white mile-post on your L. Quaint, unobtrusive and half smothered by roadside vegetation, it offers a useful reference as to your location. On its nearside it states: 'Trossachs ¾ mile, Callander 9 miles, Stirling 25 miles'; on its far side, 'Loch Katrine ½ mile, Ellen's Isle 1¼ miles'. The road then bends to the L and from here progress is made ENE to the junction with the main road, the A821, opposite the NW corner of Loch Achray. Proceed in front of a grey stone house on your L and continue E in the direction signposted to 'Callander'. Stay on the road beside the N shore of Loch Achray as far as the FC car park on the R after a further 300 m (330 yd).

Alternative routes

ESCAPES

Due to short distance and duration, escape routes other than that of retracing the course of the ascent route are neither possible nor relevant. This 'there and back' option is recommended for those without confidence on Highland terrain.

However, if you do wish to avoid excursions requiring walking boots, then consider a simple exploration of the environs of Loch Achray. Especially recommended is a visit to the tiny Trossachs Kirk, idyllically situated by the lochside at MR 515067, about 800 m (½ mile) SE from the Ben A'an car park. The view of Ben Venue, across the water, is a classic and much photographed one. Alternatively, you could amble along the roadside W into the Pass of Trossachs proper, as described at the end of the main route. This affords a pleasant stroll through deciduous woodlands, passing some rugged outcrops near the main Trossachs car park beside Loch Katrine.

EXTENSIONS

The obvious extension is that due SE into the Duke's Pass. A popular viewpoint from the heart of Achray Forest, marked on the OSLR map as such just off the A821 2 km (1¼ miles) S of Loch Achray at MR 523046, offers the visitor a memorable Trossachs panorama.

For most fit walkers, it is perfectly feasible to combine the Ben A'an route with that on Ben Venue into one day's walking (see Route 1). Allow an extra 4½ hours.

A further option is to combine Ben A'an with the Glen Finglas circuit which begins 3 km (2 miles) to the E, at Brig O'Turk (see Route 6). Allow an extra 6½ hours, including the drive between car parks.

Route 3: THE COBBLER (BEN ARTHUR)

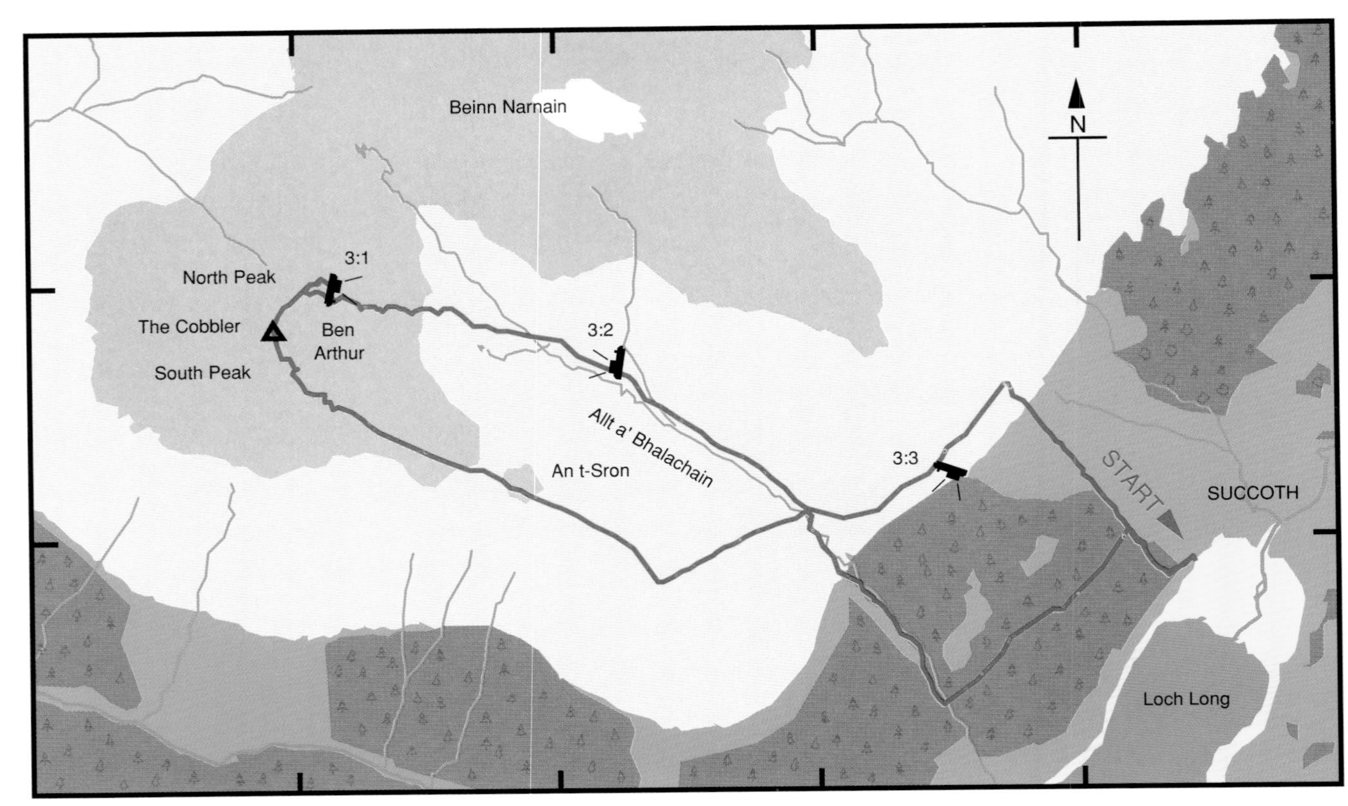

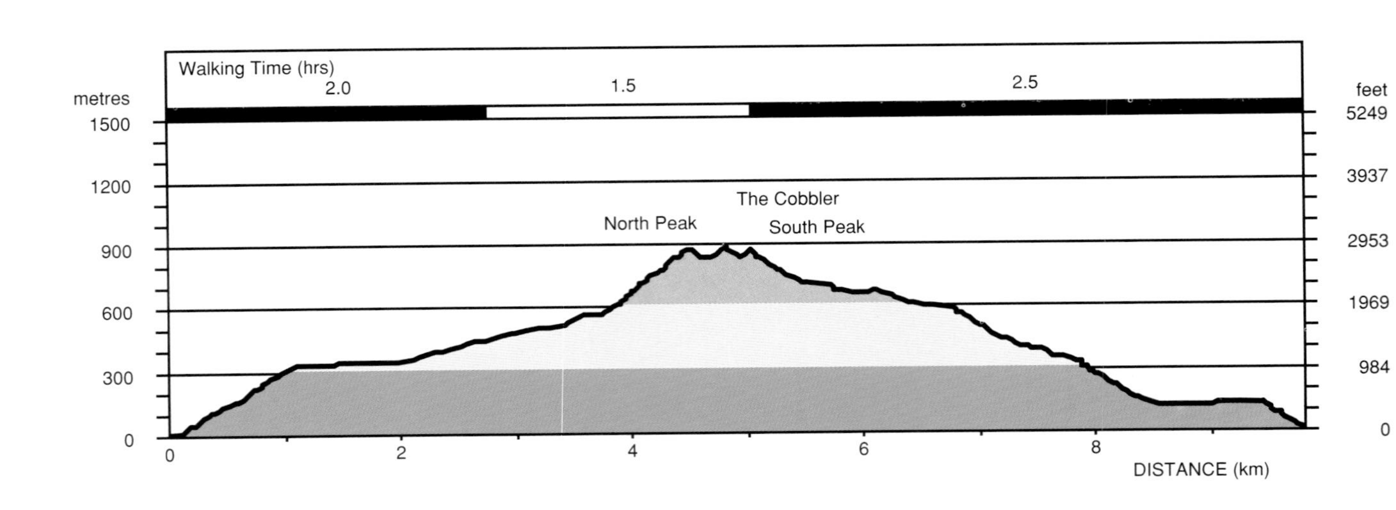

4

ARROCHAR ALPS AND LOCH LOMONDSIDE

HIGH-LEVEL ROUTE

Route 3 · The Cobbler (Ben Arthur)

STARTING LOCATION
S of Succoth, beside the A83 at the head of Loch Long.
OSLR 56 or OSPF 368/MR 295049.
Parking on verges on both sides of the road just N of the Argyll Forest Park sign.
Accommodates approximately 25 cars.

ALTERNATIVE STARTING LOCATION
Parking bay beside the A83, 300 m (330 yd) to the NE.

PUBLIC TRANSPORT
Nearest railway station – Arrochar and Tarbet.
Regular coaches and buses from Glasgow.

OVERVIEW/INTEREST
One of the most striking mountains in the Southern Highlands.
One of the most popular hill walks in the country.
Displays a distinctive alpine-like character normally attributed to much bigger hills.
Optional scrambling.
Generally straightforward route-finding.
A physically demanding route.

FOOTPATHS
No waymarking.
Seriously eroded on initial steep slopes and on ridge approach.
Obvious and well-worn on most sections.
Often waterlogged below the Coire a' Bhalachain.
Some easy free-ranging required on descent.
Part of return is via forestry track.

GRADING 4 (5, if scrambles on Central and South Peaks are included – see 'Extensions')

TIME ALLOWANCE
6 hours.

DISTANCE

Excluding Height	9.8 km	(6 miles)
TOTAL HEIGHT GAINED	960 m	(3150 ft)
PRINCIPAL HEIGHTS		
Ben Arthur:		
North Peak	866 m	(2841 ft)
The Cobbler	884 m	(2900 ft)
South Peak (not named on OS maps)	858 m	(2815 ft)

Loch Long to the Narnain Boulders

Allow 2 hours

With the exception of the tourist treadmill on Ben Nevis, the well-worn path to the Cobbler is one of the most frequented routes to a summit in all the Highlands. A striking alpine-like character coupled with its convenient proximity to Glasgow has guaranteed the mountain's popularity. The Cobbler is not a Munro, although it undoubtedly possesses finer attributes of many much bigger hills. Falling just 30 m (100 ft) short of the qualifying height of 914 m (3000 ft), ever-greater pressure from walkers is at least limited.

By the shore at the head of Loch Long, follow the road SSW to the prominent Argyll Forest Park sign and commence on the track to the R of it. For the first few metres, the track directs you gently

3.1 *Ben Lomond from the Cobbler.*

upward between deciduous trees. Pass a cairn on your L, serving as a collection box for the Mountain Rescue services, and bear R. Pass between wooden fence posts and begin a steep climb NW on the seriously eroded path through the conifer plantations. Here, on the edge of the FC's Ardgartan Forest, follow a line of concrete blocks. Now defunct, they once carried a railway used for the construction of the Loch Sloy hydro-scheme.

After approximately 150 m (165 yd), emerge above the trees to more open recently replanted ground. Proceed uphill to reach a forestry track. Turn L and then almost immediately R to continue on the steep gradient, once more alongside the concrete blocks. Height is gained quickly on what seems a hard slog up the grass and bracken-covered slopes. Glance to your rear from time to time to view, in the ESE, the distant cone of Ben Lomond. On the very edge of the Highland fault line, the mountain is the most southerly Munro.

At about the 330 m (1100 ft) contour, the path connects with another at right angles. Ignore the less worn path straight ahead, which continues NW to Beinn Narnain. Instead, turn L and proceed SW along the flank of the hillside. The views ahead SSW, beyond the Ardgartan plantations and across Loch Long, are magnificent. The loch, appropriately named, is a far-reaching channel of sea water, barely a kilometre wide, stretching out as far as the Firth of Clyde.

Continue on the agreeable path which after 800 m (½ mile) veers R. The striking profile of The Cobbler is suddenly revealed to the WNW. On encountering its jutting peaks and spines of twisted schist, so conspicuous in profile, one feels at the same time apprehensive and yet entirely compelled. Anxiety proves misplaced as there are real rewards in store for the walker as well as the scrambler. However, the fancied resemblance to a cobbler bent over his last does, to be honest, require a stretch of the imagination. Rarely referred to by its proper name, Ben Arthur, The Cobbler relates to the summit in general but also specifically to the Central Peak. Deceptively, your objective appears closer than is the reality.

At the small dam restraining the waters of the

Allt a' Bhalachain on your L, Ben Lomond warrants a retrospective appreciation. Leave the dam on a gently rising course by the path that follows the delightful Allt a' Bhalachain upstream, on its R side. Above you, to the R, the rugged slopes of Cruach nam Miseag and Beinn Narnain block the view N. Ford four consecutive burns, all easily, to reach the Narnain Boulders. A pair of huge metamorphic lumps, they provide an ideal resting place to recharge batteries. Psychologically preparing for the rigours of the final push to the summit, expect interruptions from practising rock climbers. Their preparation is likely to be for more ambitious routes on that which now lies so tantalisingly close, immediately to the W.

Narnain Boulders to the South Peak

Allow 1½ hours

Walk WNW to ford the Allt a' Bhalachain by easy boulder-hopping at a point 400 m (¼ mile) from the Narnain pair. From the opposite bank proceed W up the steep, often extremely wet, grassy slopes leading to the Cobbler. Follow the path on a beeline for the R-hand North Peak. Beyond the grass, the path becomes a rugged, crag-ridden and still steeper passage. Erosion has scarred the hill badly but in compensation you have a clearly defined route to follow. Distinctly gruelling in places, beware of loose and easily dislodged rocks.

At the corrie immediately below the peaks, the gradient relents for a while before a final demanding climb on to the ridge. The other mountains of the Arrochar Alps, revealed from the bealach, are best contemplated a little higher up. Thus, turn R from the cairn and indulge in a short walk traversing the rocks to the NE to gain the summit of the North Peak. Of the mountain's three peaks, this is the only one readily accessible to walkers. The faint-hearted would do best to stay well clear of the vertiginous rocks at the N edge of the overhang. Instead, look horizontally to a fine prospect across the Arrochar Alps as well as to the mountains beyond, including: ENE, Beinn Narnain; NNE, Ben Vorlich, Ben Vane; N, Beinn Ime;

3.2 *The Cobbler from the Narnain Boulders.*

NW, Beinn Luibhean; WNW, Beinn an Lochain; WSW, Ben Donich; SSW, The Brack; ESE, Ben Lomond.

To the S, the waves of an ocean of less lofty tops predominate. Unfortunately the view N into the Highlands is mostly obscured by the Munro, Beinn Ime.

Return to the bealach and walk out on the broad ridge SW. At first, stay on the path well to the R of the cliff edge but draw nearer to it after gaining more height. The Cobbler is the central and highest peak lying just to the L of a cairn. It is an easy walk out to the base of the rock. However, do not attempt what Campbell chiefs were once obliged to, unless entirely confident of your scrambling abilities and prepared for an exposed situation (see 'Extensions').

Leave the cairn and descend the path S. Bear SSE towards the seemingly impregnable monolith of the South Peak. This is out of bounds to all but the most nimble of crag ferrets and comes close to a rock climb (see 'Extensions'). Continue to descend to the R of the South Peak by pursuing the path that skirts the base of the rock.

South Peak to Loch Long *Allow 2½ hours*

From the rocks below the S-facing crags of the South Peak, proceed ESE towards the next protrusion of outcrops on your L. Glance back to view the peaks in an entirely new profile, now seen across the Cobbler's E-facing corrie from the S.

Descend terrain which returns to grass underfoot, now above Glen Croe on your R. Opposite, the Brack and Cruach Fhiarach form its southern boundary. Persevere by a rudimentary path, though one likely to become more worn as its popularity increases. The ground is wetter again approaching An t-Sròn. Walk on ESE on a course heading just to the R of Ben Lomond on the skyline.

Descend to a grassy plateau and then walk up the mound of An t-Sròn. Continue down the broad grassy ridge, over a small hump and then out to where the ridge falls away noticeably more steeply at MR 274048. At its near shore, a pier on Loch Long is seen below, SE. Turn sharply to your L and head ENE down the slopes, devoid of distinct paths, directly towards the dam and the Allt a' Bhalachain. The descent is easy and not steep. Only the normally saturated ground impedes progress.

Having returned to the dam, this time on its W side, turn R and walk SE. Follow a raised bank on the path downstream of the Allt a' Bhalachain. On re-entering the plantations of Ardgartan Forest, steepness increases but maintain your route upon the path close to the R side of the allt. Pursue a channel between spruce, invigorated perhaps by the fresh smell of pine – aromatherapy courtesy of the FC! A parallel burn is on your R.

At gaps in the coniferous canopy, Loch Long may be glimpsed below. At a more open glade in the forest, it is necessary to clamber carefully down one or two awkward outcrops. Deciduous trees including birch and rowan have taken advantage of this light-break between conifers. On the L side of the allt, much of the area has recently been clear-felled, an activity that always results in a scene of apparent devastation.

The ground becomes much wetter again where alder trees add botanical variety to the bankside scene. Ford the burn on your R at the rocks above its confluence with the Allt a' Bhalachain. Heading steeply downhill for a further 250 m (275 yd), pause where the path is crossed by a forestry track. Turn L and walk NE along the track and through the forest. Cross a concrete bridge over the 'Buttermilk Burn' and continue skirting the hillside to rejoin the path pursued initially, that alongside the concrete blocks. Turn R and proceed downhill SE, backtracking the final steep 300 m (330 yd) to your vehicle and the A83.

Alternative routes

ESCAPES

Effectively a figure-of-8 circuit, the route lends itself nicely to foreshortening. Those with aspirations more modest than reaching the summit can simply return having reached the dam at the Allt a' Bhalachain. Cross the allt at the dam and turn L to follow the path downhill SE back through the

3.3 *Looking* SSW *across Loch Long.*

plantation, as described at the end of the main route. Fine views across Loch Long and to Ben Lomond, as well as the memorable profile of The Cobbler, are the worthy rewards of this shorter circular option. Allow 2¼ hours in total.

Having gained the broad summit ridge of The Cobbler, there are no quicker routes off the mountain than the one described. Attempting a descent directly below the pinnacles via the very steep ascent path will prove more treacherous this way round, and is therefore inadvisable.

EXTENSIONS

The Central Peak (The Cobbler) and the South Peak (The Cobbler's Wife) are accessible only to scramblers. While adding little in total distance or height gained, both nonetheless prove significant encounters in terms of difficulty.

To sit aloft the summit block of The Cobbler, the highest point on the mountain at 884 m (2900 ft), walk out a little SE from the adjacent ridge cairn. From its base, clamber up through an obvious rock window, known as Argyll's Eyeglass, to gain access to a narrow ledge. It is then a short scramble up the L side to the flat summit top but with a drop of hundreds of feet below. You have succeeded in what was once a test of manhood for Campbell chiefs. As with all such climbs, the way down is a test of even greater nerve.

A yet more daunting prospect is presented by the South Peak. Leave the main ridge by the path off to the L to gain the first few feet of the pinnacle. Having made your own assessment of the best route up the rocks to the summit, the hard work begins. I discovered a viable route up the N side but this involved lying belly-flat at one point! Again, remember that you have to return. Allow an extra 45 minutes for both scrambles combined.

Two easily accessible and higher summits, though much less exciting ones, will be of interest to Munroists. Leave the ridge opposite the cairn where you gained it, by striking off downhill NW. Soon after, bear N and proceed on the path to the summit of Beinn Ime, 1011 m (3318 ft). Return the same way as far as the Bealach a' Mhaim, then veer L to ascend the NE slopes of Beinn Narnain, 926 m (3038 ft). Leave the triangulation pillar of this second Munro by descending generally SE, later joining the path that follows the line of disused concrete railway blocks. Allow 5 hours from The Cobbler to Loch Long via these mountains (8 hours in total for the round trip).

Route 4: LOCH LOMOND and GLEN GYLE

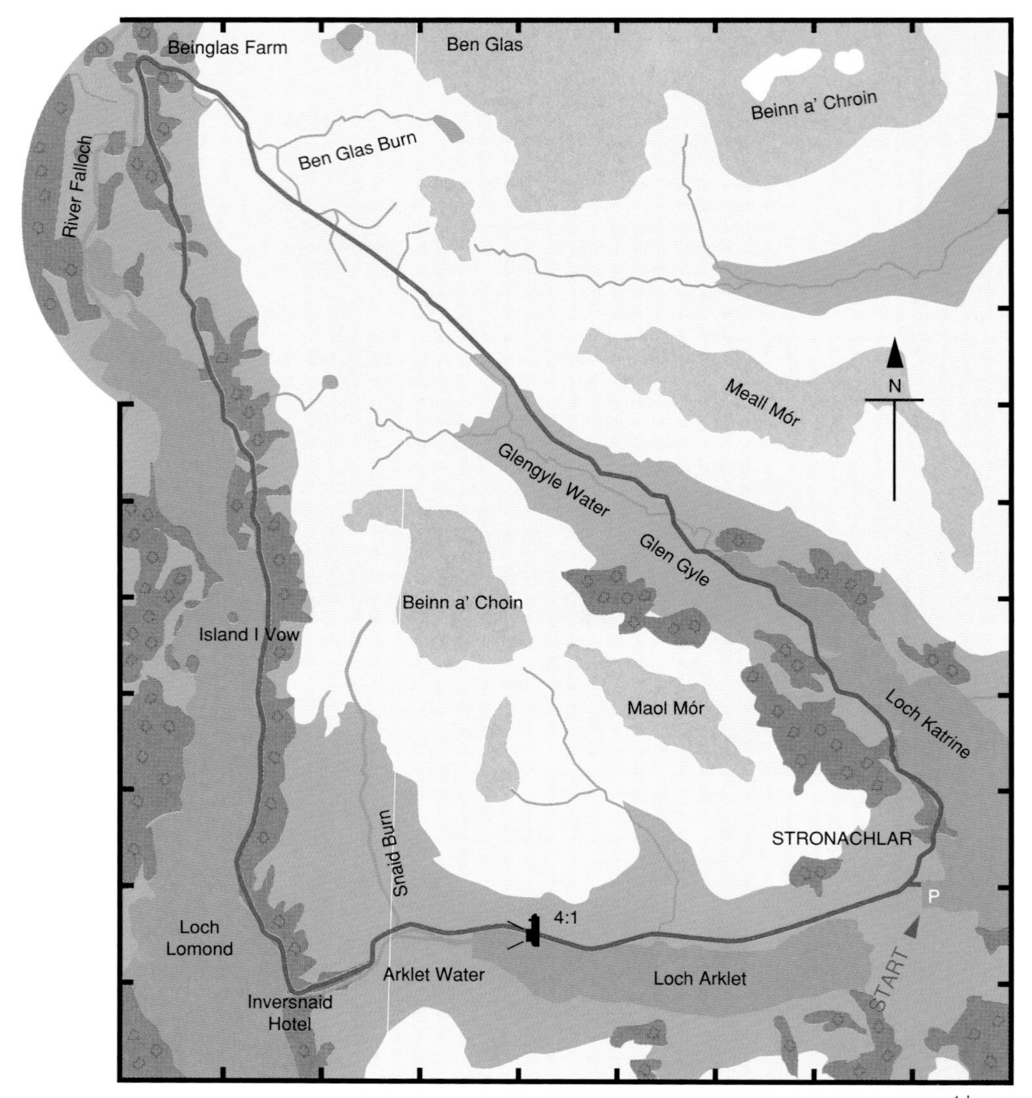

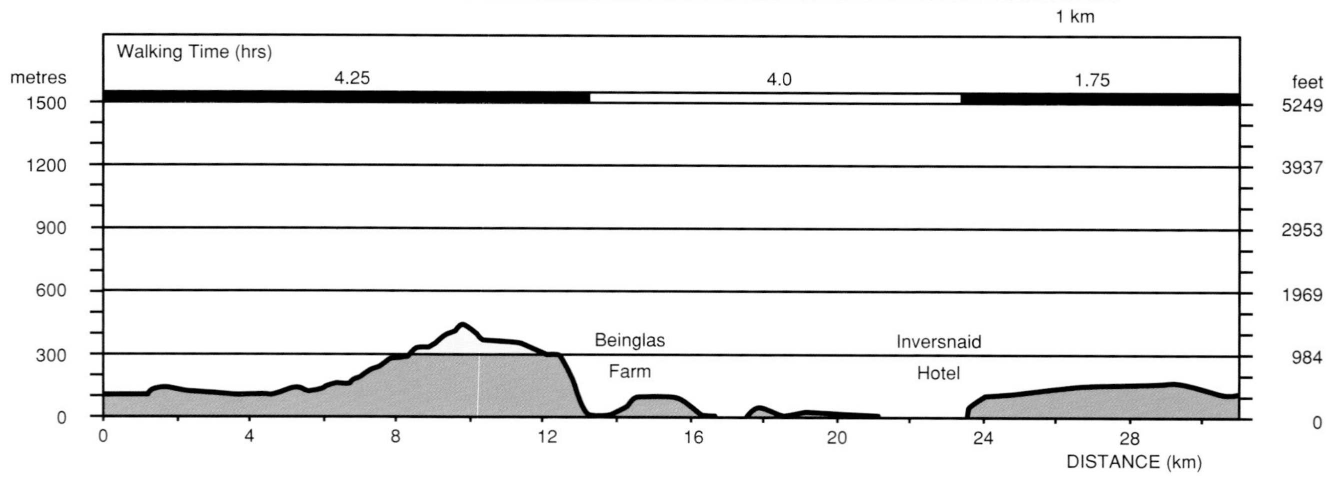

Route 4 · Loch Lomond and Glen Gyle

STARTING LOCATION
Stronachlachar Pier car park by the W shore of Loch Katrine.
OSLR 56 or OSPF 357, 358 and 368/MR 404102.
Situated 1 km (2/3 mile) WNW from the N end of the B829.
Metalled surface car park, accommodates approximately 30 cars.

ALTERNATIVE STARTING LOCATION
Inversnaid Hotel car park (open to non patrons) by Loch Lomond.

PUBLIC TRANSPORT
Nearest railway station – Stirling or Ardlui.
Regular buses Stirling to Aberfoyle.
Postbus, once daily, Aberfoyle to Stronachlachar (except Sunday).

OVERVIEW/INTEREST
Good scenic diversity.
Includes part of the WHW on the 'Bonnie Banks' of the largest area of fresh water in Britain.
Bird watchers should carry binoculars (see bird list for each route section).
Optional short detour to the Drovers Inn – one of the best pubs in the Highlands.
This is Rob Roy's country.
A lengthy and physically demanding circuit.

FOOTPATHS
Excellent metalled cycleway to Glengyle.
Good farm track thereafter by Glengyle Water.
Some free-ranging over moorland to Glen Falloch.
Severely eroded and hard going in places on WHW.
Single-track metalled road in Glen Arklet.

GRADING 4

TIME ALLOWANCE
10 hours.

DISTANCE

Excluding Height	30.9 km	(19¼ miles)
TOTAL HEIGHT GAINED	680 m	(2231 ft)

PRINCIPAL HEIGHTS
None – highest point of route at MR 346165, 440 m (1444 ft).

Stronachlachar to Inverarnan

Allow 4¼ hours

Walk W from the Pier for about 400 m (¼ mile) along the single-track road you drove in on. At a junction on the R, a white metal gate bars access to unauthorized vehicles. Walkers and cyclists are welcome. Turn R, pass through the gate and proceed NNE on the metalled road between the red-and-white Water Department buildings of Stronachlachar. What is surely one of Britain's tiniest post offices lies almost hidden beneath stands of Scots pine on your R. Walk beside the neat lochside lawns and green metal railings edging the road here. Look to your R for views E across Loch Katrine as far as the Trossachs. Ben A'an can be clearly seen on the horizon.

Beyond the last of the buildings, pass through a second white metal gate and continue on the road that serves equally as a public cycleway and footpath to the Trossachs as well as an access road for Water Department vehicles. After an incline, bear NW and simply follow the lochside road, the water being on your R. Numerous schist outcrops on your L present an interesting series of roadside rock walls.

A little beyond Black Island, where white metal railings edge the roadside, bridge a burn which drains the slopes of Maol Mór on the L. Silver birch line the gully through which it descends. Continue NW and from a large oak on the R look back at the view SE to a seemingly island-pitted Loch Katrine. Approaching the loch's far NW end, another burn is bridged at more white railings. Glengyle House lies on the opposite shore looking NE. Today a large white house in a tranquil wooded setting, it was undoubtedly the scene of a less peaceful past, being once the home of the notorious Rob Roy MacGregor!

Ignore a track that forks to the L leading up to 'The Dhu', a red-roofed cottage. Instead continue to the very corner of the loch, just prior to where the road bears R to cross Glengyle Water. Turn L to gain the farm track and walk on through a gate, making further progress NW.

Ascend Glen Gyle by following the good track below a line of electricity pylons which, thankfully, fail to detract too seriously from the beauty of the glen. Here and there, the track is surfaced with old railway sleepers to take farm vehicles across the wettest ground.

At a bridge made from railway sleepers, cross Glengyle Water and walk NW following the course of the water upstream.

The mountain increasingly prominent ahead at the top of the glen is Beinn Ducteach. Walk towards it, keeping binoculars out. Glen Gyle is an excellent place for spotting eagles. Bird species frequenting Glen Gyle and Loch Katrine include peregrine, golden eagle, whooper swan, dipper, golden plover and wheatear.

Gaining height, the track deteriorates and the surface becomes increasingly wetter underfoot. Near the top of glen, the track comes to an abrupt end. Ford the upper reaches of Glengyle Water where it flows beneath the E-facing crags of Beinn Ducteach and continue NW, free-ranging over spongy, wet ground.

Follow the line of pylons counting six from the end of the track. At 440 m (1444 ft) you have attained the highest point on the route. The view is to a sparse panorama of summits in the vicinity but includes those of Beinn Chabhair N and Ben Lui NW. Do not attempt to improve on the view by climbing a pylon: the 'Danger of Death' signs are no bluff.

Plot your own route NW over the moor, keeping just to the R of the pylons. Remember the golden rule of free-ranging in the Highlands: heather = dry, grass = wet. Pass by a line of rusty fence posts and proceed for a distance of a further six pylons. Where they start to march down across Glen Falloch, bear N away from them and cross the moorland as far as the Ben Glas Burn. Ford the burn to gain the obvious path on its N side and walk W, maintaining a gradual descent. Where you begin a much steeper decline, savour for a while the view into the delightfully wooded Glen Falloch. The River Falloch meanders its way through the glen and, in a less agreeable way, so does the busy A82.

Continue WNW on the path to the R of the Ben Glas Burn. Walk carefully down the very steep, eroded but clear path into the glen. After a series of waterfalls, cross a stile at Beinglas Farm and on level ground pass to the L of two 'wigwams' (wooden tents). A signpost indicates the junction of footpaths, having reached the WHW.

Before continuing to Inversnaid, an 800 m (½ mile) detour to the Drovers Inn at Inverarnan is highly recommended. The Drovers Inn was established in 1705, and the eccentric collection of dummies and stuffed animals crammed into its characterful hallway is renowned. Haunted bedrooms and a dark cosy lounge bar dispensing essential whiskies and beers by the fireside add to the atmosphere.

Inverarnan to Inversnaid *Allow 4 hours*

On the WHW at Beinglas Farm, cross a stile where the signpost indicates 'Inversnaid'. Walk over the wooden footbridge crossing the Ben Glas Burn and proceed S, heading up into the trees. Footpath erosion is severe in some places, which is testimony perhaps to the ever-growing pressure of boots on the WHW.

At Blarstainge, emerge on to more open ground between the ruins of a hillside settlement. Cross a wet section using the thoughtfully placed railway sleepers. The view S from here, at the far N end of Loch Lomond, is magnificent, looking out along Britain's largest expanse of fresh water. Pass to the L of the ruined buildings at Ardleish. On the opposite shore, Ben Vorlich (*not* the mountain of Route 5) dominates the view SW. Climb a drystone wall using the ladder-stile and traverse the open ground pursuing a route above the E shores of Loch Lomond.

On entering more extensive woodland, cross a fence at a stile. A path to the R connects with the lochside and the Ardlui Ferry. Walk over a footbridge and descend close to the shore. The ban on speedboats at Lake Windermere has resulted in a corresponding increase in such traffic here. Thus, in summer, your peace at Loch Lomond is too often a disturbed one.

Continue S passing Doune bothy on the R. The condition of the footpath deteriorates again on re-entering the woods.

Maintain a route of repeated undulations. When adjacent to the tree-covered Island I Vow, cross a footbridge over a burn and descend a 4 m (13 ft) ladder-stile. Walk on over yet another footbridge, which crosses the Allt Rostan, to a plaque that indicates you are entering the Inversnaid Nature Reserve. This RSPB reserve extends for 4.5 km (3 miles) as far as Inversnaid itself. These important deciduous woodlands, predominantly of oak, are significant for their breeding populations of a variety of bird species. Migrants include wood warbler, willow warbler, pied flycatcher, redstart and cuckoo, while among the resident species are blue tit, great tit, greater spotted woodpecker, buzzard, sparrowhawk and tawny owl.

Keep an eye out also for the famous herd of feral goats which roam wild in these woods.

Pass through a K-gate and persevere on the seemingly endless root-ridden path thereafter. Emerge at a pleasant beach in the clearing at Pollochro. Beyond ruins on the R continue further along these gloriously wooded 'Bonnie Banks'. The Way passes above the unremarkable Rob Roy's Cave, easily missed despite the word 'CAVE' splashed in white at its entrance.

Ignore the footpath that ascends the slopes on the L unless you can muster the energy and inclination to explore the RSPB Nature Trail (see 'Escapes'). Pass in front of a corrugated-iron boathouse.

From here, the relief of a well-surfaced footpath affords a pleasant 600 m (⅓ mile) stroll to the Inversnaid Hotel. Emerge from the trees at its large car park, a little beyond the RSPB interpretation panels on your R.

Inversnaid to Stronachlachar

Allow 1¾ hours

Walk across the car park to the S side of the hotel. Arklet Water plunges spectacularly to Loch Lomond at a waterfall that is a popular magnet for visitors. Climb the brick staircase on the L side of it. The WHW continues S from a footbridge at the top of the falls on the R. Instead, walk E up the wooded slopes to the L of the river. Pass through a rusty K-gate between rhododendron bushes and bear L where the path forks. Emerge at the single-track road opposite a white garden gate and turn R, continuing uphill by the roadside.

Walk beyond the driveway to Inversnaid Lodge on your L and proceed E, above and to the L of the attractive gorge cut by Arklet Water. Pass Arklet Bridge on your R. Beyond the tiny, well preserved church, which now doubles as a Boys Brigade Outdoor Centre, approach the cluster of buildings near Garrison Farm on the L. The road bridges the Snaid Burn, inspiration to Gerard Manley Hopkins' much celebrated nineteenth century poem, 'Inversnaid'. His environmental plea is as poignant today as ever, ending:

> "What would the world be once bereft
> Of wet and wilderness?
> O Let them be left, wilderness and wet;
> Long live the weeds and the wilderness yet."

The school on the L is staffed by one teacher and with 11 pupils is one of Britain's smallest primaries. The garrison itself, a little further up the hill and its ruins now integrated into the farm, was built by the British in the early eighteenth century. The aim of the Hanoverian authorities then was to subdue Rob Roy and the other marauding MacGregors but to little effect!

Where the dam, on the R, is reached, begin to follow the N shore of Loch Arklet. Pass a line of Scots pine on the R, between the road and the loch. Proceed E along Glen Arklet beyond the farm on the L at Corriearklet. The pure waters of Loch Arklet and Loch Katrine constitute much of Glasgow's water supply. Please do heed the warnings preventing swimming. Glen Arklet

offers yet more opportunities for observing birds with the possibility of a few rarities: winchat, curlew, buzzard, golden eagle, hen harrier, grasshopper warbler, dipper, grey wagtail, black grouse, short-eared owl, woodcock and black-throated diver.

A little beyond the farm buildings, the road bridges the Corriearklet Burn. Continue E, looking back from time to time. The memorable views of the Arrochar Alps across Loch Arklet seem reminiscent of wilder Highland scenes further N. At the E end of the loch, pass Garry Cottage on the L, just prior to the B829 Aberfoyle road on your R.

From the road junction, continue E between two white posts and walk down to Stronachlachar, bearing NE. At the third turning on the R, and immediately in front of the white gate at the beginning of the cycleway again, turn R. Retrace much earlier footsteps on the minor road to the Pier car park.

Alternative routes

ESCAPES

Apart from the section of wild moor from the top of Glen Gyle to Glen Falloch, where there is no path for 4 km (2½ miles), you should encounter few navigational problems. Options for curtailing this long route include mostly separate excursions in their own right.

If you trust your route-finding abilities, it is possible to cross the rough, steep country S from Glen Gyle. Climb the steep slopes of Beinn a Choin, free-ranging to the Bealach a' Mhaim, and then descend the Corriearklet Burn to emerge by the road in Glen Arklet. While this route reduces total distance by about half, it more than doubles the navigational difficulties!

For a circular route affording fine views over Loch Lomond, climb the steep slopes SSE from Inversnaid. Begin at the the car park on the S side of Arklet Bridge, MR 345091. Walk up on the L side of the new plantation to gain the summit of Cruachan Hill at 537 m (1762 ft). To return, continue S to Gleann Gaoithe and then descend the good track W to Cailness. Turn R and walk N on the WHW by the E shore of Loch Lomond as far as the Inversnaid Hotel. The car park is near Inversnaid church, 1 km (⅔ mile) further E.

4.1 *West from Inversnaid, across Loch Arklet to the Arrochar Alps.*

For a short and easy ramble, explore the RSPB Nature Trail in the Inversnaid Nature Reserve. To reach the trail, walk N on the WHW by the side of Loch Lomond starting at the Inversnaid Hotel car park, MR 337089. After about 600 m (⅓ mile) and near the boathouse, follow the waymarked 'nature trail' up densely wooded slopes to the R. This is a particularly good option in late spring when the oaks are alive with woodland birds. The clearing at the top of the trail affords superb views of Loch Lomond and the nearby mountains including Ben Lomond. From here, a descent to the lochside, emerging 400 m (¼ mile) further NNW along the WHW, completes the trail. Turn L and follow the WHW back to the hotel.

EXTENSIONS

Adhering to the main route ensures a long day out. Extensions are therefore not recommended. However, further days spent exploring the area are. Barely an hour by road from Glasgow, Loch Lomond is readily accessible.

Consider returning to Stronachlachar (between May and October) to board the paddle steamer, the SS *Sir Walter Scott*, departing daily at noon. The vessel has plied the waters of Loch Katrine since 1900, connecting this pier and the one in the Trossachs. After disembarking at the Trossachs end, pursue the cycleway W through Strath Gartney. Follow the N shore of Loch Katrine and eventually return to Stronachlachar, via Glengyle. Allow 6½ hours, including the boat trip.

For a pedestrian marathon lasting six or seven days, the popular WHW is the finest of all such expeditions. Begin at Milngavie, just N of Glasgow, and follow the frequently waymarked thistle symbols for 150 km (95 miles) N to Fort William. Campsites, hostels, bed-and-breakfasts and 'wigwams' provide for nightly stopovers. You can return by train to Glasgow on the scenic West Highlands line.

Route 5: BEN VORLICH

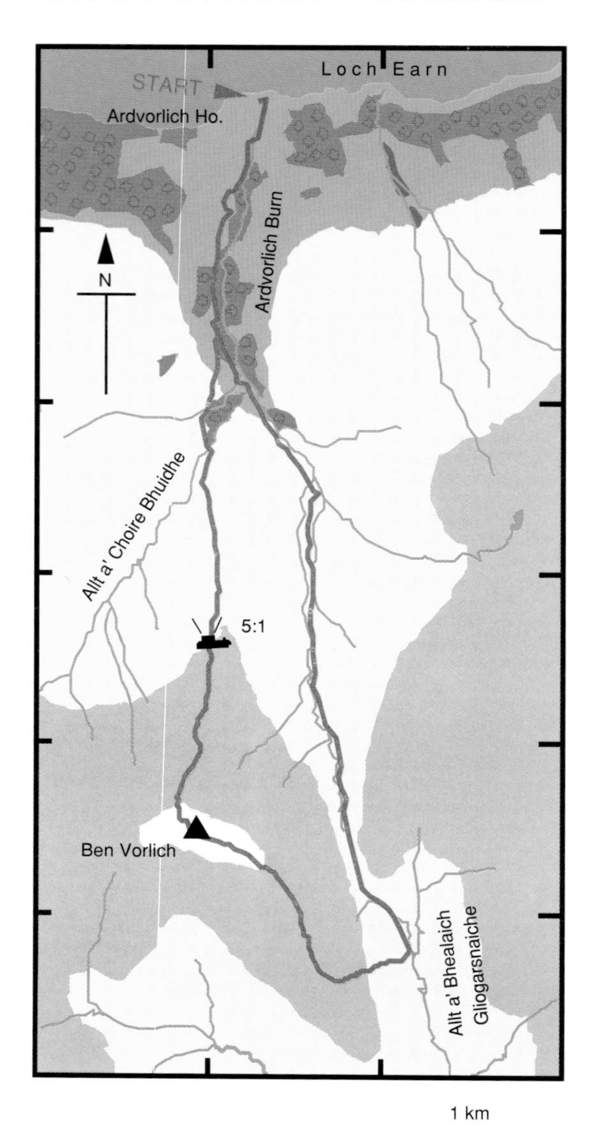

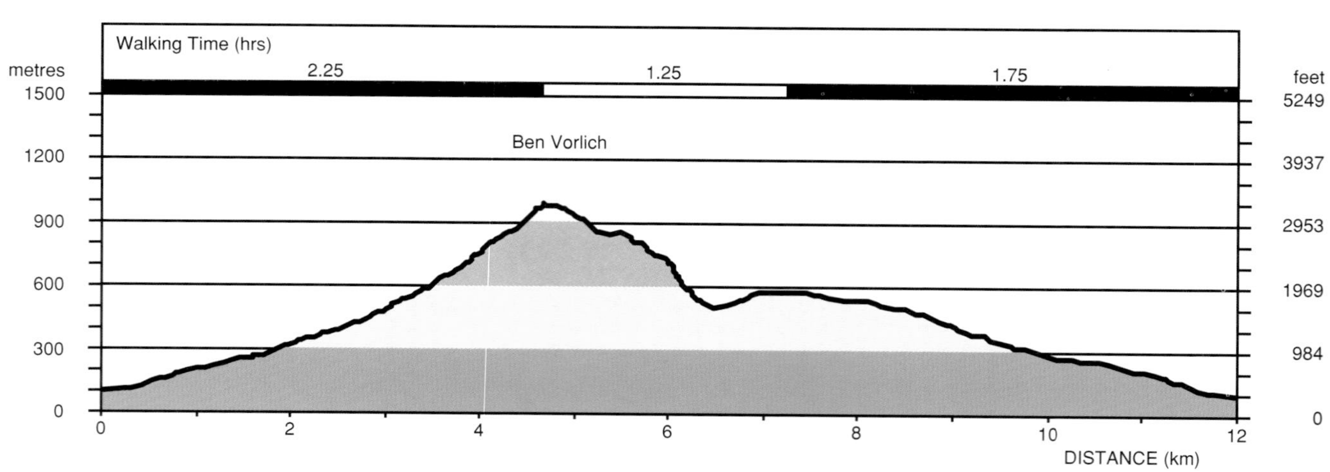

5

STRATHYRE

HIGH-LEVEL ROUTE

Route 5 · Ben Vorlich

STARTING LOCATION
Roadside parking at Ardvorlich by the S shore of Loch Earn, immediately N of Ardvorlich House.
OSLR 51 and 57 or OSPF 348 and 359/MR 633232.
On the minor road 4.5 km (3 miles) E of Lochearnhead.
Space for approximately 10 cars but more space nearby.

ALTERNATIVE STARTING LOCATION
None.

PUBLIC TRANSPORT
Nearest railway station – Stirling.
Regular buses, twice daily, Stirling to Lochearnhead.

OVERVIEW/INTEREST
A straightforward and most attractive Munro ascent with lower sections in typical deciduous Highland woodland.
Contrasting summit views – S and E across lowlands, N and W to a Highland scene.
Opportunity to bag a second Munro (if 'Extension' is included).
A physically demanding route.

FOOTPATHS
Excellent firm and dry track on lower sections.
Clearly marked, if eroded, close to summit.
Elsewhere, possibly wet and less obvious.
Access may be difficult during stalking season.

GRADING 4

TIME ALLOWANCE
5¼ hours.

DISTANCE

Excluding Height	12 km	(7½ miles)
TOTAL HEIGHT GAINED	970 m	(3182 ft)

PRINCIPAL HEIGHTS
Ben Vorlich (Mountain of the Bay)
985 m (3231 ft)

Ardvorlich to summit of Ben Vorlich

Allow 2¼ hours

From the lochside, turn R off the road, immediately after the bridge over the Ardvorlich Burn, and head off SSW down the Eastgate drive to Ardvorlich House. The burn is on the R. Here at the very start by Loch Earn, your summit objective is already clearly visible ahead.

Approaching Ardvorlich House, after crossing the bridge over the burn, turn L off the driveway and continue S. After a K-gate, the ground to the R becomes more open and on your L beech trees line the route of the burn. Where a dry-stone wall leads off (one of the more aesthetic human impositions on the landscape), cross a stile. After a second stile, the route continues to follow the excellent track through a typically sparse though very beautiful Highland woodland. The track passes over numerous babbling burns as it meanders between birch and rowan trees. In the woods the track divides. The L fork is your return route so take the track on the R without deviating from a course S. A solid wooden bridge crosses the Allt a' Choire Bhuidhe, marking an end to the deciduous tranquillity and, alas, the easy walking.

Walk S, summit bound, on a path distinctly softer and wetter as you traverse open moorland.

5.1 *Ben Lawers range from Ben Vorlich.*

Pass the grouse butts protruding above the heather on your L and continue upward, the path becoming drier as altitude and steepness increase. Behind you, NNE, Ben Lawers begins to dominate among an increasing number of intrusions on the skyline, its presence befitting the highest mountain in the Southern Highlands at 1214 m (3982 ft).

Veering slightly R, now on Vorlich's northern ridge, the view W opens up in a progressively more spectacular way as height is gained. Then, close to the summit, the ridge flattens out for a while, inviting a pause while simultaneously offering a side view L of Ben Vorlich's impressive NE-facing slopes. Catch your breath here before the final 200 m (600 ft) steep climb to the triangulation pillar at 985 m (3231 ft) marking the summit.

The view immediately ahead, looking S across to E, is impressively extensive if relatively flat. Ben Vorlich is situated close to the southern edge of the Highland fault line. However, if visibility is good, the topography between SW and NE is strikingly different in character with many of the major peaks of the Southern Highlands laid out in a wonderful panorama: SW, Stuc a' Chroin; WSW, Ben Ledi, Ben Lomond; WNW, Ben Cruachan, Ben More and Stob Binnein, Ben Lui; NNW, Ben Nevis; N, the Tarmachan Ridge; NNE, Ben Lawers.

Ben Vorlich summit cairn to the Bealach Gliogarsnaich

Allow 1¼ hours

Walk 100 m (110 yd) ESE to the cairn at the opposite end of the summit plateau. Most visitors to the summit simply retrace their footsteps from here to Ardvorlich. However, to complete the intended circuit and by so doing add interest to this route, you should not backtrack. Instead, descend to follow a line of rusty fence posts down

Vorlich's SE ridge beyond the summit cairn. A path is beginning to emerge as this route becomes more popular but it is, as yet, quite rudimentary. Navigation, however, should only be problematic in mist.

Keep to the course which descends the crest of the ridge and after approximately 1.2 km (3/4 mile), at MR 638180, strike out ENE. From here, continue down across rough grassy slopes, making for the Allt a' Bhealaich Gliogarsnaiche. The route from the ridge is without a path or any immediate obvious features to guide you, so pick your own way and be very careful to avoid potholes. This is actually far easier than it looks from a distance. On reaching the allt, after about 400 m (1/4 mile), bear 90° and head NNW, keeping to its W side, on a path that is barely a sheep track and make for the Bealach Gliogarsnaich visible immediately ahead.

Entering the bealach, the feeling is more confined and one of greater intimacy with the immediate landscape, the craggy E side of Ben Vorlich rising sharply L and the bouldery slopes of Beinn Domhnuill closing in on your R. On reaching the summit of the bealach, the unmistakable undulations on the skyline in the gap ahead of, first, the Tarmachan Ridge and then Ben Lawers beckon you northward and along Glen Vorlich.

Descending Glen Vorlich to Ardvorlich

Allow 1¾ hours

From the top of Glen Vorlich, beyond the bealach, follow the emerging Ardvorlich Burn keeping to its E side and descending N on a rough and none too obvious sheep track through the heather. Take care as the going can be wet and boggy down across the peat. The route becomes clearer 1.6 km (1 mile) from the bealach as a landrover track is gained, presumably a means of access for the grouse shooters of the estate. Continue on the track to take a NNW bearing. Loch Earn is clearly visible below. On returning to the delightful woodland, after negotiating the Allt a' Choire Bhuidhe by easy rock-hopping, the track continues to improve before rejoining the ascent route. Turn R where it joins to retrace earlier footsteps along the clear track to the road, now walking N, having returned following the Ardvorlich Burn from its source in the bealach to where it enters Loch Earn.

Where the road crosses the burn at the bridge, just before the off-road parking places, note the memorial burial stone: 'Near this spot, we re-interred the bodies of 7 McDonalds of Glencoe killed when attempting to harry Ardvorlich. Anno Domini 1620'.

Alternative routes

ESCAPES

If you get tired or into trouble anywhere on this route, remember that the nearest road and the nearest place of habitation is at Ardvorlich. The easiest and quickest descent from the summit of Ben Vorlich is simply to regain the ascent route and backtrack.

On a warm summer's day, when you might be feeling lazy, enjoy a tranquil afternoon among the birch and rowan of Ben Vorlich's lovely lower reaches, gently rising up above Loch Earn's southern shore.

EXTENSIONS

If bagging Munros is your game, then it makes sense to extend the Ben Vorlich route to take in its neighbour Stuc a' Chroin, 10 m (30 ft) its junior at 975 m (3198 ft) and 2 km (1¼ miles) to the SW.

Descend from Ben Vorlich's summit triangulation pillar following a well-worn path heading W but which a little lower down bears SW. Having descended to the Bealach an Dubh Choirein, a steep path on the R of the crest of the buttress avoids any scrambling to reach the summit of Stuc a' Chroin. Descend by its SE ridge, following it down above the Coire na Rainich. At the bottom, strike off NE for the ruined shieling at Dubh Choirein. From here, turn L walking N along the path to the Bealach Gliogarsnaich, thus later rejoining the suggested Ben Vorlich descent route at its southernmost point. Allow an extra 2½ hours.

Route 6: GLEN FINGLAS

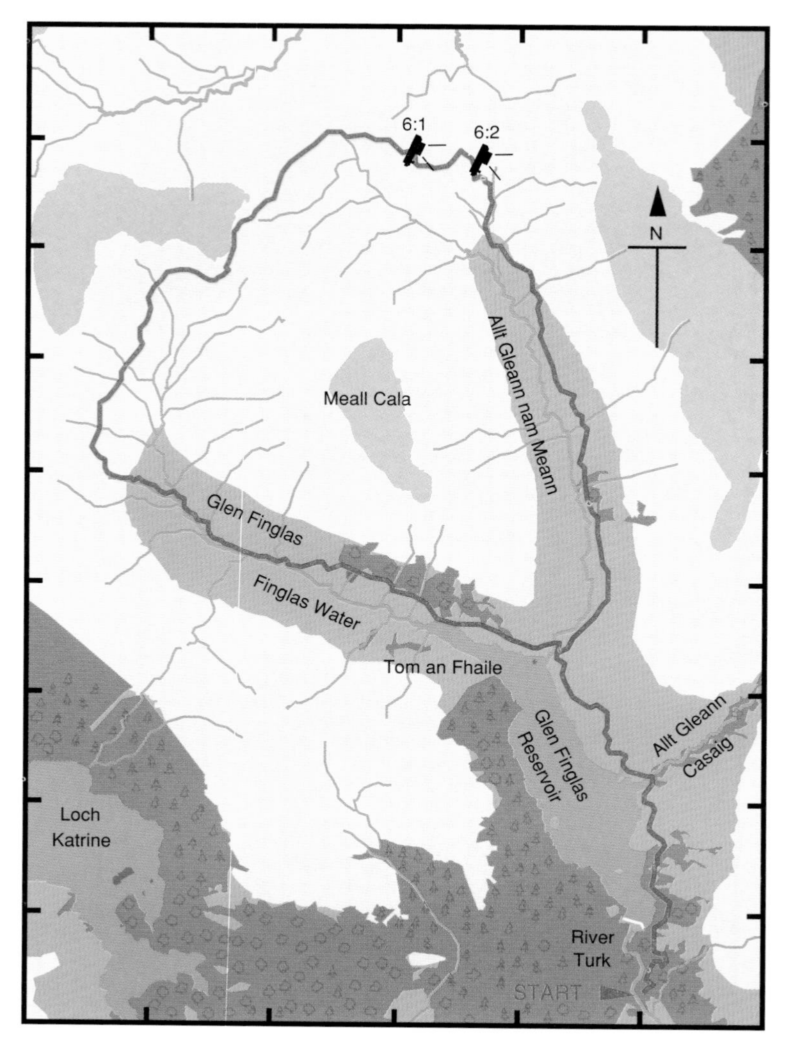

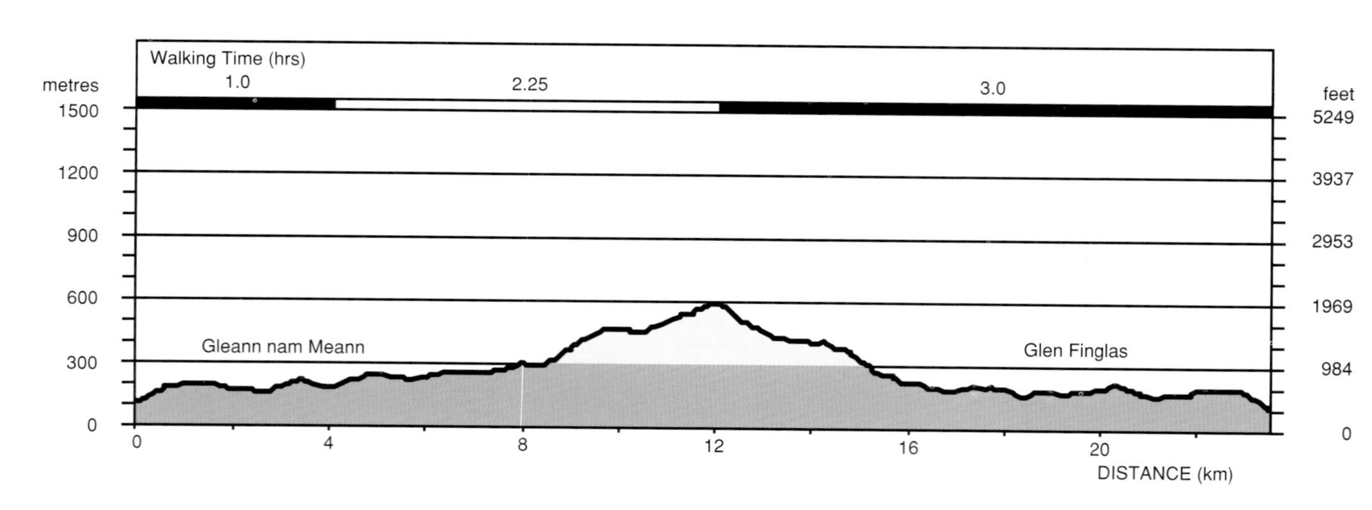

Route 6 · Glen Finglas

STARTING LOCATION
At the end of the single-track road, 1 km (2/3 mile) NNW of the A821 at Brig O' Turk.
OSLR 57 or OSPF 358 and 369/MR 532073.
Roadside parking for about 12 cars, up to the point where cars are prohibited.

ALTERNATIVE STARTING LOCATION
Further parking space at Brig O' Turk village.

PUBLIC TRANSPORT
Nearest railway station – Stirling.
Regular buses Stirling to Callander.
Postbus, twice daily, Callander to Brig O'Turk (except Sunday).

OVERVIEW/INTEREST
Completely traverses two lovely glens.
Good opportunities for observing wildlife, especially red deer and birds including golden eagles, curlew, oyster catchers and wheatear.
Upper reaches of both glens are lonely and remote.
Generally straightforward and undemanding route.

FOOTPATHS
Metalled surface for first and last 2 km (1¼ miles).
Excellent clear and generally dry track designed to take off-road vehicles elsewhere.

GRADING 2

TIME ALLOWANCE
6¼ hours.

DISTANCE

Excluding Height	23.5 km	(14½ miles)
TOTAL HEIGHT GAINED	720 m	(2362 ft)

PRINCIPAL HEIGHTS
None – highest point of the route at MR 497142, 598 m (1962 ft).

Brig O' Turk to Tom an Fhaile *Allow 1 hour*

From the parking place, beyond which unauthorized vehicles are prohibited, walk N taking the R fork in the road on the metalled track signposted 'Footpath to Balquhidder 10 miles'. The L fork is for the power station and the dam.

The route begins as a series of hairpins where the track twists its way uphill passing through an area of birch scrub. A steady, uninterrupted pace is quickly achieved and after 800 m (½ mile), Finglas dam is seen below looking W between trees. Its concrete wall pens back the water of Glen Finglas Reservoir.

Continue walking N, flanking the slopes above the E shore of the reservoir now following the shoreline along the 140 m (460 ft) contour. The track passes over some lovely burns tumbling to the reservoir below. Having walked about 2 km (1¼ miles), descend to the buildings of a farm at the lochside. Ignore the track forking to the R and walk past the farm around the inlet at the bottom of the Allt Gleann Casaig. Head generally NW on the track, the metalled surface having gradually deteriorated to gravel underfoot. Pass through a gate and continue on the lochside route in a series of gentle undulations. On your R, Ben Ledi can be clearly seen looking E.

Having descended on the track and reached a point immediately adjacent to the tiny tree-covered island of Tom an Fhaile, in the reservoir on the L, the track divides and each fork ascends a different glen.

Glen Finglas Reservoir to Carn Dubh *Allow 2¼ hours*

Turning away from the reservoir, take the R fork, the L being the return route, and walk on following the good track NE into the Gleann nam Meann. From here the route begins to follow the course of the tree-lined Allt Gleann nam Meann, upstream on its E side. 800 m (½ mile) into the glen, bear N on the track. You are walking on the glen's only blight, the track having been widened to an erosive scar. The going underfoot, however, remains easy and progress is straightforward. On two separate occasions in this glen, I have seen golden eagles scanning the high slopes of Benvane on the R. The mountain sheltering the W side of the glen, on the L, is Meall Cala and this route makes a complete circuit of it.

Continue N on the R side of the allt and towards its uppermost reaches. Cross a number of burns, the waters of which have been routed beneath the track by plastic piping. Rising gently up into the glen, you eventually reach a sheep fold on the L. On the opposite side of the Allt Gleann nam Meann, the remains of a dry-stone wall adds aesthetic appeal to a harsh environment. At the sheep fold, ford the allt and begin to climb much more steeply N, the allt now more of a small burn on your R. The track bends to the L and then veers quite sharply R near the top of the slopes. About 1 km (⅔ mile) from the sheep fold, bear W. From here, pause for a breath and to contemplate the superb view looking S back down the glen. Rising above it on the L side is Benvane.

6.1 *Benvane from the track above Gleann nam Meann.*

After the level area at Lag a' Phuill, the route climbs again. The track becomes somewhat rougher here in its highest reaches, but even when snow-covered it is easy to follow. Bear SW, for the last section involving ascent, to reach Carn Dubh. A little beyond is the very highest point of the route at 598 m (1962 ft), MR 497142. Ben Ledi's summit can be seen on the skyline SE. Benvane is now visible E and, to the ENE, the summits of Ben Vorlich and Stuc à Chroin rise up on the opposite side of Strathyre.

Carn Dubh to Brig O' Turk *Allow 3 hours*

Descend relatively steeply from Carn Dubh, heading S, and then bear R to contour along the steep slopes of Creagan nan Sgiath. As you descend again more gradually, bear L walking SSW. A number of tiny burns intersect the track on approaching the top of Glen Finglas but are all easily forded. Looking S, the view down into Glen Finglas becomes increasingly more extensive and, beyond it, Ben Venue imposes upon the skyline on the other side of Strath Gartney.

From about the 400 m (1300 ft) contour, begin a much steeper descent, while simultaneously bearing L and walking ESE down into Glen Finglas. After 1 km (⅔ mile) in this direction, and on arriving at a walled sheep fold on the L, ford Finglas Water using stepping stones, either on the L or the R side of the track. This crossing is likely to prove the only significant obstacle on the entire route. In summer at least, it should be easy enough to negotiate by the track. In winter, or when in spate, it may be necessary to venture a little further upstream or down for a convenient crossing point. Continue SE, later bearing ESE, following the route of Finglas Water downstream, on its N side. Make a steady descent down into the glen and towards Glen Finglas Reservoir. Now on the S side of Meall Cala, pass by the predominantly birch woodland that clings to the slopes on the R of the track. Directly ahead lies Ben Ledi, now dominating the view from the N end of the reservoir. Follow the track next to the shoreline on the R. When adjacent again to Tom an Fhaile, bear ENE to cross the Allt Gleann nam Meann over the solid wooden bridge. This is an attractive spot, especially looking NE and upstream from the bridge towards a series of miniature waterfalls, immediately prior to where the allt empties itself into the reservoir on the R of the track. A few paces further bring you to the junction of tracks from where, earlier, the route into Gleann nam Meann began.

Having completed a circuit, retrace earlier footsteps along the E side of Glen Finglas Reservoir to the start point beyond the dam.

6.2 *Looking* ESE *from the track above Gleann nam Meann.*

Alternative routes

ESCAPES

For a lower-level route, this walk is a relatively serious undertaking. At its highest and most northerly points above both glens, remoteness is such that at Carn Dubh the walker is five miles by path or track from the nearest habitation or road. However, from the top of Gleann nam Meann, there is the option of leaving the track on a footpath that forks R heading generally N for 5 km (3 miles) via Gleann Dubh to Glen Buckie. This is the path for Balquhidder. Total distance and time are reduced by nearly one half but you must arrange for transport at the N end. Please note, however, that the path for Balquhidder may have been re-routed since the time of writing, resulting in the departure from the main route being further S.

Another option is to pursue the good track running NE from the farm situated 1.2 km (¾ mile) N of the dam. It begins 2 km (1¼ miles) from the parking place and explores Gleann Casaig.

For walks of a completely different nature, there is a maze of good forest drives and tracks in Achray Forest S of Brig O' Turk, between the village and Loch Drunkie. Also any of the alternatives suggested in the Trossachs routes are conveniently close by.

EXTENSIONS

Although the tracks are generally dry, firm and easy to follow, the main route is nonetheless a long one. However, if you are still sound of limb and persistent of mind, then a brisk ascent of Ben A'an would be the ideal end to your day. The route begins 3 km (2 miles) to the W of Brig O' Turk on the FC path opposite the car park on the S side of the A82 (see Route 2). Allow an extra 2¾ hours including the drive between car parks.

Before leaving the Glen Finglas Reservoir road, a recommended quick sortie allows you to view the impressive and intimately tight gorge cut by Black Water, the flow of which is now controlled by the reservoir dam. From the junction of prohibited roads at the starting point, walk W for 100 m (110 yd) on a path through the woods, returning the same way.

Route 7: BEN CRUACHAN HORSESHOE

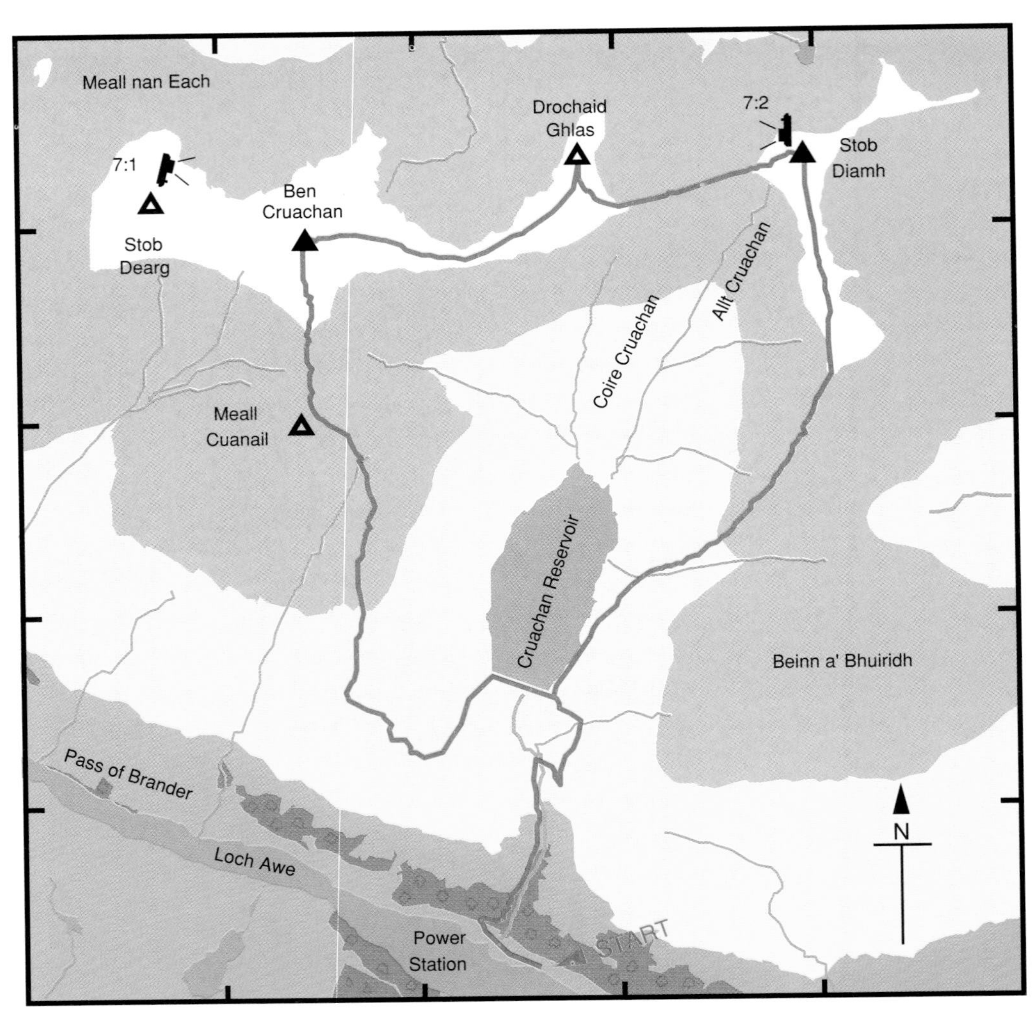

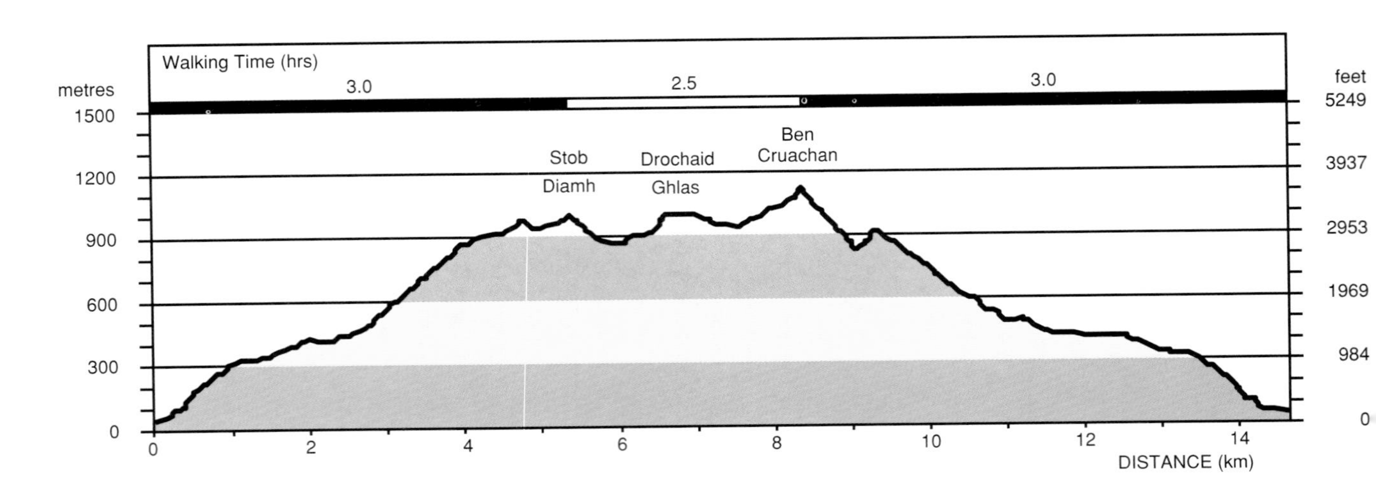

6

ARGYLL

HIGH-LEVEL ROUTE

Route 7 · Ben Cruachan Horseshoe

STARTING LOCATION
Roadside parking 100 m (110 yd) SE of Cruachan power station on N side of A85 in the Pass of Brander.
OSLR 50 or OSPF 332 and 345/MR 080267.
A space cut into the verge accommodates approximately 20 cars.

ALTERNATIVE STARTING LOCATION
Cruachan Power Station Visitors' Centre car park, if you can return by 4.45 p.m.

PUBLIC TRANSPORT
Nearest railway station – Falls of Cruachan.
Postbus, once daily, from both Bridge of Orchy and Inverary to Dalmally (except Sunday).

OVERVIEW/INTEREST
One of the classic high-level ridge traverses of the Central Highlands.
Breathtaking views in all directions from the ridge that forms the skyline above Coire Cruachan.
Includes two Munros and at least three more 'Tops' (other summits over 3000 ft).
Arduous and extremely demanding route.

FOOTPATHS
Eroded, though clear and easily navigable on lower, wooded slopes above Falls of Cruachan.
Good tracks close to dam.
Often wet and peaty between reservoir and ridge.
Ridge itself mostly boulder-strewn and quite hard going in places, requiring some easy scrambling near Ben Cruachan.

GRADING 6

TIME ALLOWANCE
8½ hours.

DISTANCE

Excluding Height	14.6 km	(9 miles)
TOTAL HEIGHT GAINED	1410 m	(4626 ft)

PRINCIPAL HEIGHTS

Ben Cruachan (Mountain of the Mounds)	1126 m	(3694 ft)
Stob Dearg (Red Peak)	1104 m	(3622 ft)
Drochaid Ghlas (Grey Bridge)	1009 m	(3310 ft)
Stob Diamh (Stag Peak)	998 m	(3274 ft)
Meall Cuanail (Hill of the Flocks)	918 m	(3011 ft)

Cruachan Power Station to Stob Diamh

Allow 3 hours

Walk NW beside the A85 until opposite the Cruachan power station. From here, turn R on to a smaller road, passing railway arches seen between trees on the R. After a wooden K-gate, cross the railway near a set of old type signals at the track side and then pass through a metal K-gate on the other side.

Begin walking NNE on a steep path up through oak woodland. The path is rough and rooty but clearly seen. Gradually, views S reveal Loch Awe below, visible at first in the Pass of Brander and then SSE to its many tiny islands and, from higher slopes, a more extensive panorama opens up across Britain's longest stretch of fresh water.

In places, the footpath is badly eroded and deeply pitted but the going is straightforward, though often leaving you breathless through such exertion so early on! However, this at least allows you time to enjoy the interest all around, as you ascend immediately L of the wooded gorge cut by the Allt Cruachan and the Falls of Cruachan. The trees here include some weird and twisted gnarled oak trunks, sculptured this way perhaps by growing in defiance of adversity.

Height is gained quickly. Having emerged from the trees to less steep grassy slopes, continue N walking on wetter ground to pass beneath power cables and beyond pylons which run NW to SE across the hillside. On arriving at the metalled single-track road, used for access by Scottish Power vehicles, turn R. Cruachan Dam is clearly visible immediately N from here. Follow the road to walk over a concrete bridge heading SE for 200 m (220 yd) to a junction with another access road and by a sign on the left indicating 'Cruachan Dam'. From here walk N on a gentle ascent for 600 m (1/3 mile) to meet the dam at its E end. Access through an iron gate allows one to walk on the dam wall. The view N across the reservoir displays the prospect ahead, the ridge roughly spread out in skyline profile before you.

From the dam, continue NNE on the single-track road after passing through an iron gate. The metalled road terminates after 200 m (220 yd) on the E side of the reservoir as the entrance to a mountain tunnel on your R emerges, one which channels water through part of the mountain Beinn a' Bhuiridgh to Cruachan Reservoir. Pass through yet another iron gate to cross this narrow waterway and walk NNE on a rough peaty path just above the reservoir shoreline. Continue on the path that gradually bears NE turning away from, and rising above, the reservoir. On reaching the burn which flows from the Lairig Torran, marked by rowan trees in a gorge, turn more sharply R to follow the burn upstream on its L side. The path becomes much steeper again, and, as you gain height, wetter! Continue on the grassy slopes gradually bearing NNE. Views S beyond the dam become increasingly accessible though the route of the path becomes a little less distinct. Close to MR 093292, pass just to the R of what looks like a triangulation pillar with an iron pole stuck through its top. Then beyond a series of outcrops, an obvious ridge is gained where suddenly impressive views E along the Strath of Orchy to Ben Lui and beyond provide revitalization for the final rocky stretch to the summit cairn of Stob Garbh at 980 m (3215 ft). Walk N to the summit where at once your first views N beyond the ridge of Stob Diamh demand a well-earned savouring. On a clear day, Ben Nevis dominates the distant skyline N. Continue from here on an obvious route N for 800 m (1/2 mile) to Stob Diamh along the narrow but easy ridge path enjoying spectacularly precipitous views into the E-facing corrie.

The summit cairn on Stob Diamh marks the first Munro of the day and offers a superb immediate prospect of the narrow ridge route to Ben Cruachan 3 km (2 miles) W along the back of the horseshoe above exciting and dramatic corrie scenery. Distant mountain views looking N out across Coire Lochain are breathtaking, as is the skyline to the E beyond Strath of Orchy and the panorama S across Loch Awe.

The ridge from Stob Diamh to Ben Cruachan

Allow 2½ hours

From Stob Diamh, walk W, on at first relatively easy ground, descending to a saddle before ascending again along the rim of the corrie, a dramatic glacial bite out of the mountain rock immediately to your R. The path climbs steeply on increasingly harder terrain, Ben Cruachan's distinctive twin summit on the skyline nearly 3 km (2 miles) away inspiring you on along this wonderful high-level ridge path. One feels here that you are on a ridge that crosses what seems an entire mountain range.

Ascend with increasing steepness, approaching the summit of Drochaid Ghlas, negotiating with care its bouldery top, coming close to a scramble in places. On reaching a small cairn, turn R and walk N, away from the main ridge to reach its summit at 1009 m (3310 ft). You will be aware, as you progress W along the ridge, that views N to Ben Nevis improve still further as you come to observe a more complete profile. The view W across Coire Caorach is memorable for me as one of the most impressive in Scotland – superb mountain scenery preluding a backdrop of the two summit masses of

7.1 *The summit of Ben Cruachan from Stob Dearg.*

Ben Cruachan, seen from here in classic cone-like profile.

Return to the cairn, turn R and continue walking W along the ridge to descend across bouldery outcrops for about 500 m (⅓ mile). Then begin the hardest work of the day up along Ben Cruachan's E-facing ridge. Walk with great care between and over large boulders. The route at this stage, with tiring limbs, begins to feel like a scramble! Only the last 50 m (160 ft) require scrambling abilities; however, it is without difficulties and nowhere seriously exposed. A triangulation pillar is reached on the tiny rock platform which constitutes Ben Cruachan's summit. As you would expect of a mountain of 1126 m (3694 ft), it affords extensive views in all directions. The views W must be one of the best from the mainland of the island of Mull, whose single Munro, Ben More, can be seen on the seaward horizon. Beyond and NW even the Cuillin Hills of Skye can be sighted on particularly clear days. From N to E, the following mountains can be seen: E, Ben More and Stob Binnien, Ben Lui; ENE, Beinn Eunaich, Bein Dòrain; NE, Beinn nan Aighenan; NNE, Ben Starav; N, the Mamores, Ben Nevis; NNW, Kintail and Torridon mountains.

From Ben Cruachan to Cruachan Power Station

Allow 3 hours

It is well worth making the excursion out to Stob Dearg, Ben Cruachan's second summit (see 'Extensions'). This finishes in a return to the main summit.

Descend S on a steep, rubbly and often difficult path from the summit. Walk across the boulder field, frequently using hands to steady yourself if need be. Before the Bealach an Lochain, below Meall Cuanail, the terrain becomes more scree-like. On reaching a stile on the L at the top of Coire Dearg, cross to the other side of a line of rusty fence posts and wires and turn R. Continue walking S to begin the last ascent of the day, a prospect which will undoubtedly seem tortuous. Walk steadily on the clear path that follows to the L of the line of rusty fence posts. The posts thus mark the route of the short climb to the large summit cairn of Meall Cuanail whose best views are W and S, those N to E now obscured by the Ben Cruachan ridge. Descend by walking SSE and then continue to follow the fence posts across rock-strewn terrain. These slopes soon give way to easier grassy ground, but going underfoot becomes peaty and noticeably wetter and on a less clear path. From here the fence immediately on your R improves in condition, coinciding with the uppermost browsing range of the ubiquitous black-faced sheep.

Continue L of the fence line. Steepness gradually relents until, after 2 km (1¼ miles) of knee-grinding downward progress, you gain a gravel track at a point a little W of an obvious transmission station (masts not marked on OSLR maps). Turn L on to the track and walk ESE to pass just L of the masts along an approximation of the 460 m (1500 ft) contour, zigzagging as you proceed. The track begins to descend where it turns NNE. Walk down towards the dam to meet it at its W end. Turn R and walk ESE along the concrete top of the dam to gain the access road on the other side. At its E side, turn R at the metalled road, retracing your route and finally descending on the steep path down to the Pass of Brander, thus returning to the start point near Cruachan power station.

7.2 *Drochaid Ghlas and Ben Cruachan's twin peaks from Stob Diamh.*

Alternative routes

ESCAPES

If the prospect of the ridge seems too daunting upon reaching Stob Garbh or Stob Diamh (and you don't have the encumbrance of returning to a car), then you can descend the grassy E-facing slopes from either of these first two summits to the Strath of Orchy and Dalmally. Otherwise, simply retrace your route to return to Cruachan power station.

It should be stressed that the Ben Cruachan Horseshoe traverse is a serious undertaking as there are no quick or easy escapes once on its ridge.

EXTENSIONS

Having reached Ben Cruachan, if time and energy allow, it is also worth extending the excursion to embrace Stob Dearg, Ben Cruachan's more westerly twin peak. At 1104 m (3622 ft) it is 22 m (72 ft) its junior and 800 m (½ mile) to the WNW around Coire Chat. This allows you to prolong a day of memorable views. At the summit of Stob Dearg, look down and along the finger of water that is Loch Etive stretching NNE. It points almost directly to Ben Nevis on the skyline beyond. This optional appendix to the ridge crosses equally bouldery granite terrain and involves a further 400 m (¼ mile) of ascent and descent before returning to Ben Cruachan. Allow an extra 1 hour for this but do not embark upon it if, on first reaching Ben Cruachan, you have less than 3 hours until sunset.

If you enjoy scrambling, then you can add to your thrills by descending the N ridges of either Ben Cruachan or Drochaid Ghlas. Be warned that these options have the additional inconvenience of landing you in the remote Glen Noe.

The main route is in itself physically very demanding. Extensions, other than the short one to Stob Dearg, are not recommended.

Route 8: STRATH of ORCHY

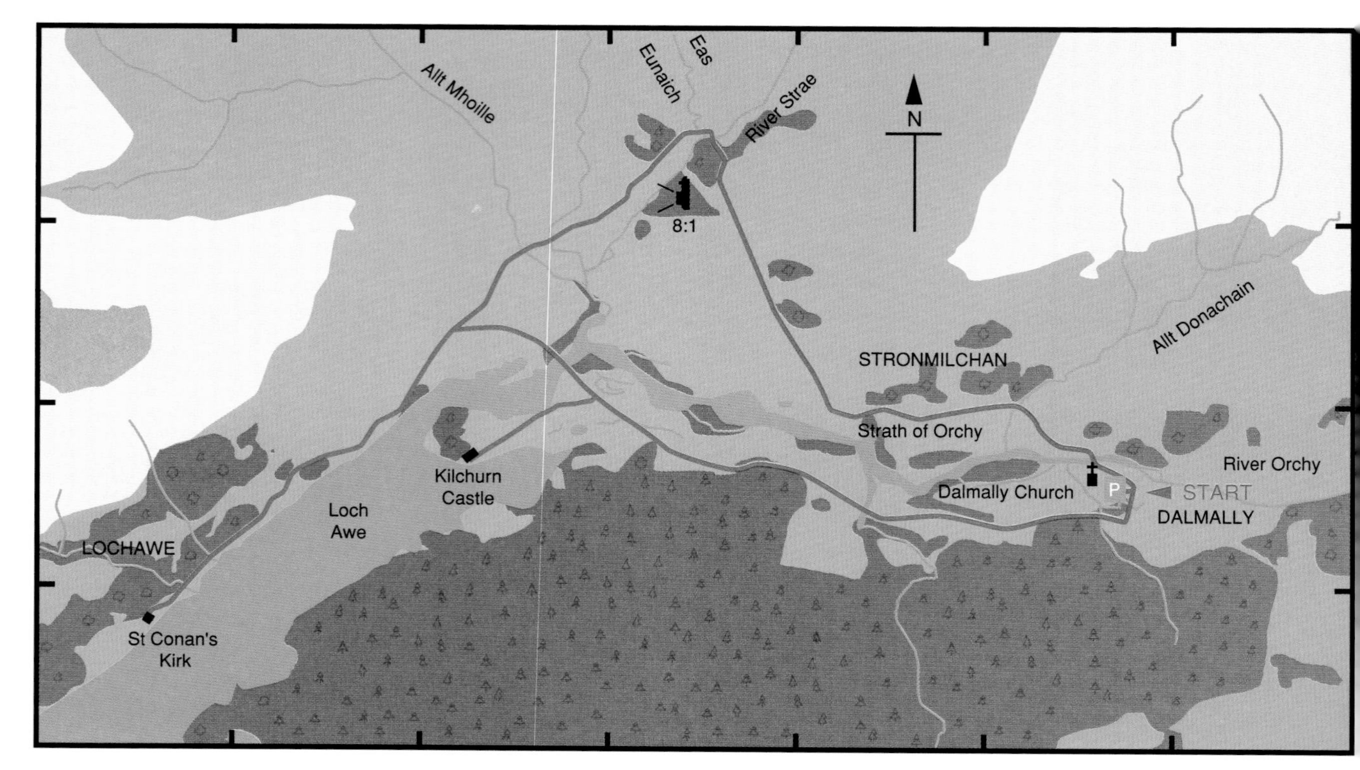

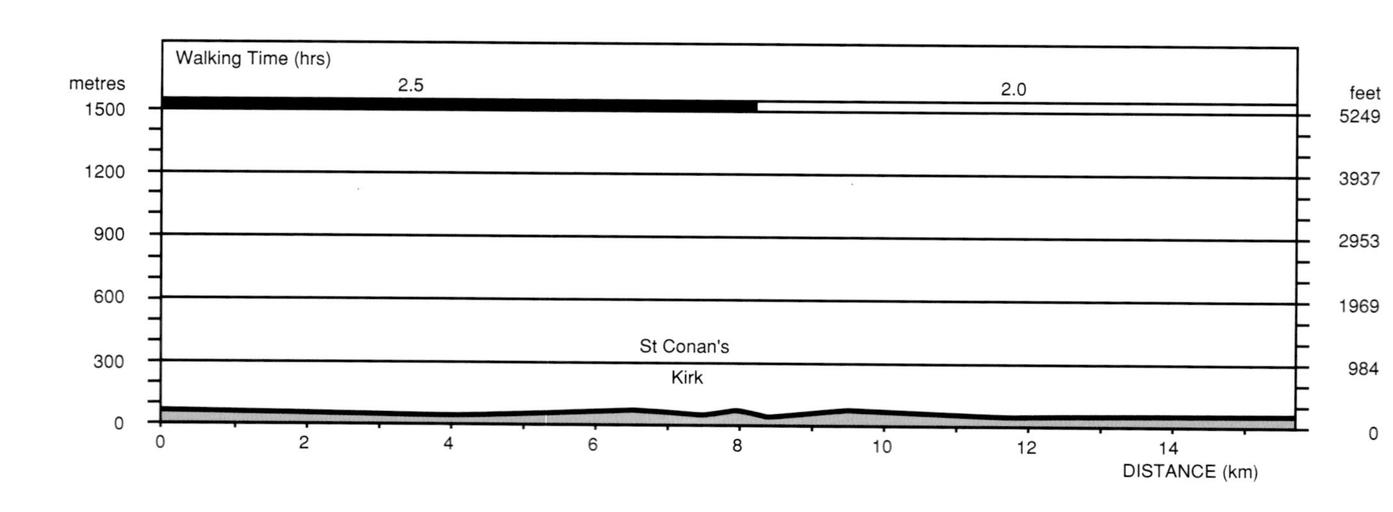

Route 8 · Strath of Orchy

STARTING LOCATION
Dalmally Church car park off the B8077 at Dalmally, 150 m (165 yd) N of junction with A85.
OSLR 50 or OSPF 345/MR 167274.
Accommodates approximately 20 cars.

ALTERNATIVE STARTING LOCATION
Elsewhere in Dalmally.

PUBLIC TRANSPORT
Nearest railway station – Dalmally.
Postbus, once daily, from both Bridge of Orchy and Inverary to Dalmally (except Sunday).

OVERVIEW/INTEREST
Beautiful and impressive architecture of two unusual churches including one of the 'show places' of Argyll.
Explores the photogenic ruins of a castle, once a Campbell headquarters, beside Scotland's longest loch.
Serene lochside and riverside views.
Easy and undemanding route.

FOOTPATHS
Obvious roadside verges and pavements.
Good track on approach to Kilchurn Castle.

GRADING 1
TIME ALLOWANCE
4½ hours.
DISTANCE

Excluding Height	15.8 km	(10 miles)
TOTAL HEIGHT GAINED	60 m	(197 ft)

PRINCIPAL HEIGHTS
None.

Dalmally to St. Conan's Kirk *Allow 2½ hours*

If only to be viewed from the outside, Dalmally church is well worth a visit before leaving the car park. The building sets the tone for the main purpose of this route, which is primarily its architectural and historical interest. As such it is quite unlike any other of the Highland routes in this book. Natural wilderness is for once substituted by human creativity and achievement, although the roadside views are far from devoid of scenic splendour.

Walk over to the gate at the N end of the car park for access to the churchyard. Dalmally Church, with its clean white walls and Italianate style, is a surprise in a Highland village. Originally, a fifteenth century church was built here on what was then an island. Today, the River Orchy flows just to the N, affording a pleasant prospect when seen between trees from the churchyard. The present building was designed in 1810 to a buttressed octagon plan by Edinburgh architect James Elliot. Its roof timbers are said to incorporate the last remnants of the forest of Glen Strae.

The church's interior is less visually striking, a stained-glass window depicting the Good Samaritan being its most impressive feature. At the entrance, in the tower, a scroll amusingly offers visitors 'a choice of Graces':

Church of England:
Oh Lord, grant we may not be like porridge – stiff, stodgy and hard to stir, but like cornflakes – light, crisp and ready to serve.

Church of Scotland:
Oh Lord, grant we may not be like cornflakes – lightweight, empty and cold, but like porridge – warm, comforting and full of natural goodness.

Having thus confirmed your allegiance, turn R on to the road from the car park and walk S over the bridge that crosses a backwater to the River Orchy. After 100 m (110 yd), at the road junction opposite a hotel, cross the A85 to turn R and proceed W along the pavement. Pass by the holding pens of a cattle market on the R and then Dalmally railway station on your L, followed by Glen Orchy Hotel, also on the L.

Beyond a small white farmhouse on the R at Upper Kinchrackine, the pavement terminates. Continue on the grass verge on the L side of the road. Pass a railway embankment on your L and then skirt beside a crash barrier near a burn prior to Kinchrackine Kennels. Dalmally Golf Club is opposite on the R side of the road. At the road junction, cross the A819 Inveraray road. Walk on, gradually bearing NW, and continue on the L-side verge by the A85. Then turn L and pursue a track SW towards Kilchurn Castle. It begins opposite the golf course, now 3 km (2 miles) from Dalmally Church. After 100 m (110 yd), pass through two sets of iron K-gates to cross the railway and continue SW towards the remains of the castle 700 m (⅓ mile) ahead.

Historic Scotland (an Executive Agency of the Scottish Office) manages the monument, now a sad yet beautiful arrangement of ruins and once the Campbell's headquarters. Interpretation panels divulge information regarding the structure of the ruins, but disappointingly little on the castle's history. The best appreciation of this idyllic situation is gained from a climb up the steps of the highest tower. Situated at the far N end of Loch Awe, Scotland's longest loch, the view SW across the water appears studded by numerous wooded islands, the biggest of which are Inishail (Isle of Rest) and Innis Chonain (St. Conan's Island). The buildings of Lochawe dot the steep wooded slopes down to the loch-shore on the R. Ben Lui is seen on the skyline looking E and the three great glens of Glen Lochy, Glen Orchy and Glen Strae radiate NE from the Strath of Orchy.

From Kilchurn Castle, retrace your footsteps to the A85, turn L and walk NW by the L-side verge. Cross the River Orchy by a concrete bridge and then cross the road to the wider grassy verge on the R side. Proceed as far as the road junction with the B8077 on your R. From here, turn SW and walk on the path by the A85 along the N shore of Loch Awe. A detour L to the Driseig Lochside Tearooms can be recommended for refreshments.

Walk on, by the remains of a dry-stone wall, R, below the slopes of Monadh Driseig. Ahead, the large turrets of Cerraig Thura Country House decorate the first building of the hamlet of Lochawe. From here you have the option of crossing the road to gain the pedestrian way on its L side, thus being that bit nearer to the lochside.

Pass a house 'Tower of Glen Strae' and, further down on your L, the multi-turetted Loch Awe Hotel. Soon after, walk to the R of Lochawe station and pier, to the L of a pub and on to Lochawe Stores. Kilchurn Castle can be seen again across the water looking E.

Continue SW and pass other residences along this pleasantly wooded road, coming next to the railway and loch-shore. One cottage is named 'Corries', a reminder of wilder expeditions perhaps. The statue of a soldier on a plinth pays tribute to the memory of the 'Glorious Dead'. Inscribed is the quote : 'Death is swallowed up in Victory.' I doubt that the 'Glorious Dead' would agree! In the trees beyond lies the architectural masterpiece that is the St. Conan's Kirk.

St. Conan's Kirk to Dalmally *Allow 2 hours*

St. Conan's Kirk has acquired a considerable reputation as one of the 'show places' of Argyll. It has a definite air of antiquity despite being quite modern – it was dedicated for worship as recently as 1930. Undeniably elaborate and beautiful, inside and out, the place deserves a visit.

The devoted builder, Walter Campbell, dedicated his many talents to the kirk. He was an unorthodox architect employing many different styles, although most of the kirk is in a Norman or Romanesque tradition. It appears he deliberately tried to include examples of every type of ecclesiastical architecture found in Scotland, more anxious to achieve beauty rather than consistency. After his death in 1914, his sister, and later their Trustees, completed the work. The result is a unique church of elaborate stonework, beautiful interior woodcarvings, stained-glass windows and intricate roof work. It is a peaceful, solemn haven, with a S-facing sundial terrace purposely situated for some of the finest of West Highland views.

From the kirk, turn R on to the A85 and retrace your previous route beside the road for 2 km (1¼ miles). Return to the first junction with the

8.1 *Stob Diamh and the Dalmally Horseshoe from the River Strae near Stronmilchan.*

B8077, where the sign points to 'Stronmilchan, 2 miles'. Then continue NE along this quietly rural single-track road. Cross a bridge over a burn and walk on as if entering Glen Strae ahead. Pass a private estate track on the L and then under power lines to cross hump-back bridges, over first the Eas Eunaich and then the River Strae. The road bears sharply R. Proceed SSE through a plantation area edged in places with deciduous species. A track on the R, through the trees heading SW, follows the River Strae on its E side for a few hundred metres. This recommended detour is rewarded with fine views to an attractive arrangement of mountains to the NW known as the Dalmally Horseshoe.

Back on the B8077, continue SSE along the edge of the broad Strath of Orchy – a scene of rural serenity extending as far as Kilchurn Castle. In spring, cuckoo-flower (lady's-smock) provides floral warnings of wetter ground on the R.

At Stronmilchan, bear L and walk E in front of its quaint cottages on the L. Ben Lui can be seen directly ahead. When opposite an idyllic cottage in a woodland setting, bear sharp R on the road, cross Dalmally Bridge over the River Orchy and pass a war memorial on your R. Proceed a little further ESE to Dalmally Church and your car.

Alternative routes

ESCAPES

Navigational problems should not present themselves on this most civilized route. The only potential dangers are from traffic on the fast A85, which can be busy in summer. The route is quite long and can be shortened by omitting visits to either of the two churches or to Kilchurn Castle. However, visits to them all are recommended, even if you have to drive between them. For itself, the unfrequented B8077 makes for a glorious evening stroll.

EXTENSIONS

Two obvious and rewarding extensions are possible from the Strath of Orchy. Consider pursuing the track NE into Glen Strae beside the River Strae. Turn L off the B8077 at MR 145294. Alternatively, explore Glen Orchy on the track leaving Dalmally Bridge at MR 166277. Walk E and then veer NE along the L side of the River Orchy.

Route 9: BUACHAILLE ETIVE MÓR

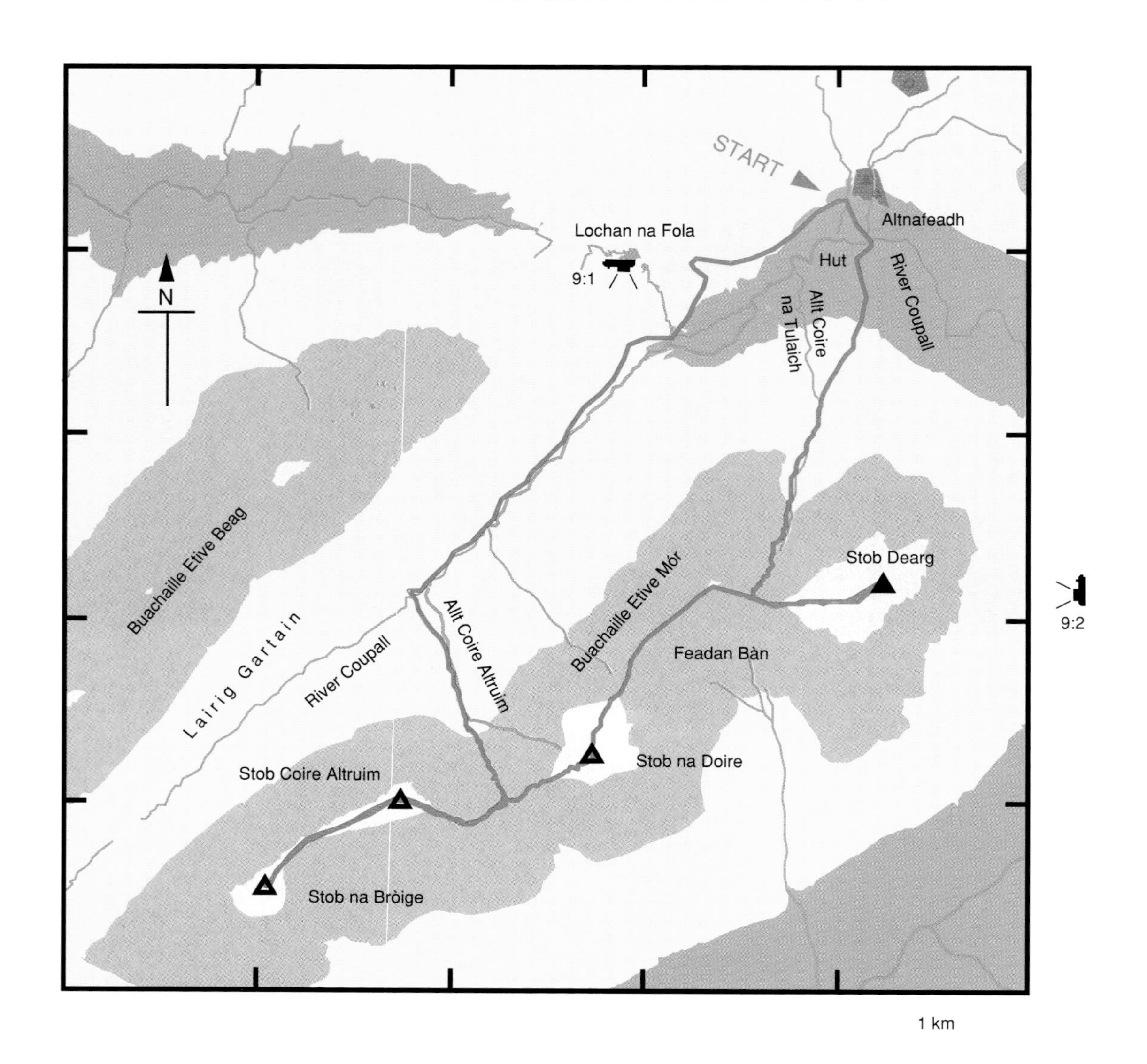

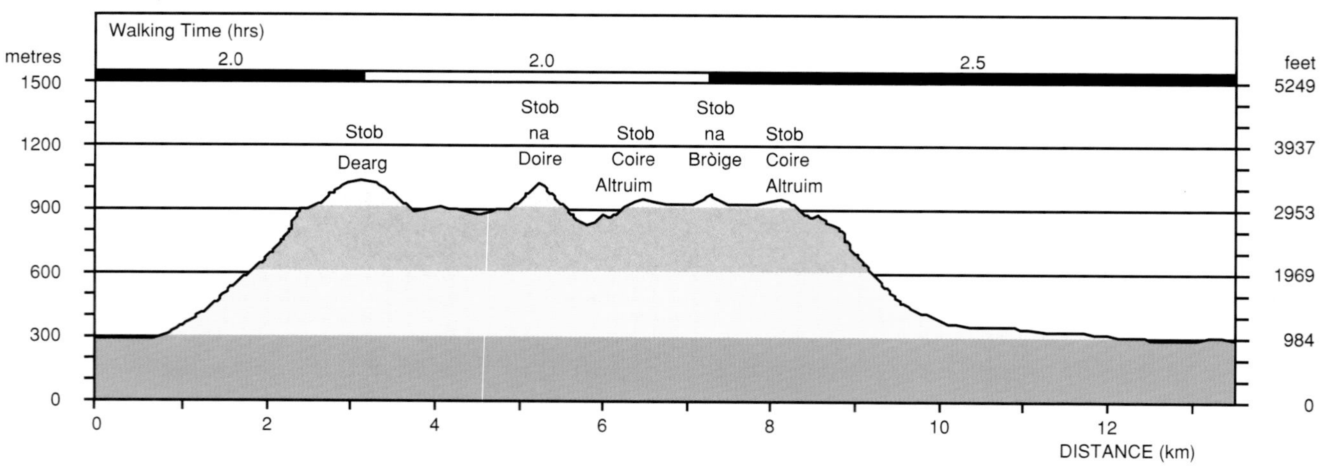

7

GLEN COE (SOUTH)

HIGH-LEVEL ROUTE

Route 9 · Buachaille Etive Mór

STARTING LOCATION
Altnafeadh on the A82 Glen Coe road 5 km (3 miles) WNW of King's House Hotel.
OSLR 41 or OSPF 305 and 306/MR 220563.
Verges on both sides of the road.
Accommodates approximately 20 cars.

ALTERNATIVE STARTING LOCATION
Alternative roadside parking 1 km (⅔ mile) WSW of Altnafeadh (see Route 10).

PUBLIC TRANSPORT
Nearest railway station – Bridge of Orchy or Fort William.
Regular buses, five daily, Glasgow to Glencoe or Fort William to Glencoe.
Postbus, once daily, from Fort William and Glencoe along A82 to Glen Etive (except Sunday).

OVERVIEW/INTEREST
High-level ridge traverse on one of Scotland's finest mountains.
Outstanding views across Rannoch Moor, Glen Coe and beyond.
Includes one Munro – Stob Dearg.
Steep ascent and descent to and from the ridge.
Navigational difficulties likely in mist.
Physically very demanding over often difficult terrain.

FOOTPATHS
No waymarking.
Wet and peaty on descent from the ridge and in the Lairig Gartain.
Arduous, well-worn but generally dry in the Coire na Tulaich.
Obvious and mostly dry and sure on the ridge.

GRADING 5

TIME ALLOWANCE
6½ hours.

DISTANCE

Excluding Height	13.6 km	(8½ miles)
TOTAL HEIGHT GAINED	1130 m	(3707 ft)

PRINCIPAL HEIGHTS
Buachaille Etive Mór (Big Shepherd of Etive):
Stob Dearg (Red Peak) 1022 m (3352 ft)
Stob na Doire (Peak of the Grove) 1011 m (3316 ft)
Stob Coire Altruim (Peak of the Corrie of Rearing) 939 m (3080 ft)
Stob na Bròige (Peak of the Hoof) 955 m (3133 ft)

Altnafeadh to Stob Dearg *Allow 2 hours*

A much favoured subject for the camera, adorning countless postcards, calendars and book covers, Buachaille Etive Mór is the mountain sentinel at the eastern approach to Glen Coe. As a huge rock cone, it rears up above the wet desert of Rannoch Moor. Appearing entirely impregnable, the cliffs and buttresses of Stob Dearg are nonetheless considered by climbers as some of the best routes in the Highlands. Contrary to first impressions, the Buachaille is not beyond the capabilities of walkers. This finest of mountains has but one significant weakness in its defences: the climbers' descent route via the Coire na Tulaich. Those inexperienced on highland terrain, however, would be advised to ensure that Route 11 is completed without difficulty before attempting Buachaille Etive Mór.

Strike off from the S side of the road at Altnafeadh and head SSE on the good track. Cross the River Coupall via a sturdy wooden footbridge

and immediately bear R to pass the Lagangarbh climbers' hut, on your R. Walk S from the hut by the obvious path leading to the base of Buachaille Etive Mór. The track divides after a further 250 m (275 yd). Take the R fork and pursue the well-worn path over the moor, heading SSW towards the corrie ahead. Gently rising at first, glance to your R to view the ridge profile of Buachaille Etive Beag (Little Shepherd of Etive).

From the bottom of the Coire na Tulaich, cross boulder-strewn ground and then commence a steep ascent alongside the Allt Coire na Tulaich. Stay on a SSW bearing, without deviating from the path that rises up along the R wall of the corrie. The allt is on your L and should be followed upstream as far as its source. Steadily gaining height, persevere on a rugged and arduous course between tapering rock walls, inducing a sense of being increasingly enclosed. An expanding vista to your rear reveals the commanding summit of Ben Nevis as well as many of the Mamores. As you proceed deep into the coire, ever more steeply, expect an eerie accompaniment from the ravens. Near the top of the corrie, take to the unavoidable shifting scree which litters the final gruelling approach to the ridge. It seems that for every two steps forward you take a sliding one back!

Even as late as July, the gully at the very head of the corrie may be snow-filled. In summer, however, this is unlikely to impede progress. On gaining the large cairn on the ridge, turn L and walk E, pursuing less demanding slopes thereafter. Continue your ascent along the more stable ryolite of the ridge to the appropriately named Stob Dearg (Red Peak). Small cairns depict the route of a path over the bare rock. On approaching the summit, veer L and proceed along a narrowing ridge as far as the two large cairns. One of these rock piles has been fashioned to serve as a weather break, much welcomed in gales for quieter contemplation of your hard-won reward: an all-encompassing panorama. Breathtaking in extent, some noteworthy mountains in view include: E, Schiehallion; SE, Stob a' Ghlais Choire, Meall a' Bhuiridh; SSW, Ben Starav, Ben Cruachan;

9.1 *Buachaille Etive Mór from Lochan na Fola.*

W, Bidean nam Bian; WNW, Sgorr nam Fiannaidh, Meall Dearg; NNW, Ben Nevis, Carn Mór Dearg; N–NW, the Mamores.

Dramatic and always solemn, the glacial trough of Glen Coe (Glen of Weeping) dominates the view below to the NW. By contrast, the near landscape to the E is strikingly different in character. Rannoch Moor, over 300 m (1000 ft) above sea level, is a vast, flat, peaty wilderness of endless hags, lochans and bogs. On close acquaintance, this wasteland possesses a stark and desolate beauty of a kind one might encounter on another planet. Rannoch Moor is proof indeed that flat terrain is not necessarily ideal walking country.

Stob Dearg to Stob na Bròige *Allow 2 hours*

Leave the summit and walk back along the ridge, returning to the cairn at the top of the Coire na Tulaich. On the skyline ahead, alpine-like and inspirational, the beautiful peaks of the Bidean nam Bian group are the making of a mountain lover's day.

Walk on W, gently rising for a while to reach a cairn at 902 m (2960 ft). Turn L and follow the ridge SW, here grass-covered and indented by dark peaty pools. Seen across the Lairig Gartain on your R, Buachaille Etive Beag echoes a parallel SW running ridge in more modest terms.

Descend a few metres to the foot of the next peak. Then, from the last sizable water-filled hollow, walk uphill on tougher terrain again. After more than 100 m (330 ft) of re-ascent, pause at the tiny summit cairn of Stob na Doire. Fine views into Glen Etive add to the memorable rewards of this ridge. On a distant horizon SSW, Ben Cruachan refuses to be ignored.

Leave the summit of Stob na Doire by pursuing the continuing ridge path WSW. Clamber down, enduring an awkward descent. Walk between the Coire Altruim on your R and the Coire na Doire on your L to reach the lowest point in the ridge after Stob na Doire. A cairn indicates your point of departure from the mountain top via the slopes to the R. However, your immediate objective is to complete the ridge traverse.

9.2 *Buachaille Etive Mór from the River Coupall in Glen Etive.*

From the cairn in the bealach, ascend to a point where the ridge broadens. Veer R and follow the path WNW up around the rim of the Coire Altruim. Reduced to a pleasant uphill stroll, the summit cairn on Stob Coire Altruim is quickly gained. Looking NW beyond Buachaille Etive Beag and the Three Sisters, the notorious dizzy ridge of the Aonach Eagach teases.

Leave the summit and resume your orientation WSW. Descend gentle grassy slopes before re-ascending towards the conspicuous summit cairn ahead. Invariably, this southern section of the mountain is noticeably less busy than the Munro end. In summer, sheep find the happy combination of high-level grazing and the infrequency of walkers much to their liking: you can expect to startle a blackface on your approach to Stob na Bròige. Its very large summit cairn adorns the southern extremity of the ridge. Not surprisingly, it is a superlative vantage point to Loch Etive with Ben Starav now that little bit nearer.

Stob na Bròige to Altnafeadh

Allow 2½ hours

Turning away from Stob na Bròige, pursue the ridge path in reverse. After less than a mile, regain the cairn at the bealach below Stob na Doire. Depart from the ridge by turning L on to the rough steep slopes at the top of the Coire Altruim. Apply a cautious approach down the first few awkward metres before encountering a more conventional, though still very steep, path. Continue your descent NNW to pick up the course of the emerging Allt Coire Altruim on your R. In clear conditions, Ben Nevis should be obvious on the skyline directly ahead.

On the way down, all intervening tributary burns flowing in from the L are easily forded. Relief from constant knee-jarring is enjoyed on the gentler gradients of the lower slopes. However, care is again required as the ground leading into the Lairig Gartain is especially wet and slippery. Where the Allt Coire Altruim divides, stay beside the L-hand watercourse as far as its eventual confluence with the River Coupall. Ford the River Coupall to the L of the Allt Coire Altruim via a rudimentary weir or by boulder-hopping at any other convenient point. If the river is running high, it may be necessary to seek a narrower, shallower crossing point further upstream.

From the N side of the river, climb up the grassy bank to gain the main Lairig Gartain footpath. Turn R and follow the gently descending path NE. In a reverse of the first 4 km (2½ miles) of Route 10, pursue where possible the undulating raised peat bank on the W side of the River Coupall. Between the two 'shepherds' (Buachailles) at their Glen Coe ends, veer L a little away from the river. The tranquil sound of water is given up for the less agreeable tone of traffic ahead.

In early summer, orchids and butterwort offer botanical interest, diverting your attention perhaps while traversing a series of loathsome peat hags. Ford a burn between them. Where the path divides, take the peaty one to the R. Bear NNE, after 400 m (¼ mile) emerging at the S side of A82. Turn R and walk along the busy road for 1 km (⅔ mile) to your car at Altnafeadh. Glance back to view the classic U-shaped valley of the Lairig Gartain.

Alternative routes

ESCAPES

Having 'bagged' Stob Dearg, Munroists need go no further on Buachaille Etive Mór. The other three peaks over 914 m (3000 ft) on the mountain are merely 'Tops' in Munro's Tables. Simply return to Altnafeadh back down the Coire na Tulaich. At the top of the coire, even greater care is required on the descent. Returning by the ascent route is also advisable should you get misted-out on Stob Dearg. Allow 4 hours overall. If such conditions seem likely from the outset, the lower-level route would be a far safer and more rewarding option.

It is feasible to descend from the bealach below Stob na Doire by the S-facing slopes to Glen Etive. A more rugged option to Glen Etive is SW from Stob na Bròige. Neither route seems logical for those with a car at Altnafeadh, however they allow for the quickest descent to the road from the S end of the ridge.

EXTENSIONS

Further extensions are not recommended due to the rigours and physical demands of the main route. In any case a continuation is not possible without first descending and re-ascending elsewhere as Buachaille Etive Mór is a detached mountain.

Very energetic walkers have the option of combining both the high-level and lower-level routes suggested for Glen Coe (South). Having descended the ridge as described, turn L at the River Coupall and proceed via the Lairig Gartain and the Lairig Eilde, finishing the day as for Route 10. Allow an extra 3 hours.

Other opportunities for expeditions around Glen Coe and Glen Etive are infinite and the area could easily justify several chapters. For strong walkers, with well-practised scrambling skills, the Aonach Eagach ridge traverse offers the greatest challenge.

Route 10: LAIRIG GARTAIN and LAIRIG EILDE

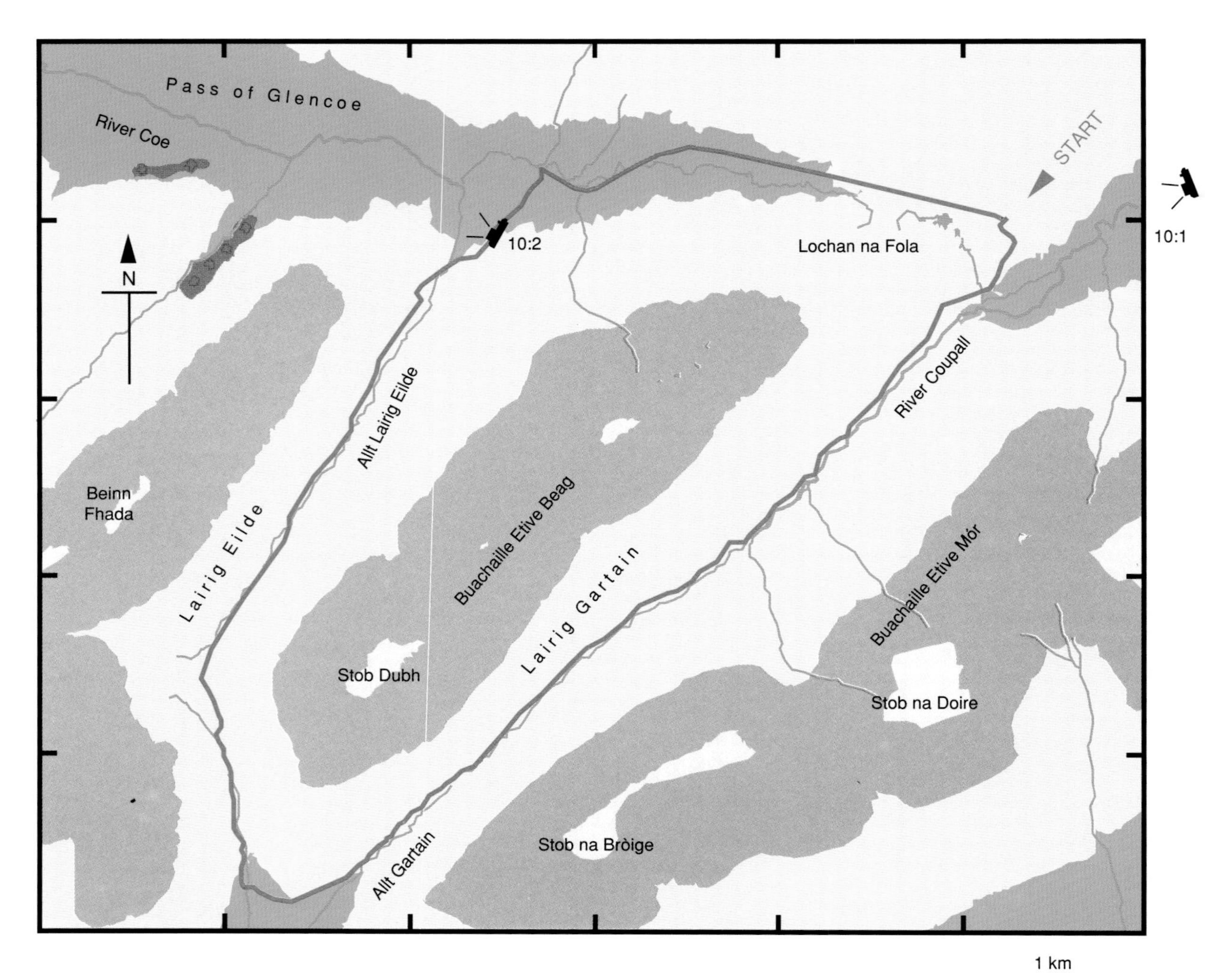

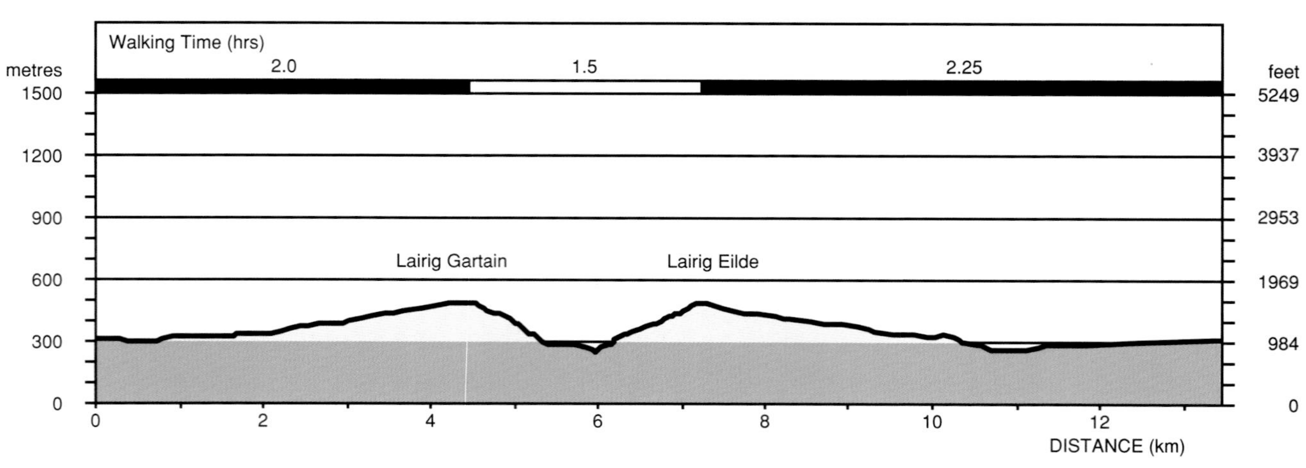

Route 10 · Lairig Gartain and Lairig Eilde

STARTING LOCATION
Parking bay on S side A82 in Glen Coe, 1 km (2/3 mile) WSW of Altnafeadh near River Coupall.
OSLR 41 or OSPF 305 and 306/MR 213559.
Accommodates approximately 25 cars.

ALTERNATIVE STARTING LOCATION
Parking at Altnafeadh and at the area known as The Study, near the waterfall.

PUBLIC TRANSPORT
Nearest railway station – Bridge of Orchy or Fort William.
Regular buses, five daily, Glasgow to Glencoe or Fort William to Glencoe.
Postbus, once daily, from Fort William and Glencoe along A82 to Glen Etive (except Sunday).

OVERVIEW/INTEREST
Important historical significance as centuries-old mountain passes, both Lairigs, were used frequently by the MacDonalds.
Glen Coe itself, site of the notorious 1692 massacre of the MacDonald clan by the Campbells.
Dramatic mountain scenery in the environs of Scotland's most famous glen.
Physically quite demanding.

FOOTPATHS
Wet and muddy in places, especially in Lairig Gartain.
Drier, rocky terrain near Lairig summits.
Steep at the Glen Etive end.
A final flat section by the roadside.
Few navigational problems.

GRADING 3

TIME ALLOWANCE
5¾ hours.

DISTANCE

Excluding Height	13.4 km	(8½ miles)
TOTAL HEIGHT GAINED	490 m	(1608 ft)

PRINCIPAL HEIGHTS
Lairig Gartain (Gartain is a man's name) 490 m (1608 ft)
Lairig Eilde (Pass of the Hinds) 496 m (1627 ft)

Altnafeadh to the summit of the Lairig Gartain *Allow 2 hours*

On a path that begins immediately R of the parking bay, walk SSW towards the entrance of the obvious U-shaped glacial valley, the Lairig Gartain. The going underfoot normally commences in a wet and muddy way but persevere across the peat hags, between which numerous tiny burns must be negotiated. Ascend gradually to where, after about 400 m (¼ mile), the path becomes more clearly marked and the ground somewhat drier. Walk towards the sound of more prominent water coming closer to the River Coupall.

Continue SW on the path up into the Lairig Gartain, a once important mountain pass sheltered on the L by the mountain of Buachaille Etive Mór and on the R by Buachaille Etive Beag. Even after long dry spells you may not escape the wet

10.1 *Buachaille Etive Beag from Altnafeadh.*

areas of grass and peat. However, navigation is never a problem. Simply follow the route of the River Coupall upstream to its source on higher ground in the Lairig. The river is always on your L.

Progressing gradually along the pass the terrain becomes rather featureless. Continue walking in an undulating way along a high bank where the preserved root systems of Scots pines protrude from the peat. Near to where they flow into the river, ford numerous small burns which drain the steep slopes of Buachaille Etive Beag, on your R. Maintain a SW bearing.

About 3 km (2 miles) up into the Lairig, approach the edge of a rocky little gorge above the river to view a particularly spectacular water shoot at the top of a waterfall. Follow the route of the river which, soon after, becomes more of a trickle. On nearing the crest of the pass, its numerous feeder-burns have now been left behind. Close to the source of the river, the path becomes less clear again but a series of prominent cairns mark the route. Walk on to the last and largest of them. This one marks the crest of the pass at 490 m (1608 ft), close to its S end and above that loveliest of glens, Glen Etive. The view SW along the River Etive to distant Loch Etive, beyond Glen Etive Forest, is superb. Its mountain sentinel, the huge mass of Ben Starav, rises up above the N end of the loch.

The summit of the Lairig Gartain to the summit of the Lairig Eilde *Allow 1½ hours*

Walk on SW, descending steeply to the R of the Allt Gartain and soon crossing a particularly bouldery section. This would seem to be an entirely unplanned obstacle adding some difficulty to the route, although a path is quickly being worn across it. However, exercise caution in your footwork. To the R, high upon slopes below Stob Dubh, Buachaille Etive Beag's southernmost peak, a huge scar provides evidence of the dramatic landslide that deposited thousands of tons of rock along a previously good path. Traverse carefully the interruption, which lasts for about 30 m (30 yd), and then continue descending on the clear path again SW towards Dalness. Dalness House lies one mile ahead at the roadside below in Glen Etive. Where the path forks at about the 250 m (820 ft) contour, turn R to skirt the steep southern slopes of Buachaille Etive Beag and walk W away from the Allt Gartain. Descend into a depression to cross the burn from the Lairig Eilde, bearing NW as you do so. If in spate, the water-course should be forded further downstream. Climb the opposite bank, quickly joining a good path from Dalness from the L. Turn R on to the path and walk N, keeping L of the burn, followed upstream, and ascending the Lairig Eilde. The path is steep but in relatively good condition. From here, look behind you S for an impressive view of Beinn Ceitléin that rises up steeply opposite, constituting the mountain wall which shelters Glen Etive on its E side at Dalness. An attractive waterfall is passed before fording the upper reaches of the burn. On reaching the crest of the Lairig Eilde, about a mile up into the pass, a large cairn marks the summit on ground that has become increasingly bouldery after passing below the steep craggy slopes of Stob Coire Sgreamhach, L.

The summit of the Lairig Eilde to Altnafeadh *Allow 2¼ hours*

From the cairn, walk NNE on a clear path that soon joins the route of the Allt Lairig Eilde, following it along its E side. After 800 m (½ mile), ford the allt by rock-hopping and climb up the bank on the other side to continue along the path on the W side of the Allt Lairig Eilde. The Lairig Eilde is sheltered on its W side by Beinn Fhada, the most easterly of the Three Sisters of Glencoe, and on its E side by the gentler slopes of Buachaille Etive Beag.

Walk on the clear path immediately below the steeply rising slopes of Beinn Fhada on your L. The route continues NNE to the L of the Allt Lairig Eilde, descending gradually. Emerging at the N end of the pass, ford the allt again to regain the E side and walk NE, while contouring for a short distance the NW slopes of Buachaille Etive Beag and leaving the allt behind you. A good path should be followed which bears NNE again. Before descending more steeply, take time to contemplate one of the finest views of Glen Coe, seen from here as a dramatic but broad glacial trough. The glen lies between the Three Sisters, a trio of high rocky protrusions in a line E to W, and a seemingly unbreachable mountain wall on the R. The high-level ridge that connects these mountains on the N side of the glen is the Aonach Eagach, laying claim to being the finest ridge on the Scottish mainland and the most sensational of scrambles. The high peaks above Glen Coe are often obscured, typically shrouded in low clouds and swirling mist, which can nonetheless add to an atmosphere of drama and mystery.

With the busy A82 again visible, descend heathery slopes and continue on a path NNE. The path emerges at the road opposite a large precision-made cairn looking like a dry-stone igloo. Cross the road, turn R and walk E by the roadside for 2.5 km (1½ miles) to return to the start point, taking care as this is one of the fastest and busiest roads in the Highlands.

Having almost completed a low-level circuit of Buachaille Etive Beag, make time for a final pause at Lochan na Fola. The car park is a further 400 m (¼ mile) on the R.

Alternative routes

ESCAPES

The route can be just as easily walked in an anticlockwise direction.

There are no escapes from either the Lairig Gartain or the Lairig Eilde other than by descending from them N into Glen Coe for the A82 or S into Glen Etive to gain the minor road. If you are not confident about contouring the steep slopes from the Lairig Gartain, then descend all the way to Dalness before ascending in the Lairig Eilde. You could effectively reduce the total distance and time of the route by about half by terminating at Glen Etive, that is assuming you can arrange transport from Dalness.

Alternatively, you need not strike out at all from Glen Coe. The glen itself has many low-level tracks and paths. In particular, consider the Pass of Glen Coe immediately W from where the Allt Lairig Eilde joins the River Coe.

10.2 *Looking WNW into Glen Coe from the bottom of the Lairig Eilde.*

A descent NW along the Lairig Gartain from near its summit to Glen Coe is the return route from Buachaille Etive Mór (see Route 9).

EXTENSIONS

Possibilities for low-level extensions are numerous within Glen Coe itself. If energy permits after having made a descent from the Lairig Eilde to the A82, turn L and walk W into Glen Coe exploring the roadside paths as described above. This will simply leave you with a longer roadside walk E before returning to the start point. At the S end of the main route, the beautifully scenic Glen Etive is also well worth exploring.

Having completed the main route, the footpath from Altnafeadh to the top of the Devil's Staircase, 1.5 km (1 mile) N, is highly recommended. The views N from it to Ben Nevis and the Mamores and S to Buachaille Etive Mór are exceptionally impressive. At 550 m (1800 ft), this is the highest point of the 150 km (95 mile) West Highland Way, Scotland's first long-distance footpath. Allow an extra 1½ hours for this.

The section of the WHW that traverses the western edge of the remote Rannoch Moor is also a rewarding expedition, best saved for another day. Walk S on the track from the King's House Hotel.

Route 11: PAP OF GLENCOE and SGORR NAM FIANNAIDH

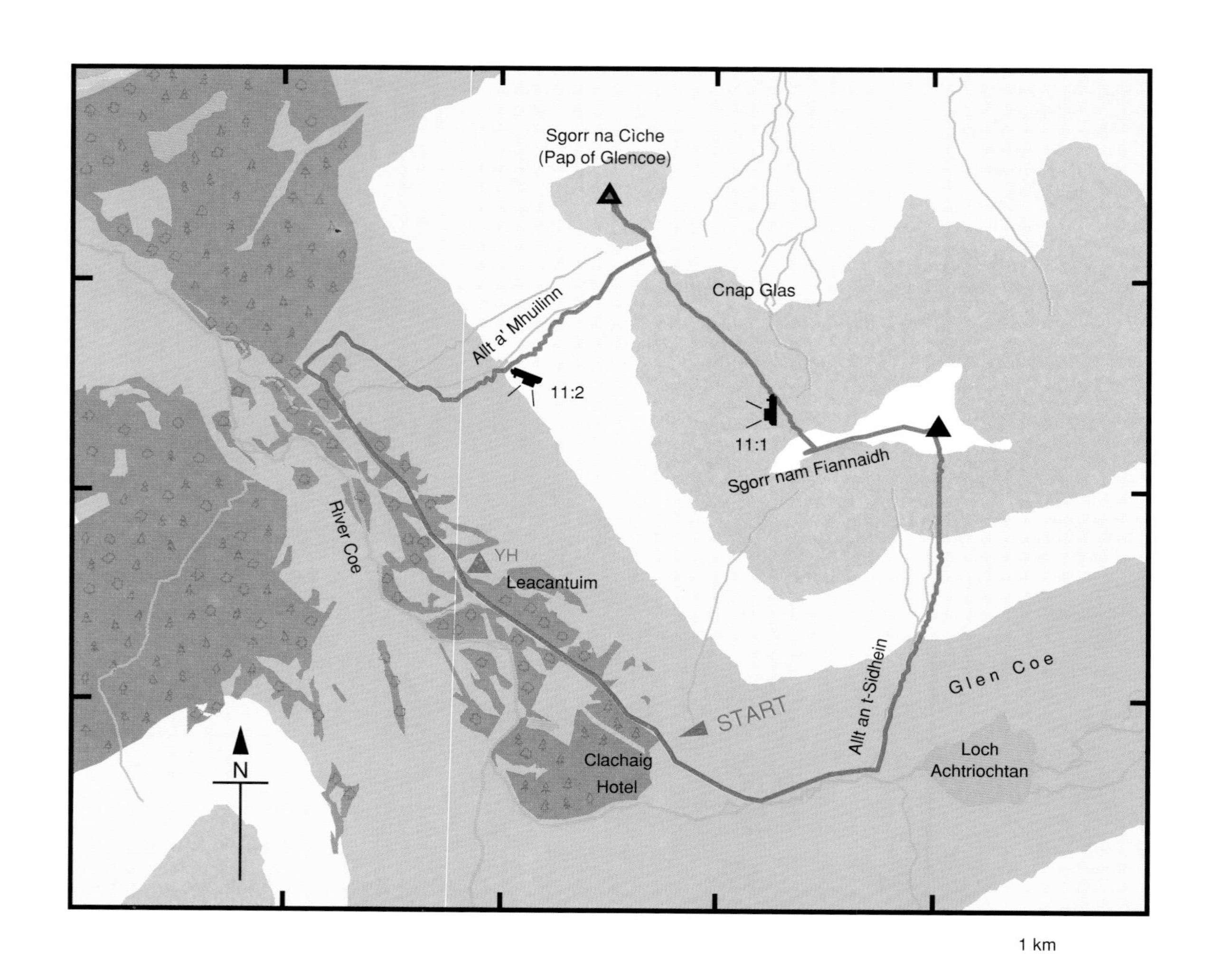

Walking Time (hrs)

2.5 | 1.5 | 1.5

metres: 0, 300, 600, 900, 1200, 1500

feet: 0, 984, 1969, 2953, 3937, 5249

Sgorr na Cìche (Pap of Glencoe)

Sgorr nam Fiannaidh

0 2 4 6 8 10

DISTANCE (km)

8

GLEN COE (NORTH)

HIGH-LEVEL ROUTE

Route 11 · Pap of Glencoe and Sgorr nam Fiannaidh

STARTING LOCATION
The Clachaig Inn, on the minor road which serves Glencoe, 1.2 km (3/4 mile) W of its junction with the A82.
OSLR 41 or OSPF 305/MR 128567.
Car park at the Inn or by the roadside thereabouts. Non patrons to the Inn are advised to seek permission.
Accommodates at least 25 cars.

ALTERNATIVE STARTING LOCATION
Car park at the NTS Visitors' Centre, 400 m (1/4 mile) S of the Inn.

PUBLIC TRANSPORT
Nearest railway station – Bridge of Orchy or Fort William.
Regular buses, five daily, Glasgow to Glencoe or Fort William to Glencoe.
Postbus, once daily, from Fort William and Glencoe along A82 to Glen Etive (except Sunday).

OVERVIEW/INTEREST
A good introduction to high-level walking in the Glen Coe area.
Outstanding views across Loch Leven, the Mamores and Glen Coe.
Includes one Munro summit.
Extremely steep descent.
Route-finding problems likely in mist.
A physically demanding route.

FOOTPATHS
No waymarking.
Minor road at lowest levels.
Ascent to ridge by rough track and path.
Eroded and steep on summit cone.
Mostly unpathed but easy going on traversing the broad ridge.
Loose, scree-ridden and potentially treacherous at first on descent.

GRADING 4

TIME ALLOWANCE
5 1/2 hours.

DISTANCE

Excluding Height	10.2 km	(6 1/4 miles)
TOTAL HEIGHT GAINED	1110 m	(3642 ft)

PRINCIPAL HEIGHTS
Pap of Glencoe or Sgorr na Cìche (Peak of the Breast)
742 m (2434 ft)
Sgorr nam Fiannaidh (Peak of the Fians)
967 m (3172 ft).

Clachaig Inn to the Pap of Glencoe

Allow 2 1/2 hours

Head off NW from the Clachaig Inn, along the minor road which serves Glencoe village. Pass an enclosure of conifers on your L. Soon after, deciduous species predominate by the roadside and a burn is never far away on your L.

After the campsite, the road bears R as you pass a youth hostel on your L. Continue NNW, beyond the driveway, to the bunkhouses at Leacantium. The distinctive pale summit of your first objective, the Pap of Glencoe, reveals itself between gaps in the trees on the skyline, looking NNE. Draining the hill slopes on your R, numerous tiny burns pass under the road. Since the A82 replacement on the W side of the River Coe, this now mostly redundant thoroughfare is blissfully unfrequented. Wriggling between ash, alder and pine, the road retains a delightful rural charm.

A noticeable black gate on your L bars the top of a driveway to a house 1.2 km (¾ mile) from Leacantium. Just beyond it stands the large grey Glencoe Hut, also on your L. Strike off R from the road 50 m (55 yd) further on, passing through a K-gate and then sheep pens. Leave them behind after a metal gate and pursue the rough service track up the hill NE. The summit of the Pap lies directly ahead.

Where after about 300 m (330 yd) the track comes next to a burn on your R, turn R and ford it easily. The track veers uphill off to the L. Instead, proceed across the flank of the hillside SW, following the course of a gently rising path. Somewhat optimistically, OS maps represent this as a track. Ahead, the commanding height of Bidean nam Bian competes for your attention with views emerging to your rear over Loch Leven. Ford a second burn after 500 m (⅓ mile) and then the Allt a' Mhuilinn (possibly dried up in summer).

Having gained the R side of the gully through which the allt flows, bear L and begin on a much steeper gradient. At first, the going underfoot is wet and peaty. Higher up, progress is continued over an agreeably firmer surface. Maintain a route NE, immediately above the R side of the stony gully, gaining height quickly if tiringly. At MR 119586, cross a line of old flattened fencing and continue up the bracken-covered slopes. Here and there, the path veers off a little to the R for a while, inevitably returning alongside the course of the Allt a' Mhuilinn.

On nearing the top of the gully, traverse drier heathery ground and then dip into the gully itself. Follow the line of scree between its banks to a cairn on the L. Walk on up through the broadening cleft. Head for the low point on the ridge ahead, between the Pap's summit cone on the L and the less distinct mound of Cnap Glas on the R.

At the top, the view across the Coire na Cìche displays new and fascinating sights to the E and NE. Turn L at the cairn and follow a succession of similar such stone piles directing you NW towards the summit. From the base of its quartzite summit cone, you must negotiate a route twisting steeply between boulders, at times coming close to a scramble. Clamber up the final few metres and walk out over the top to enjoy your just earnings for the rigours of the climb. Two summit cairns stand about 10 m (30 ft) apart. Most of the mountains on the S side of Glen Coe are, from here, blocked by the other peaks on this northern boundary. At 742 m (2434 ft), the Pap of Glencoe, rarely known by its Gaelic name of Sgorr na Cìche, is a junior to most of them. However, perched here on its summit above the waters of Loch Leven, the feeling of height is marvellously exaggerated. The panorama is simply magnificent, the horizon quite as far-reaching as that from many a loftier mountain. Clockwise, the mountains in view include: SE, Sgorr nam Fiannaidh; SSE, Bidean nam Bian; S, Stob an Fhuarain, Sgor na h-Ulaidh; SW, Fraochaidh; WSW, Beinn a' Bheithir (Ben Vair); NNE, Ben Nevis. Views of the Mamores include: N, Mullach nan Coirean; NNE, Stob Ban, Sgurr a Mhàim, Sgor an Lubhair; NE, Am Bodach, Binnein Mór, Na Cruagaichean. To the E is Garbh Bheinn. The distant mountains of the Morvern peninsula, seen across Loch Leven, extend W to NW across a seaward horizon.

Pap of Glencoe to Sgorr nam Fiannaidh

Allow 1½ hours

Reverse back down the summit cone SE, returning to the cairn in the saddle between the Pap and Cnap Glas. Extra care is required on descent. Head off from the cairn SE, up the broad ridge to Cnap Glas. There is no path at first, but it is difficult to lose your way. Although steep in places, the grassy slopes and outcropping rocks can be traversed without any cause for concern. After a while, small cairns may be encountered indicating the course of a faint path, though proving unimportant as an aid to route-finding. The gradient relents at Cnap Glas. Beyond the insignificant mound, maintain a route SE, keeping just R of the rim of the Coire an Lochain while resuming a steeper course. Again, there are cairns to guide

11.1 *Westwards across Loch Leven from the ridge between the Pap of Glencoe and Sgorr nam Fiannaidh.*

you. The views out across Loch Leven provide the best kind of excuses for attentive pauses. At looser, rocky ground higher up, gradually bear L a little. On gaining a cairn at the top, turn R and walk out to a vantage point about 150 m (165 yd) to the W. An awe-inspiring landscape is revealed.

There can be few better viewpoints for contemplating the high drama of the area's topography. From here Glen Coe exhibits most spectacularly its great yawning, glacier-scraped trough. A diminutive river and a road snake along its bottom towards the huge mound of Stob Dearg. Seen through the glen, a few miles to the E, Stob Dearg is also Buachaille Etive Mór's northern extremity. A pyramidal monolith on a grand scale, it guards the glen's western approach (see Route 9).

To reach your even higher objective, just a few hundred metres away, turn back and pursue the E-running ridge as far as the triangulation pillar on Sgorr nam Fiannaidh. As many do, you may find the large encircling summit cairn a useful shield from the ceaselessly blasting westerly winds. At 967 m (3172 ft), Sgorr nam Fiannaidh is the

11.2 *Looking SSW into Glen Coe and (left) to Bidean nam Bian, from the lower slopes of the Pap of Glencoe.*

Munro which marks the westernmost point of the infamous Aonach Eagach traverse. Held in great esteem in mountaineering circles, it is widely regarded as the most sensational ridge scramble on the Scottish mainland (see 'Extensions'). Fear not, for our route ventures no further in this direction, but do pause to take in the magnificence all around. The mountains on the southern boundary of the glen, those denied you from the Pap, now figure memorably: ESE, Stob Dearg (Buachaille Etive Mór), Buachaille Etive Beag; SE, the Three Sisters (Beinn Fhada, Gearr Aonach, Aonach Dubh); SSE, Stob Coire nan Lochan, Stob Coire Sgreamhach.

Bidean nam Bian continues to dominate the skyline S. Seen at near its best from here, it rises higher than any other mountain in Argyll.

Sgorr nam Fiannaidh to the Clachaig Inn

Allow 1½ hours

Leave the triangulation pillar by walking back W. After 50 m (55 yd) or so take the path which departs from the ridge to your L. Exercise great care down the very steep so-called path, in reality a channel of shifting quartzite scree. At first, follow a succession of cairns, heading directly S towards a diminutive and distant Loch Achtriochtan. Mossy ground immediately to the R of the scree may provide surer footholds. Emerging on the eastern skyline, the dizzy profile of the Aonach Eagach is worthy of your passing attention.

About halfway down, loose scree is succeeded by much more stable ground. At a small cairn, veer L to gain an orthodox path traversing grass-covered slopes by the E side of the Allt an t-Sidhein. Follow the watercourse downstream making a beeline for the W end of Loch Achtriochtan. Pass a waterfall on your R, after which the gradient gradually relents. The path finally deposits you at the junction of the A82 with the older Glencoe road. Turn R and walk W along the minor road alongside the River Coe on your L. Where the road bends away from the river, continue WNW for the final 500 m (⅓ mile) to the Clachaig Inn and much deserved refreshment.

Alternative routes

ESCAPES

Both the Pap of Glencoe and Sgorr nam Fiannaidh can be scaled separately as straightforward there and back routes, if so desired. Eliminating the easy ridge between the two seems futile, however, given the little extra time and effort involved. Nonetheless, the descent from the Pap is undoubtedly less severe than that from the higher top. Allow 4 hours for the return journey to either peaks.

Warning: no matter how great your need for sustenance, on no account attempt the dangerous and direct descent to the Clachaig Inn from Sgorr nam Fiannaidh.

EXTENSIONS

Having reached the summit of Sgorr nam Fiannaidh, you are at the western end of a high-level ridge widely regarded as the finest on the Scottish mainland. Only expert scramblers with a very good head for heights should attempt negotiating those dizzy pinnacles to the E. 'Daunting', 'intimidating' and even 'despicable' are all words that have been used to define the Aonach Eagach. To crag-ferrets and adrenalin addicts, however, its traverse represents a sensational route of unequalled excitement. If you have decided this is definitely for you, then from the Pass of Glencoe gain the ridge at Am Bodach and traverse E to W. Finish the day by descending from Sgorr nam Fiannaidh, as described in the main route. Remember, unlike all other scrambling options described in this book, there is no bypass path or feasible escape route. Allow 8 hours.

After a break at the Clachaig Inn, walkers of average ability might find the easy stroll around the Hospital Lochan, near Glencoe village, a very fitting end to their day in the hills (see Route 12). Allow an extra 2 hours including the walk between start points.

Visitors to this most famous of Highland glens need not look far for a reason to prolong their stay. High drama and superlative views await the mountain walker on routes on both sides of Glen Coe – an outdoors-lover's playground supreme!

Route 12: LOCH LEVEN

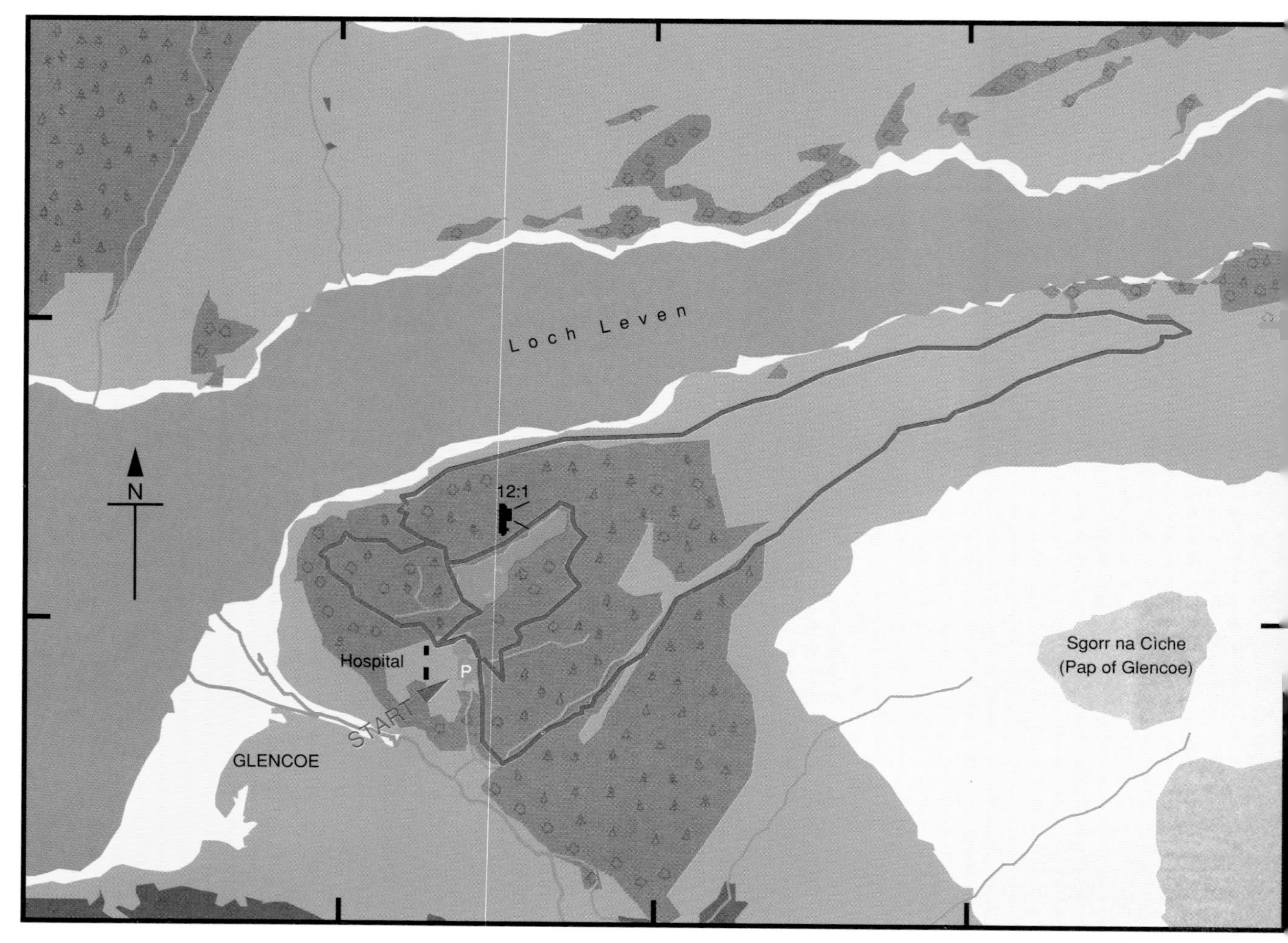

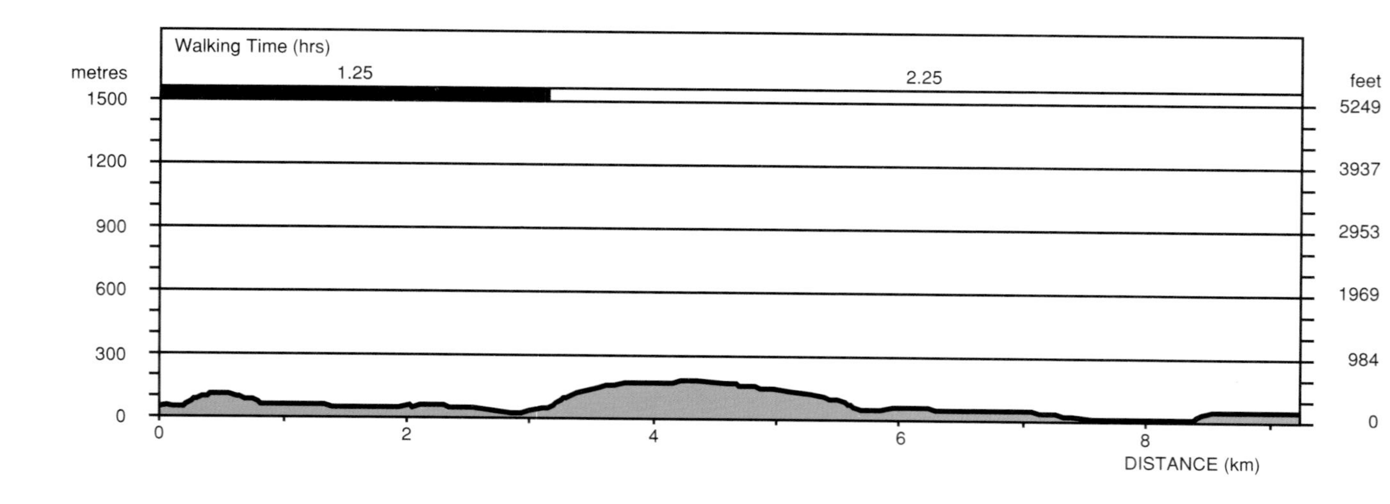

Route 12 · Loch Leven

STARTING LOCATION
In the forest near the Hospital Lochan immediately NE of Glencoe village.
OSLR 41 or OSPF 305 and 290/MR 104594.
FC car park at the end of the hospital drive, 600 m (⅓ mile) N of the Bridge of Coe.
Accommodates approximately 20 cars.

ALTERNATIVE STARTING LOCATION
Further parking in Glencoe village, 1 km (⅔ mile) SW of above map reference.

PUBLIC TRANSPORT
Nearest railway station – Bridge of Orchy or Fort William.
Regular buses, five daily, Glasgow to Glencoe or Fort William to Glencoe.
Postbus, once daily, from Fort William and Glencoe along A82 to Glen Etive (except Sunday).

OVERVIEW/INTEREST
Includes a tranquil woodland stroll beside a lochan – a refuge from the high drama of Glen Coe.
Fine views over Loch Leven.
Few route-finding problems.
Generally straightforward and undemanding route; easily curtailed.

FOOTPATHS
Colour-coded waymarking on FC Woodland and Lochan Walks.
Excellent and well-maintained paths in the vicinity of Hospital Lochan.
In places, rugged and wet on the slopes above the FC walks.
Follows the unfrequented B863 by the shore of Loch Leven.

GRADING 2

TIME ALLOWANCE
3½ hours.

DISTANCE

Excluding Height	9.2 km	(5¾ miles)
TOTAL HEIGHT GAINED	320 m	(1050 ft)

PRINCIPAL HEIGHTS
None – highest point on the NW slopes flanking the Pap of Glencoe, 186 m (610 ft).

From FC car park via Hospital Lochan and Woodland

Allow 1¼ hours

Of the two waymarked paths which depart from the N end of the car park, take the R-hand one coded blue. The one on the L is coded blue, red and yellow, being a path that serves all three of the FC's walks. Wooden waymarking posts display the appropriate colours.

Walk uphill between rhododendron bushes in proliferation. Initially head SSE on forested slopes. After 50 m (55 yd) pass a bench on your L and then go through a metal gate. Carry on up the winding path to the viewpoint looking out W across Loch Leven. There is a bench here on your R. The ascent thereafter takes you under an increasingly dense forest canopy.

On reaching a plantation of Scots pine, picnic tables on your L tempt an early pause. Close to the highest section of the FC designated walks, it is a fine vantage point. The view W, across Loch Leven, is a reward quite out of proportion to the little effort so far invested. To the SW, above Ballachulish, the commanding height is Beinn a' Bheithir (Ben Vair). On the other side of Loch Leven, plantations to the NW carpet the slopes of Tom Meadhoin and Creag Bhreac.

Continue on the easy path heading NE between Scots pine. Pass a bench on your R, at the first corner, heading downhill. A more diverse mix of trees heralds new delights. Further blue-coded posts direct you down quite steeply towards the lochan. First, cross a tiny burn and then walk on through a 'tunnel' of conifers. The lochan is a little beyond an open glade at the last of the blue-coded posts.

Having joined the red-coded walk that encircles the lochan, turn R and proceed by the obvious path skirting around its E shore. In the shallow water on your L, note the splayed roots of trees drowned during the creation of this artificial lochan.

Beyond another picnic bench, pass a red-coded post on your R. Continue on the excellent path, bearing L to walk SW along the N side of the lochan. Scots pine cloak the slopes on your R. At a gap in the rhododendron by the loch-shore on your L, glance back across the water. Rising above the forest to the E, the Pap of Glencoe appears impressive and fully deserving of its name – 'pap' meaning 'breast'. At the NW corner of the lochan, pause to enjoy an idyllic scene of the mountains of Glen Coe to the S reflected in its waters.

After a bench on your R, the path divides. Take the path off to the R, heading N away from the lochan. Pass a yellow-coded post on the L, indicating the Woodland Walk. Ignore the less defined path off to the R and walk on, shifting generally W. The path maintains an undulating course amid a variety of deciduous tree species. A worthy and quick detour is to take the second path on the R. It leads out to a bench after about 15 m (15 yd), from where there is a good view N across Loch Leven. Soon after, back on the 'yellow' walk, the path narrows and becomes wetter underfoot. At yet more picnic tables there is another viewpoint on the R. Walk generally SE from here to reach a junction with a better path. Turn R on to it but then, almost immediately, bear L around a hairpin corner. The hospital is beyond the trees to your R but a Scottish Ambulance Service building is clearly visible.

12.1 *Eastwards across Hospital Lochan to the Pap of Glencoe.*

Follow the 'tri-colour' path down ENE bearing R at the edge of a tiny lily-smothered lochan. After a wooden K-gate, the path terminates at the FC car park and the starting location. If you have walked enough, then you can finish here.

From FC car park via Loch Leven

Allow 2¼ hours

Walkers who wish to see more should, at this stage proceed through the car park to pick up the unmetalled track that you drove in on. Walk S to join with the metalled hospital drive after about 120 m (130 yd). Continue in this direction until the road bends to the L. Where it subsequently bends to the R, strike off L and pass through a chicken-wire gate between the trees. Pursue a relatively rugged path up the hillside. This is steep, rooty and in places wet; head NE. Fallen trees may cause one or two obstructions on this obviously neglected route but progress is generally straightforward.

At the top of the steepest section, gaps between the Scots pines afford views W down to Glencoe village and Loch Leven. Follow the course of a tiny burn on your R. Then pass through a rusty metal gate between a line of old fence wires. The Pap of Glencoe rises up to the E. A more significant clearing in the forest opens up and running through it are poles carrying electricity transmission lines from Kinlochleven. Follow a succession of them NE, traversing ground invariably wet underfoot. Come alongside a line of birch trees bordering the edge of the plantation on your R. Further on, leave the forest's eastern boundary through a gap in a rusty wire fence.

Continue NE across the open moor which flanks the NW facing slopes of the Pap of Glencoe (Sgorr na Cìche). At MR 115599, the path reaches the very highest point of the route at 186 m (610 ft) above sea level, providing the best vantage point on the entire route. Views extend W beyond the forest and Loch Leven to the Ballachulish Bridge and the Morvern mountains. Dominating the scene across the E end of Loch Leven are the mountains of Mam na Gualainn to the N and Beinn na Caillich to the NE. The mightier and more distant mountain Am Bodach rises with the Mamores above Kinlochleven.

Gently descend with Loch Leven below on your L. Gradually bear ENE, staying near the transmission lines. A burn, which flows from a birch-strewn gully on your R, is easily forded. Pass beneath the transmission lines at a cairn. Soon after, ford a burn and proceed across the heather moor. On your R a few desperate birches cling to outcropping rocks. As the path veers slightly away to the L of the transmission lines, begin a steeper descent. Garbh Bheinn is the mountain newly revealed ahead of you to the E. OS maps indicate a path off to the L and down to the road but I have found no evidence of this. Therefore, without deviating, continue ENE to gain the B863 below. Turn sharp L on to the road, walking on the R side against oncoming traffic. Although a B road, it is rarely busy now, mostly serving Kinlochleven only. Carry on W above the pleasantly wooded shore of Loch Leven, the water on your R.

After 2 km (1¼ miles) the road skirts the bottom of the FC forest on your L. Pass over a burn via an attractive stone bridge, then on past a path off to your R which offers an optional diversion to the loch-shore. Having reached a boathouse with a slipway on your R, walk on 10 m (10 yd) further and then cross the road. Go through a chicken-wire gate and head away from the road on an ascending path through the trees. Cross a timber bridge over a tiny burn to join up with the yellow-coded path, trailed earlier in the day. Turn L and return to the NW corner of the Hospital Lochan at the next junction of paths.

Turn R on to the red- and yellow-coded path heading S for a short distance. Stay alongside the W shore of the lochan by crossing the dam where a path on the L leads to a picturesque timber boathouse-type shelter. Turn R and join the tri-colour-coded path. Keep with it to the car park, retracing again your earlier footsteps downhill via the hairpin bend in the path near the hospital.

Alternative routes

ESCAPES

The complete route can be treated as two shorter routes combined. It is a simple matter to make separate circular routes out of either the inner lochan and woodland walks circuit or the outer Loch Leven section. In both cases the starting location is the FC car park.

On its own, the Hospital Lochan and woodland circuit is Grade 1, for which walking boots are not essential. Allow 1¼ hours.

Those wishing to bypass the lochan, by pursuing only the more rugged route above Loch Leven, should allow 2¼ hours.

EXTENSIONS

An easy extension would be to include Glencoe, 1 km (⅔ mile) SW of the FC car park. From the starting location, walk S back along the hospital drive to the Bridge of Coe. At the junction with the old Glencoe road, turn R and walk W over the bridge and into the village, which still retains some of its character. A few hundred metres W of the village, on the N side of the A82, a small pier jutting out into Loch Leven affords a fine view E. The distinctive profile of the Pap of Glencoe can thus be seen across the water. Allow an extra hour.

More capable walkers would do well to consider combining the lower-level Route 12 with the high-level Route 11. Only 1 km (⅔ mile) of tarmac separates the two routes. Allow an extra 5½ hours for Route 11.

Route 13: BEN NEVIS and CARN MÓR DEARG

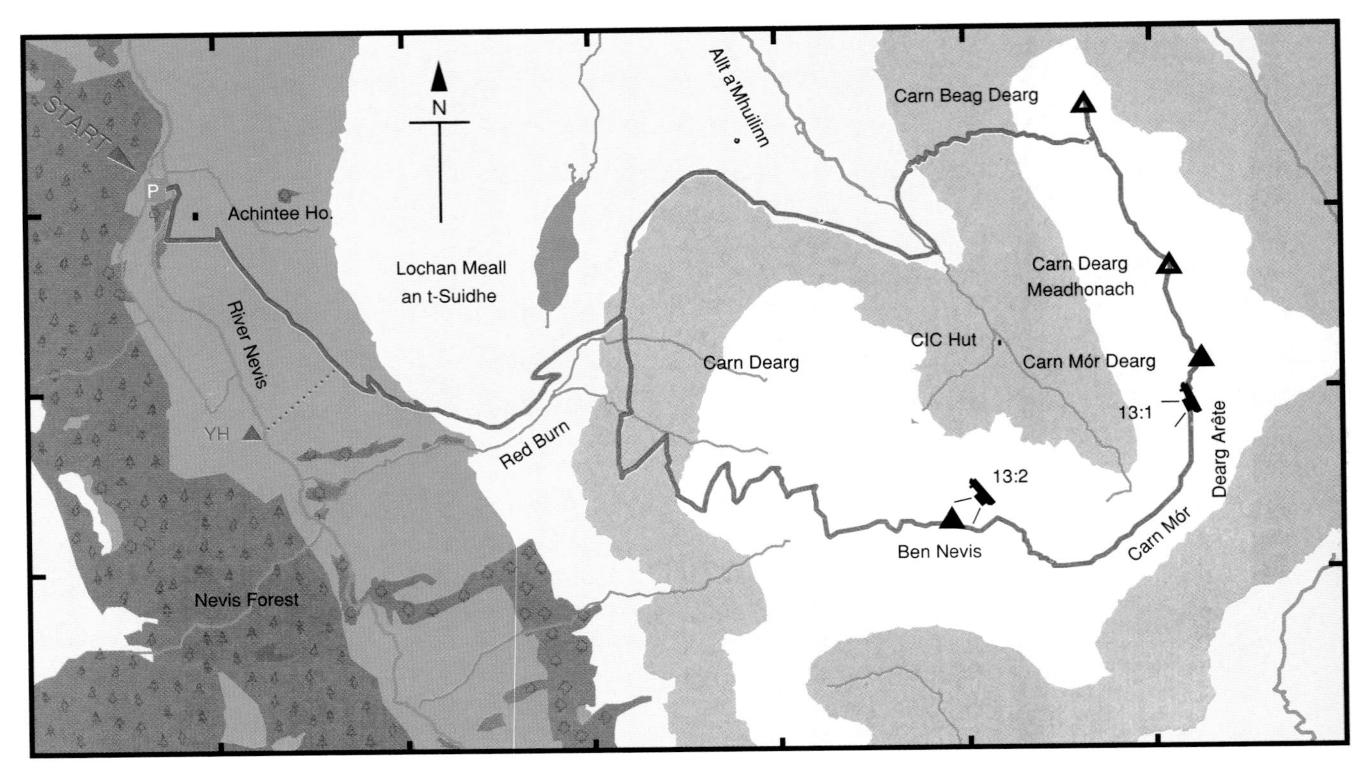

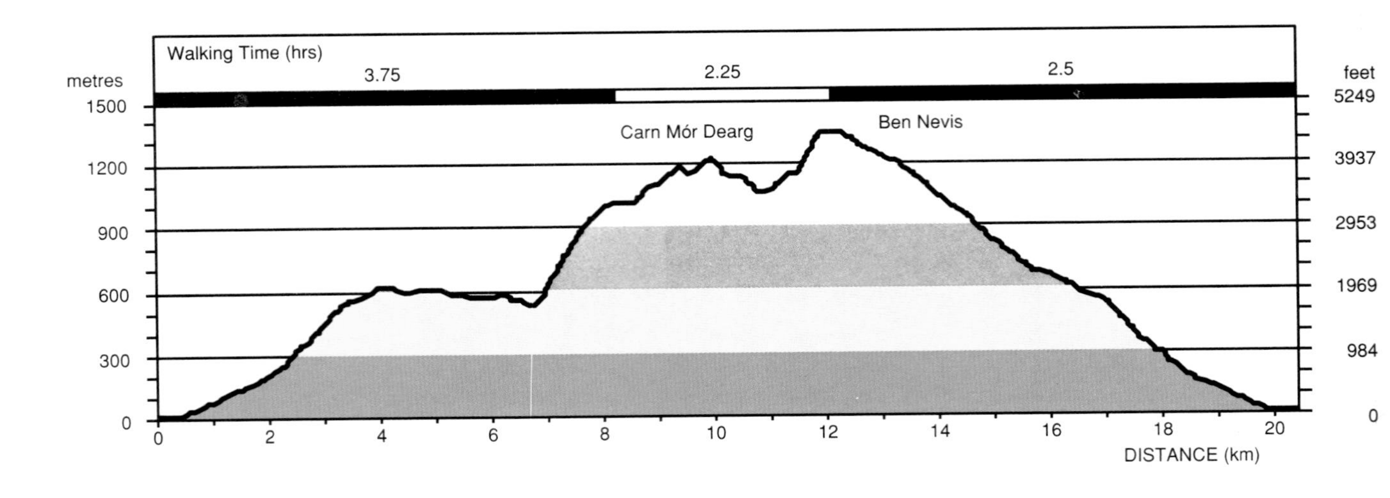

9

LOCHABER

HIGH-LEVEL ROUTE

Route 13 · Ben Nevis and Carn Mór Dearg

STARTING LOCATION
VC car park just off the Glen Nevis road, 1.2 km (3/4 mile) SE of Fort William.
OSLR 41 or OSOL 32/MR 123731.
Large car park on the W side of the River Nevis near Achintee House.
Accommodates approximately 40 cars.

ALTERNATIVE STARTING LOCATION
Car park at the youth hostel, 1.6 km (1 mile) further S on the same road. A footpath from here leads up the hill NE to join with the one from Achintee.

PUBLIC TRANSPORT
Nearest railway station – Fort William.
Regular buses, five daily, Glasgow to Fort William and eight daily, Inverness to Fort William.

OVERVIEW/INTEREST
Unfrequented ascent route on Britain's highest mountain. Enthralling ridge walk via a narrow arête – some scrambling involved.
Summit approach affords unique views to the Ben's spectacular NE-facing cliffs.
Extensive summit plateau with many features – a superb vantage point.
Takes in two Munros, both over 1200 m (4000 ft).
Competence with map and compass essential.
Arduous and extremely demanding route.

FOOTPATHS
Minimal waymarking.
Seriously eroded on tourist path but wide, obvious and much frequented.
Peaty and wet near Lochan Meall an t-Suidhe.
No path on steep slopes to Carn Beag Dearg.
Rugged traversing the ridge – a bypass path avoids awkward sections of the narrow Carn Mór Dearg arête.

GRADING 6
TIME ALLOWANCE
8½ hours.
DISTANCE
Excluding Height 20.4 km (12¾ miles)
TOTAL HEIGHT GAINED 1630 m (5348 ft)
PRINCIPAL HEIGHTS
Carn Beag Dearg (Little Red Cairn) 1010 m (3314 ft)
Carn Dearg Meadhonach (Middle Red Cairn) 1179 m (3868 ft)
Carn Mór Dearg (Big Red Cairn) 1220 m (4003 ft)
Ben Nevis 1344 m (4406 ft)

Visitor Centre to Carn Beag Dearg

Allow 3¾ hours

From the E end of the car park, cross the River Nevis by the suspension footbridge. Turn R and walk alongside the river for about 300 m (330 yd). The VC is among the trees opposite, possibly worth a diversion before leaving the car park. Turn L and walk up the path E. Cross a stile at the top on reaching a junction in paths, approximately 150 m (165 yd) S of a small plantation near Achintee House.

Cross a ditch using a footbridge made of railway sleepers, pursuing the path opposite which is the tourist route to Ben Nevis. Bear R and ascend steadily SE along grassy slopes below Meall an t-Suidhe. In places, the path is in a severely eroded state but good maintenance has made for an agreeable surface. All burns are crossed by footbridges. Cross a stile between sheep fencing after 500 m (1/3 mile) and carry on up a hillside swathed in bracken. One or two of the Mamore peaks emerge on the horizon beyond Glen Nevis.

Soon, on your R, the path is joined by one coming up from the youth hostel. Continue SE, engaging in a series of zigzags as steepness increases. On bearing ESE higher up, two aluminium footbridges cross feeder burns to Red Burn. Curve around the S side of Meall an t-Suidhe, keeping to the clear path which comes above a grassy ravine. Red Burn flows through it, below on your R. Walk NE and on reaching a sign 'To the Top', hairpin L. At a cairn soon after, hairpin R to resume a course NE. The substantial hill slope on your R is topped by Carn Dearg and beyond, out of sight, Ben Nevis. After 600 m (1/3 mile) on a pleasant gradient-free path over softer ground, the tourist path turns sharp R at a large cairn. Instead, turn L and proceed N on a wilder moorland path about 400 m (1/4 mile) E of Lochan Meall an t-Suidhe. Cairns depict a route that roughly follows the 600 m (2000 ft) contour around to the R. One or two intervening burns introduce a degree of peaty wetness to the going underfoot but these are easily forded. Continue NE and pass between a line of rusty fence posts. Fort William is easily discernible to the NW but the skyline emerging to the E is far more inspiring.

The path bears sharply R having come directly above the Allt a' Mhuilinn. Further to your R the first of a series of impressive buttresses and cliffs are encountered at Castle Ridge. Stay on the path into the Coire Leis which gently brings you down nearer to the allt on your L. There are in fact two paths but it makes little difference whether you choose the higher or the lower one.

A short distance before the path meets the allt, leave the path by heading E across country and down to ford it. Pick up the good path on the other side, turn L and walk NW. After about 300 m (330 yd), strike off from the path to ascend the very steep slopes on your R. Find your own way up over the boulders and moss and maintain progress generally E. A stone gully, conspicuous earlier on from the other side of the Allt a' Mhuilinn, may be as good an ascent option as any. The gradient is severe and unremitting but the grandeur of the scene looking S into the Coire Leis more than compensates. Look out for pairs of long ears dashing across the slopes ahead of you – mountain hares are frequently seen here.

Approaching the ridge, gentler slopes bring welcome relief from the rigours of the climb. Head towards the lowest point on the ridge. Once there, turn L and make the short walk out to Carn Beag Dearg at 1010 m (3314 ft). Looking E, new delights now figure in a day where everything is big. Aonach Mór and Aonach Beag are the peaks that rise high and remote above the Allt Daim, the latter mountain being the sixth highest in Britain.

Carn Beag Dearg to Ben Nevis

Allow 2 1/4 hours

Turn and walk SSE back down along the ridge and then continue on an easy ascent passing a couple of cairns up to Carn Dearg Meadhonach at 1179 m (3868 ft). The views are yet more extensive. To the SW the great armchair of Coire na Ciste separates the huge buttresses of Carn Dearg on the R and Ben Nevis on the L.

Descend S from Carn Dearg Meadhonach then bear SSE again on a re-ascent towards the next summit ahead. Stay immediately above the crags on your L. Higher up, rubbly slopes lead on to the summit cairn on Carn Mór Dearg at 1220 m (4003 ft). In contrast to the dark andesite of the Ben, pink granites constitute Carn Mór Dearg. It is these rocks that give it, and the peaks on the ridge running N of it, their names.

From this first Munro of the route you have the reward of one of the finest views possible of Ben Nevis. Towering buttresses and 600 m (2000 ft) cliffs attribute the mountain with an identity unique in the British Isles, and one that is unseen and unimaginable from the tourist path. The Ben's NE buttress, and to the R of it Observatory Ridge and Tower Ridge, can easily be identified. They are

13.1 *Ben Nevis – the summit and the NE Buttress, looking WSW from Carn Mór Dearg.*

13.2 *The summit cairn and triangulation pillar on Ben Nevis.*

all highlighted especially well by summer sunlight from the S (at midday). Causing perhaps more apprehension, though, is the narrow rocky crest that curves around the rim of Coire Leis: the Carn Mór Dearg (CMD) arête.

Proceed SSW from the summit cairn on to the CMD arête, where both sides of the ridge fall away on either side with severe steepness. The result is a sharp, narrow rocky crest enclosing Coire Leis. Whilst boulder-hopping along the crest can be immensely enthralling, to some it will prove an unnerving experience. A path lower down on the L allows you to bypass all the awkward scrambles.

The arête curves around to the R and dips down to its lowest point at 1058 m (3471 ft), where it becomes extremely sharp. Proceed SW ascending a little to where rising ground on the L brings relief to the sense of exposure. Pass an Abseil Post on your R and continue round the corrie rim. Commence a steep ascent up over boulders on a rugged path following a line of marker posts WNW. On your L, the Ben's S-facing slopes drop abruptly away for thousands of feet into Glen Nevis. For the final 90 m (300 ft) of ascent, bear NW.

The summit is at 1344 m (4406 ft) above sea-level and suddenly it seems you have emerged into a different world. It is a vast 36 ha (90 acre) boulder plateau which on a fine summer's day is a positively crowded place! However, there is much of interest here, apart from a substantial cairn hosting the triangulation pillar. In fact there is a large array of memorial cairns of all kinds paying tribute to the victims of war or commemorating the casualties of the mountain. There is a prominent emergency shelter as well as the ruins of an observatory. Alas, it is also Britain's loftiest rubbish dump, a despicable littering of tin cans, plastic bags, polystyrene, broken glass and just about everything else. However, there is undoubtedly a wonderful feeling of achievement standing on the roof of Britain. Having done it the hard way, by the mountain lover's route, you have every reason to be satisfied with yourself. On a clear day your just reward is a far-reaching view apparently over all the Highlands. It is a prize you will have to no doubt share but there is plenty to go around.

There are mountains in almost every direction. On a western horizon, far out to sea, some claim even to have seen Northern Ireland. However, those mountains in the distance, as well as in the vicinity, and easily identifiable in clear weather include: S, the Mamores, the mountains of Glen Coe, Ben Starav, Ben Cruachan; SSE, Ben Lui, Ben More and Stob Binnien; SE, Ben Lawers; ESE, Schiehallion; E, Aonach Beag; ENE, Aonach Mór, the Cairngorms; NNW, the Torridons; NW, Kintail Hills, the Cuillin of Skye.

Ben Nevis to Visitor Centre *Allow 2½ hours*

Walk SW across the summit plateau from the triangulation pillar, keeping well away from the cliff edge. In adverse weather conditions, see recommendations included in 'Escapes' for the exact compass bearings. More walkers wander dangerously astray here than anywhere else on the mountain.

After 150 m, turn R at the top of Gardyloo Gully and walk W to pick up the well-worn tourist path across the bouldery plateau. As you begin slowly descending, there is a noticeable bright orange emergency shelter a few hundred metres away towards Carn Dearg. Once on the path, it is difficult to get lost. There are cairns to guide you over an otherwise quite featureless, almost quarry-like terrain.

A steeper descent ensues on commencing the first of an endless succession of zigzags. Those who savour the best of a mountain will be grateful not to have suffered so on the way up. Loch Linnhe to the W and the Mamores range to the S do their best for you in providing a degree of interest on the way down. Eventually, the barren rock-strewn slopes give way to a green carpet of rough grass.

Beyond the last zigzag, pass further cairns and walk N along the path. Cross the Red Burn by a rough stone bridge and then proceed to where a sign ('Danger Eroded Ground. Path This Way') directs you safely away from the old route. A large cairn where the path bears sharply L signifies your return to the point where you much earlier deviated from it, close to Lochan Meall an t-Suidhe. Stay on the tourist path and walk back to the car park at the VC, in reverse of the upward route.

Alternative routes

ESCAPES

Those who doubt their abilities on narrow ridges and on unpathed, steep terrain should use the tourist path, up and down. Allow 6 hours. This makes for an easy ascent, without obstacles, but whichever way you do it, Ben Nevis is always a serious undertaking. Once on the ridge, there are no viable escapes, especially from the arête. On no account attempt the positively dangerous descent on the S-facing slopes of the mountain!

There are more fatalities each year on Ben Nevis than on any other mountain in Britain. Most serious accidents befall climbers attempting routes on the challenging cliffs above the Coire Leis. However, of particular danger to walkers is bad visibility on the summit. OSOL map 32 (1994) recommends the following in such conditions:

Recommended Bad Visibility Descent Route from the Summit of Ben Nevis

1. From the triangulation pillar, walk for 150 m (165 yd) on a *grid* bearing of 231°.
2. Then follow a *grid* bearing of 281° to clear the plateau and gain the path.

NOTE: Magnetic north currently lies about 6° W of grid north, decreasing by about 1° every six years. To obtain a *compass* bearing *add* this value to the grid bearing.

Accuracy and competence with a compass is vital for safety in such conditions. Remember to keep the compass well away from metal objects and electrical gadgets, such as cameras and watches, which will invariably cause needle deflections.

The summit of Ben Nevis is obscured by cloud nine days in every ten and the average mean temperature is just below freezing.

EXTENSIONS

Due to the physical demands of the main route and the detached nature of this group of summits, extensions are not recommended.

On the S side of Glen Nevis, the high-level possibilities on the attractive peaks of the Mamores easily justify a few days' further exploration of the Lochaber hills. Most of the mountains of the Mamores range are accessible from starting locations in Glen Nevis.

Other worthy contenders on the N side of the glen include Aonach Mór, Aonach Beag and the Grey Corries. The scaling of these mountains is best initiated from the N, if possible, avoiding the ski tows and chairlifts.

Route 14: GLEN NEVIS

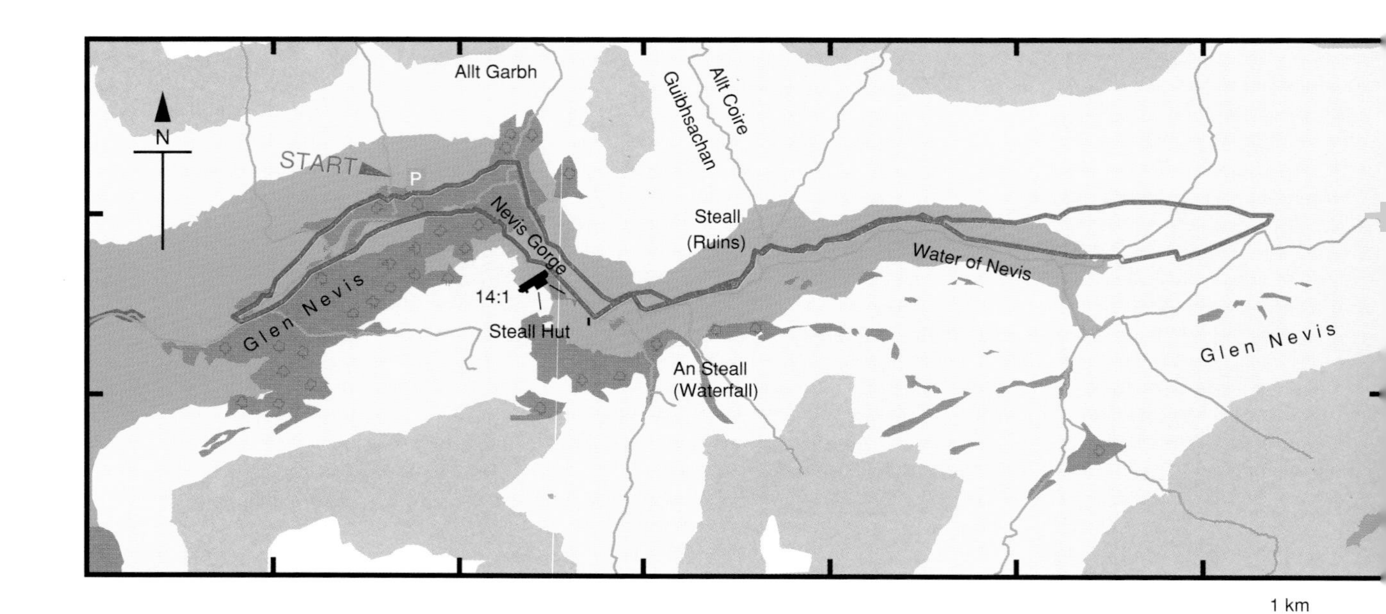

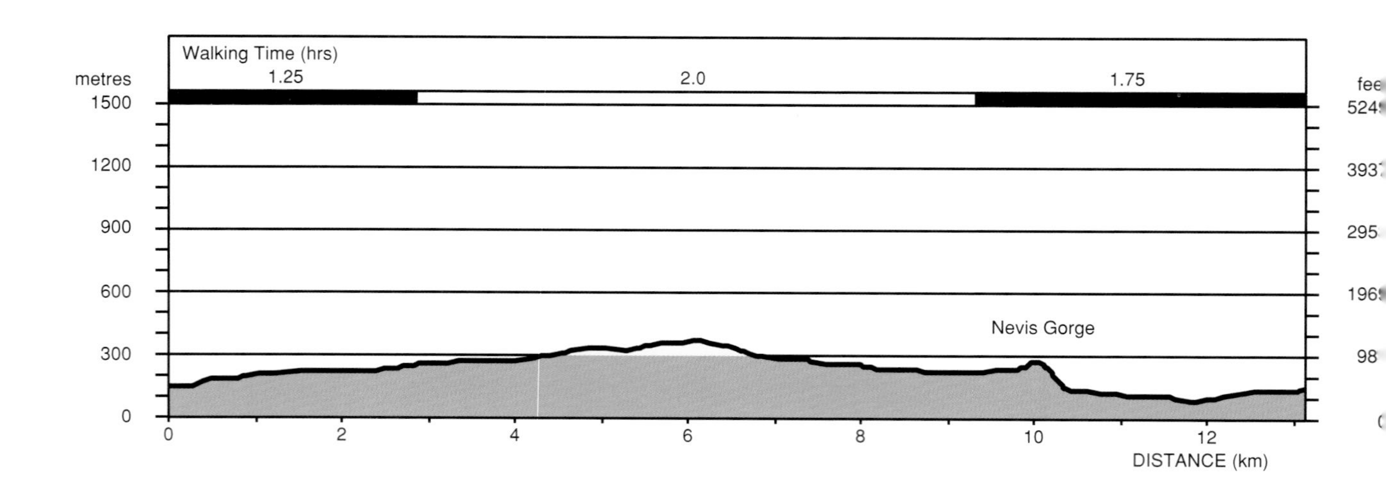

Route 14 · Glen Nevis

STARTING LOCATION
At the end of the Glen Nevis road from Fort William.
OSLR 41 or OSOL 32/MR 167691.
Car park located below a long waterslide descending the lower slopes of Ben Nevis.
Accommodates approximately 40 cars.

ALTERNATIVE STARTING POINT
Car park by the bridge over the Water of Nevis at Polldubh, 3 km (2 miles) ESE from end of Glen Nevis road.

PUBLIC TRANSPORT
Nearest railway station – Fort William.
Regular buses, five daily, Glasgow to Fort William and eight daily, Inverness to Fort William.

OVERVIEW/INTEREST
Breathtaking scenery in possibly the most beautiful of Scottish glens; frequently described as 'Himalayan' in character.
A spectacular gorge set between the magnificent Mamores range and Britain's highest mountain.
A river crossing via a footbridge made of just three cables! Timid walkers, see 'Escapes'.
Possible route-finding problems on S side of the Water of Nevis.
Quite demanding physically.

FOOTPATHS
Minimal waymarking.
Obvious but quite rough through the Nevis Gorge.
Even and level near An Steall Waterfall.
Wet and peaty at the E end of the route.
Rugged and effectively unpathed descending through woods on S side of Water of Nevis.
Finishes via a narrow single-track road.

GRADING 3
TIME ALLOWANCE
5 hours.
DISTANCE

Excluding Height	13.1 km	(8¼ miles)
TOTAL HEIGHT GAINED	340 m	(1115 ft)

PRINCIPAL HEIGHTS
None – highest point above the W side of Nevis Gorge, 275 m (902 ft).

End of the Glen Nevis road to the Steall Ruins

Allow 1¼ hours

A long waterslide cascades from a high rock face immediately N of the car park. Leave the far end of the car park by walking E along the path sign-posted 'Public Footpath to Corrour 15 and Rannoch 25'. You begin above the N side of the Water of Nevis.

After 50 m (55 yd), pass a large boulder displaying a fascinating layered texture. Walk on ENE into denser woodland, an attractive mix of birch, young oak, rowan and pine, gently rising above the water on the well-maintained path. After fording a small burn, the path divides. Take the L fork, keeping to the well-trodden route which crosses the Allt Garbh by a footbridge. Bear R and continue on the path, now much rougher underfoot, heading SSE. A gap in the trees on your R affords a fine view along the Water of Nevis, seen twisting its way W between beautifully wooded slopes.

Having clambered over the exposed roots of a contorted Scots pine on your R, you come closer to the spectacular Nevis Gorge. Directly below, the water forces a course through a labyrinth of channels and holes and then, bursting out into fierce cauldrons, it rushes on. In this impressive place, over the years, rocks have been eroded smooth and into weird shapes. Suddenly, on coming closer to the water, you are released from the confines of the gorge.

A long grassy meadow stretches out before you, backed by the distant pale cascade of the An Steall Ban (waterfall) – a tranquil scene where the Water of Nevis flows slow and sure, in great

contrast to the hectic confines of the gorge. Follow the path SE up the L-hand edge of the meadow, coming nearer to the long, graceful fronds of the Steall Falls. For the time being, ignore the path on your R leading out to a cable footbridge. Turn L and pause to enjoy the loveliest of waterfalls, the Allt Coire a' Mhail, terminated by perhaps the finest example of a hanging valley in the Highlands. Surpassed in height only by Eas a' Chual Aluinn and the Falls of Glomach (Route 20), the An Steall Ban is a good deal more accessible.

Follow the path ENE alongside the Water of Nevis, at the same time skirting below the crags of Aisridh Mairi Bhan on your L. Where the river turns sharply to the R, walk E along the edge of a gravelly plateau formed from river deposits. The ground then becomes wetter, more typical of the open moor.

Proceed, gradually bearing L. After about 200 m (220 yd) of further progress NNE, turn R on to a footbridge ('Erected by the RE troop of Oxford UOTC 1982') which crosses the Allt Coire Giubhsachan. From the opposite bank, pass to the R of Steall (Ruins). Those with geological interests, will no doubt enjoy the prominent angled strata exhibited in the mountain rocks on both sides of the glen.

Steall (Ruins) to Steall Hut *Allow 2 hours*

Head off from the Steall (Ruins) pursuing a less agreeable and less frequented path E. To your R, above the Water of Nevis, rise the mountains on the E side of the Mamores range. Those in view include An Gearanach to the S, Binnein Mór to the SE and the distinctive cone of Binnein Beag looking ESE. Rising still higher and to your L, Ben Nevis towers above the Coire Giubhsachan.

Maintain a course on the L side of the Water of Nevis. At first about 100 m (110 yd) away, come closer to it after fording an intervening burn. Further on the path divides at a cairn. Head off on the less well-trodden path to the R, that closest to

14.1 *The An Steall Ban (Steall Waterfall) from the Water of Nevis.*

the water; the L-hand one is your return route. Proceeding E over increasingly wet ground, ford a tiny burn and then continue between bracken and bog myrtle. Look to your rear for a magnificent view of the ravine, the Steall Hut now dwarfed by the grandeur of its mountain backdrop. Years ago a hydroelectric scheme had been planned for the area. A public enquiry came out in favour of the conservationists and a crime against the landscape was averted.

Come adjacent to the Water of Nevis where it squeezes through a mini gorge. Ford a small burn and carry on by the N bank of the water on the path, for a while little more than a sheep track. The banks of the water widen again and further burns must be forded. Here and there, scatterings of white quartzite do their best for you as a surface. Where the water turns abruptly away to the R, ignore the path that continues alongside it. Instead, continue E pursuing the L-hand fork.

After a few hundred metres, bear L and traverse the moor ENE towards a relatively substantial burn. Without crossing it, turn sharply L, in effect a hairpin, to gain a more obviously worn path. Walking back roughly parallel to the lower one, head W. The view ahead into Glen Nevis, as well as up to Ben Nevis, provides lasting pleasures.

You are now some way distant from the Water of Nevis on your L. Ford again the same burns encountered lower down. After 2 km (1¼ miles) by the better path, return to the cairn where the paths earlier diverged at the beginning of the loop. Walk back on previous footsteps making for the Steall Hut. After the footbridge adjacent to Steall (Ruins), a path immediately alongside the Water of Nevis avoids a repetition of the route in reverse. Such a course also brings you that little bit nearer the Steall Falls.

Soon after regaining the main path, walk out SW to reach the cable footbridge. The bridge itself extends for about 30 m (100 ft) and is merely three suspended cables, one to walk on and two above to grab. Crossing this way is easier than it looks and the water is neither deep nor very far below you. Those not convinced can attempt to ford the water further upstream. In summer this alternative should be quite feasible. Otherwise, simply return through the gorge, by the path on its E side.

Steall Hut to the Glen Nevis road

Allow 1¾ hours

Having made the crossing and gained the opposite bank, you will notice that the Steall Hut (Mountain Rescue Post) is in a clearing on your L. However, turn R away from the bridge and up on to the path. Follow the Water of Nevis downstream, on its L side.

Walk NW along the wet bankside path where birch and alder trees line the way. Keep a look out for dippers, grey wagtails and kingfishers. After about 400 m (¼ mile), clamber over an outcrop to emerge at a clearing by the water. Cross the grass and bracken to the N end of the clearing and then turn L on to the open hillside. Ascend a steep, rough path heading W. On the way up, pass a large conspicuous boulder on your L and then rusty fence posts on your R. The path veers R after approximately 40 m (130 ft) of ascent.

Resume a course NW over the grass, continuing to gain height above the outcropping rocks which demarcate the W side of the gorge. Cross a line of rusty fence wires beyond an insignificant three-stoned cairn protruding from the top of a large boulder. Soon after, commence a difficult descent through an overgrown bouldery cleft that leads down through the woods. There is no obvious path but those with some familiarity of Highland terrain should have few problems. Stay on a NW bearing and to the L side of a line of rusty fence posts. At gaps in the trees, the long waterslide above the car park can be seen.

On nearing the Water of Nevis, now downstream of the gorge, begin to bear L. At the bankside, on your R, the rusty remains of old fencing is again encountered. Continue W over more level ground, now below the predominantly deciduous wood. Interspaced with a few fine stands of Scots pine, the glen here is a joy with much to commend it for aesthetic appeal.

From the open ground at Blàr Bàn, curve round on a SW course coming away from the water for a short distance. Ford a tiny burn as you approach the corner of new deer fencing, crossing a subsequent burn by a miniature concrete bridge. Resume a course alongside the rusty deer fencing next to the water. A post mysteriously marked 'P' is on your R. Carry on past an especially attractive copse of Scots pine and then ford another burn before reaching a small hut, the property of 'Highland Region, Department of Water and Sewage'. Passing in front of it, turn R to cross the water at the footbridge. Bear L, up a track on the other side, to meet the Glen Nevis road.

Turn R and proceed NE along this delightfully wooded lane. Head upstream of the water, now on your R. The road squeezes between an archway of Scots pine where two have grown together in the weirdest way. Two '3 Tonne Limit' bridges later, return to the start point at the end of the road.

Alternative routes

ESCAPES

Effectively an elongated figure-of-8 circuit, the route is easily shortened by omitting the paths in the glen to the E of the cable bridge. Allow 2½ hours in total.

Timid walkers may well be alarmed at the prospect of having to cross the Water of Nevis with only three simple cables for support. Also, it is important to bear in mind that the return via the S side of the water is, for a few hundred metres, especially rugged and demanding. Those unfamiliar with Highland terrain are advised to return by the well-worn path on the E side of the gorge. Settling for the 'there and back' option does not deny you the best of this route – the An Steall Ban and the Nevis Gorge. If omitting the return section on the S side of the Water of Nevis only, then allow 3½ hours.

EXTENSIONS

A straightforward and very worthwhile extension is to prolong the walking on the S side of the Water of Nevis. Continue W, bypassing the first bridge over the water, to cross via the next one at Polldubh. This involves a longer walk back over tarmac on the single-track road on the N side of the water. Allow an extra hour.

Alternatively, at the other end of the route, continue E through Glen Nevis as far as you desire before returning. Those without their own transport can keep going by making the remote Corrour station their objective. The station, on the Glasgow–Fort William line, is a tough 24 km (15 miles) from the end of the Glen Nevis road. Allow 9 hours for the one-way trip.

For one of the finest circuits in the Mamores range, high-level walkers and Munroists should save a clear day for the so-called 'Ring of Steall'. From the same starting location at the end of the Glen Nevis road, walk out over the cable bridge and strike off up the slopes SSW behind the Steall Hut. On gaining the ridge at Sgurr A' Mhaim, four Munros can then be picked off on a horseshoe of peaks. Follow the ridge round anti-clockwise, finishing the day by descending N from the Munro An Gearanach. Allow 8 hours.

Those hoping to scale Ben Nevis, see Route 13. You would be well advised to heed warnings on ascending via the mountain's S-facing slopes.

Route 15: LOCHNAGAR

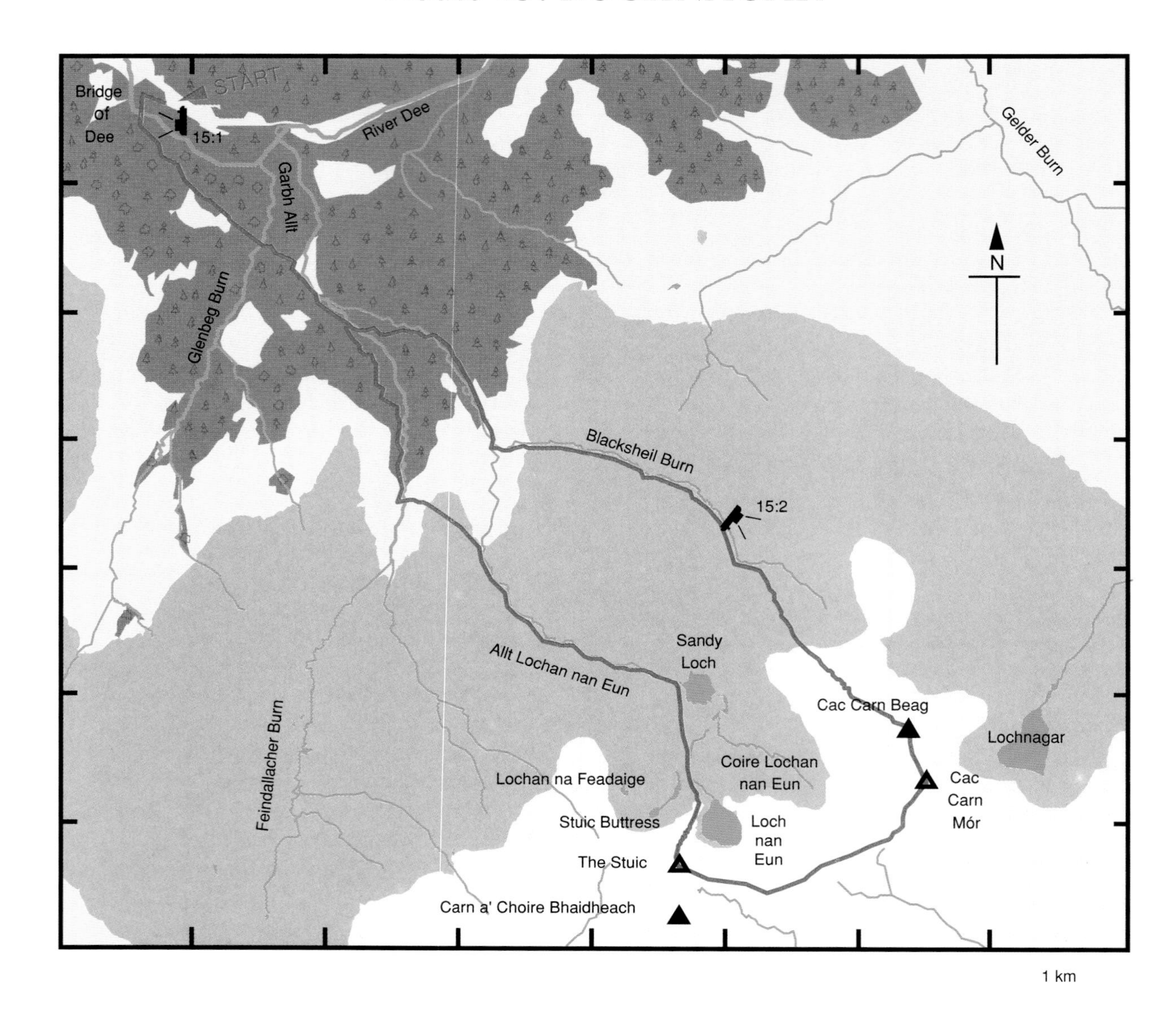

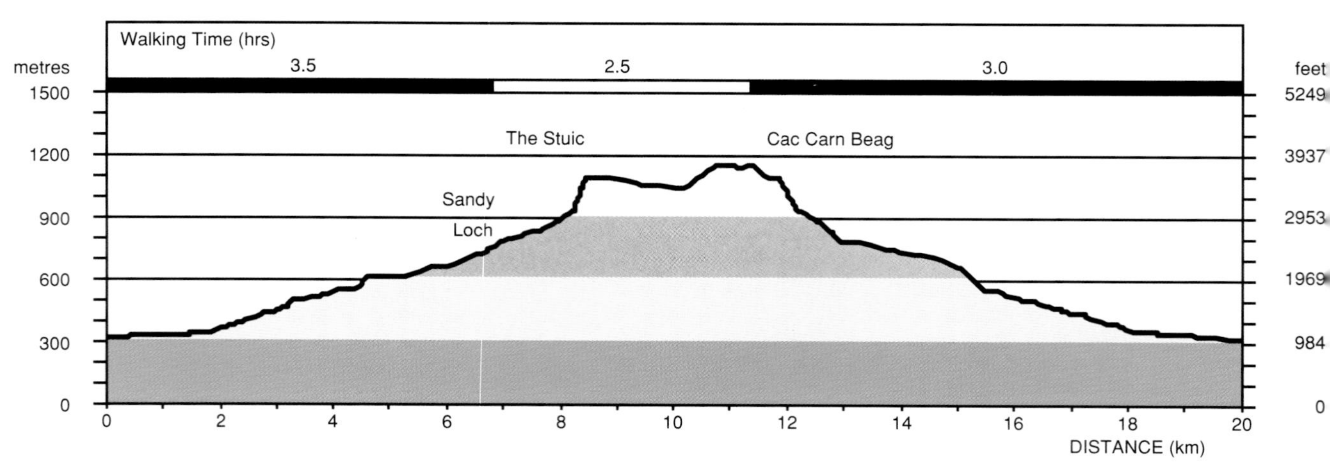

10

DEESIDE

HIGH-LEVEL ROUTE

Route 15 · Lochnagar

STARTING LOCATION
Invercauld Bridge on the A93, 5 km (3 miles) E of Braemar.
OSLR 43 and 44 or OSPF 255, 269 and 270/MR 188911.
Park on the verges at the junction of the minor road with A93, 250 m (275 yd) E of Invercauld Bridge and the Old Bridge of Dee.
Accommodates approximately 10 cars.

ALTERNATIVE STARTING LOCATION
Alternative parking on the A93, 2 km (1¼ miles) to the E, or at Braemar.

PUBLIC TRANSPORT
Nearest railway station – Blair Atholl or Aberdeen.
Regular buses, four to six daily, Aberdeen to Braemar.

OVERVIEW/INTEREST
A river of celebrated scenic splendour in beautiful Scots pine forests.
Two impressive corries; that of Lochnagar ringed by vertiginous cliffs.
Far-reaching panorama from the northern edge of the White Mounth.
Exciting scramble along a rocky buttress – avoidable.
Some free-ranging over long distances necessary.
Physically very demanding route.

FOOTPATHS
Good tracks in Ballochbuie Forest.
Awkward traversing unpathed moorland.
Rugged up along the Stuic Buttress.
Rough though undemanding on the White Mounth plateau to Lochnagar.

GRADING 5

TIME ALLOWANCE
9 hours.

DISTANCE

Excluding Height	20 km	(12½ miles)
TOTAL HEIGHT GAINED	920 m	(3018 ft)

PRINCIPAL HEIGHTS
The Stuic (The Pinnacle) 1093 m (3585 ft)
Lochnagar:
Cac Carn Mór (Big Shit Carn) 1150 m (3772 ft)
Cac Carn Beag (Little Shit Carn) 1155 m (3789 ft)

The Old Bridge of Dee to Sandy Loch

Allow 3½ hours

Walk WNW by the A93 towards Braemar. Turn R after 200 m (220 yd) and proceed S on the track that leads on to the Old Bridge of Dee. There is a gate-house on your L. Cross the River Dee and go through a wooden gate on the other side, just prior to a junction with a forest track. At the track, turn L and pursue the route SE into the beautiful Ballochbuie Forest. Though not quite the largest, it is nonetheless the finest stand of Scots pine in the Highlands. Beyond the trees, the wedge of the Stuic and Lochnagar are prominent on a distant skyline.

When 300 m (330 yd) beyond the bridge, walk straight on at a crossroads of tracks. All around, the forest is an attractive mix of birch and pine. Here and there, conspicuous protrusions of pine needles and earth from prolific carpets of mature

15.1 *The Old Bridge of Dee and Ballochbuie Forest from the north bank of the River Dee.*

heather betray the presence of wood-ants. It is marvellous to contemplate such regimented rivers of insects flowing in and out of their colonial mounds – common purpose and the division of labour, identified long before Marx!

After passing through a wooden gate between deer fencing, continue SE at a crossroads of tracks. Walk over the wooden bridge that crosses the Glenbeg Burn and then come to a line of deer fencing on your R. At the next junction of tracks, bear R through a K-gate adjacent to a large gate. Carry on gently uphill on the track that winds its way beside the Garbh Allt. Where the track hairpins R, stay above its R bank on a path off to the L. Soon you reach a green metal footbridge on your L, at the top of a waterfall, and from here you should keep to the path heading SE through the forest. The path is wet in places, but nowhere uncomfortably so. Approximately 400 m (¼ mile) from the waterfall, emerge at a forest track. Turn R on to it but then almost immediately L at its junction with a still better one.

Continue steadily uphill, now bearing SSE. Between the trees to your rear, beyond the Dee Valley, looking NW, the vast Cairngorm tableland dominates the horizon. Increasingly wider gaps between the pines suggest a thinning out of the forest on coming above the Feindallacher Burn on your L. Follow it upstream, bearing R and S. Close to the southernmost edge of the forest your first objective on the White Mounth, The Stuic and its distinctive buttress, now seems well within striking distance.

Emerging from the trees entirely, pass through a K-gate on the L side of a larger deer fencing gate. About 100 m (110 yd) further on, strike off from the path down a heathery bank on the L to gain the level ground in front of a distinct meander in the burn. Then ford Feindallacher Burn and commence a course ESE, free-ranging up over the moor and on to the broad ridge of Druim Odhar. From the top, curve down SE towards the W bank of the Allt Lochan nan Eun. On a route upstream of the allt, stay close to it all the way.

Progress is slow at times, over numerous heather banks and uneven grassy tussocks. Coming around on the S side of the large mound on your L, Meall an Tionail, you arrive eventually at Sandy Loch. From here, the magnificent Coire nan Eun and the Stuic Buttress are revealed at close quarters.

Sandy Loch to Lochnagar *Allow 2½ hours*

If on your assessment of The Stuic from Sandy Loch you would rather not confront its buttress head-on, then instead make for the easier slopes leading above the W side of Coire nan Eun (see 'Escapes'). Otherwise, walk S from the loch-shore on a beeline for The Stuic. A gradual ascent continues over the now boulder-cluttered landscape of the corrie, a wide bowl seemingly divided into two by the buttress. Soon, you are above and between Lochan na Feadaige on your R and the more substantial Loch nan Eun on your L.

Attack the buttress head-on, following a path up its narrowing crest SSW. Steepness increases until the ground falls away quite sharply either side. There is a definite feeling of exposure to the situation but the scrambling proves safe and easy, the granite blocks secure. In summer, common gulls may share your air space. High up in this corrie, they were for me an unexpected sight. I have since learned of a well established high-nesting colony at Loch nan Eun. On the wing, they make manoeuvering up and down seem so easy.

A final bit of clambering brings you at last on to The Stuic. A small cairn marks its summit at 1093 m (3585 ft) and, as you might expect, the view is extensive. It seems more fitting, however, to describe the panorama from Lochnagar where there is a convenient view indicator.

Leave the cairn and walk E by the well-worn path near the rim of the Coire nan Eun. Its high N-facing crags on your L may, at any time of the year, exhibit at least one or two pockets of snow. Below them, it would not be unusual to make out moving white blemishes, those of high-grazing sheep, characteristically oblivious to the inhospitable terrain.

After about 800 m (½ mile), having lost a little height, the path swings to the L. Continue along it, soon ascending quite steeply again. Resume a gentler ascent across the plateau while following a succession of small cairns towards the summit tor of Cac Carn Mór at 1150 m (3772 ft). Tentative gazes over the edge of the Corrie of Lochnagar, on your R, may well tempt you a little further round the rim to attain a better view of its spectacular cliffs (see 'Extensions'). The corrie buttresses are famous to climbers for challenging routes; equally loved by poets are the dark waters of the loch below. You cannot fail to be stirred in some way here.

From the tor of Cac Carn Mór, walk N towards the higher of Lochnagar's two summits. The rock mound of Cac Carn Beag lies at the other end of a pinkish granite path. On top, there is a triangula-

15.2 *The summit of Cac Carn Beag (Lochnagar) from the Blacksheil Burn.*

tion pillar at 1155 m (3789 ft) and a view indicator close by. On a clear day, the mountains of a far-reaching panorama are easily identified: W, Ben Nevis, Buachaille Etive Mór; WSW, Schiehallion; SW, Ben Lawers, Ben More, Ben Lomond, Ben Vorlich; S, Mayer; SSE, Driesh; E, Mount Keen; NW, Cairn Gorm; WNW, Ben Macdui.

Many more mountains are in view besides and the prospect across the Dee Valley, from Braemar to Balmoral, is superb.

Lochnagar to the Old Pridge of Dee

Allow 3 hours

Leave the summit behind heading WNW, in a line with Meall an Tionail. Initially, the gradient is easy but caution and concentration are demanded of you further down. Shift to a NW bearing on slopes generously strewn with boulders. Sandy Loch is now just over 1 km (2/3 mile) away to the W.

When below the most hazardous section of the moss-clad rocks, continue over difficult, unpathed terrain towards the visible origins of the Blacksheil Burn. The craggy protrusion to the N is the Prince's Stone. Typically moorland in character, the ground becomes noticeably softer and wetter approaching the burn. It is a while before a noticeable channel in the watercourse provides a descent reference point. Nevertheless, continue downstream heading NW.

To your rear the summit of Cac Carn Beag now resembles a broad cone, a new perspective on Lochnagar. As you slowly bear more W, curving around the N side of Meall an Tionail, the topography is prolifically punctuated by peat hags, bogs and lime green sphagnum mosses. Simply do your best to minimize the ordeal. Bog-asphodel, cotton-grasses and sundew add to the botanical interest of this section, as do the ghostly pale stumps of the remains of Scots pines. It is difficult to imagine a forested landscape at such high altitudes, before insatiable timber demands banished it from its natural home.

Keep to the L side of the Blacksheil Burn. The gradient becomes appreciably steeper and the potholes more numerous nearing Ballochbuie Forest. At the confluence of the Blacksheil Burn with the Allt Lochan nan Eun, the trees of the forest begin to amass in front of you. Turn R to ford the Blacksheil Burn, then walk NNW along the E side of the Allt Lochan nan Eun, pursuing a rudimentary path. Follow the allt downstream, into the depths of the forest, to a deer fence which blocks further progress.

I have only ever once glimpsed that most elusive and rare creature, the capercaillie, and it was here. My companion and I startled it from the heather from which the bird, at first appearance an agitated mass of dark feathers, made a clumsy flight for better cover. In Britain, these Highland forests are its last remaining stronghold.

Undeniably, deer fencing is important to allow regeneration of the forest and at Ballochbuie fluorescent ribbons placed along it are an unsightly attempt to alert birds to it. Fencing is a hazard to other low flyers too. In some places, foxes have learned to patrol the perimeters for easy pickings. However, since we exterminated the wolf, deer numbers have reached destructive levels. In such ways does our species mess with the balance of nature.

Turn L and walk down alongside the fencing to come next to the Allt Lochan nan Eun. Ford the allt and then head up a steep bank on the other side to reach a gate. Pass through it and then follow the path NW, now on the L side of the allt. It soon joins with another leading up from a footbridge on the R. Proceed W on the obvious path through the trees to cross the Feindallacher Burn via a wooden footbridge. Pursue the track up on the other side. Before reaching better tracks, turn R and pursue again the path beside the Garbh Allt waterfalls. From here, continue in reverse of the route through the forest to return to the Old Bridge of Dee.

Alternative routes

ESCAPES

The ascent of Lochnagar is most frequently made from the E, beginning at the Spittal of Glenmuick, just N of Loch Muick. This shorter option avoids any scrambling and there is a path all the way. Also, the starting location at the end of the minor road from Ballater is a little higher above sea-level than that from the Old Bridge of Dee. However, by this far less interesting route you miss out on the wonderful Ballochbuie Forest as well as the Stuic. Allow 6½ hours.

Non-scramblers can avoid The Stuic Buttress and still enjoy the Scots pines by following the broad crest of the SE ascending ridge from Druim Odhar. After 2.5 km (1½ miles) of free-ranging, this connects with the rim of the Coire nan Eun at its far western edge. The walk above the corrie can also be pursued from this end as far on as Sandy Loch: strike off SW from the lochside to come above the W wall of the corrie. In adverse weather, use the ridge to Druim Odhar for the safest and fastest descent from The Stuic.

The beautiful forests of Ballochbuie and the chocolate-box scenery of the River Dee can be explored by the more leisurely on a maze of excellent tracks. Poets, artists and wildlife enthusiasts will all be in their element.

EXTENSIONS

If only a short detour is made from Cac Carn Mór, all visitors should at least walk a little way around the rim of the Corrie of Lochnagar to contemplate its staggering rock scenery. Those prepared for a trek as far around as Meikle Pap will be rewarded with perhaps the finest view of the corrie – a vantage point which reveals the overwhelming extent of its buttresses and precipitous gullies.

Munro-baggers should head S from The Stuic for a short, easy stroll across the high moor to the uninspiring summit of Carn a' Choire Bhaidheach, before continuing E. Allow an extra ½ hour.

The main route represents a long and tiring day and therefore further extensions are not recommended.

Route 16: GLEN QUOICH and GLEN LUI

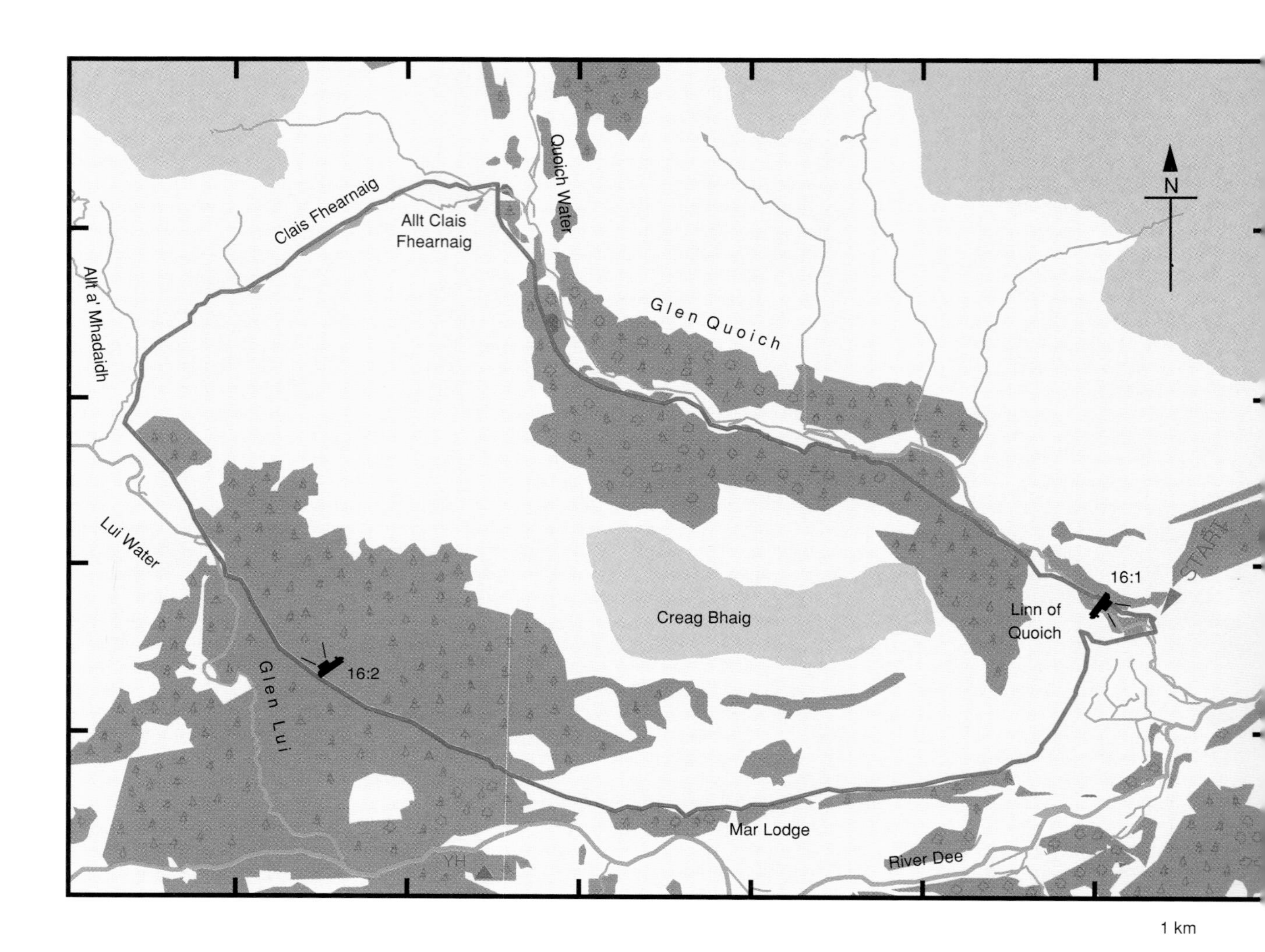

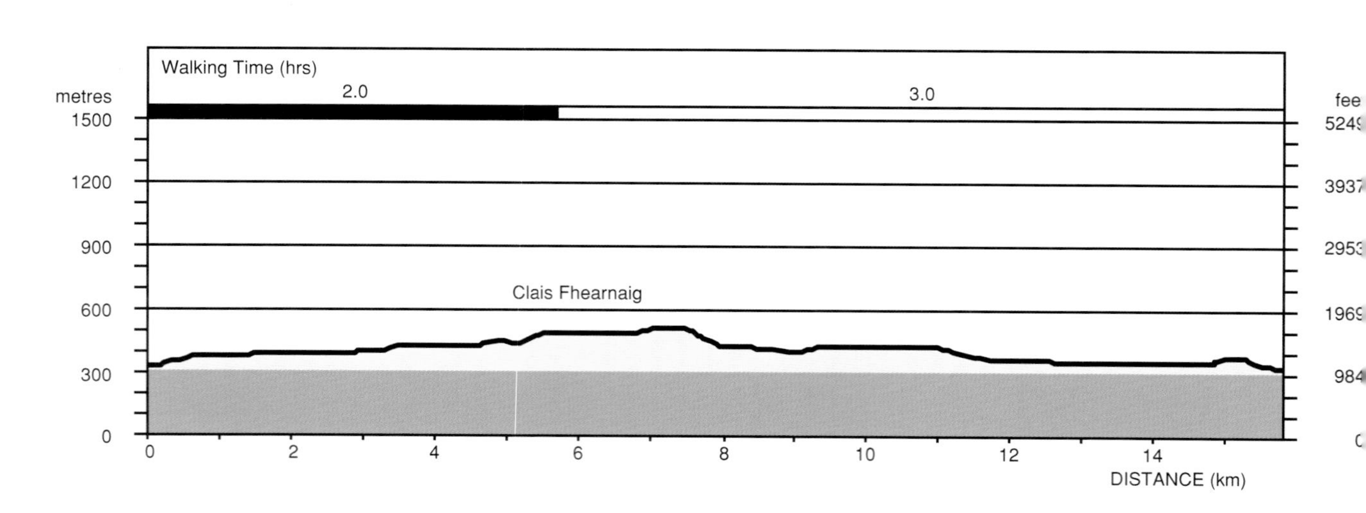

Route 16 · Glen Quoich and Glen Lui

STARTING LOCATION
Allanaquoich, in the Dee Valley, 3 km (2 miles) W of Braemar as the buzzard flies or 16 km (10 miles) from Braemar by road.
OSLR 43 or OSPF 255/MR 118912.
Bankside car park at Quoich Water, by the bridge at the end of the minor road from Braemar.
Accommodates approximately 20 cars.

ALTERNATIVE STARTING LOCATION
Alternative parking at the Linn of Dee; adds 4 km (2½ miles) to route distance.

PUBLIC TRANSPORT
Nearest railway station – Blair Atholl or Aberdeen.
Regular buses, four to six daily, Aberdeen to Braemar.
Postbus, once daily, Braemar to Allanaquoich (except Sunday).

OVERVIEW/INTEREST
Two scenic glens below the southern edge of the Cairngorm plateau.
Follows a delightful river amid beautiful Scots pine, larch and birch woods.
Passes through the tranquil, rocky defile of Clais Fhearnaig.
Few, if any, route-finding problems.
A generally straightforward and undemanding route.

FOOTPATHS
Excellent tracks in Glen Quoich and Glen Lui.
In places rough, though clear and easy to follow between the glens.
A metalled minor road in the Dee Valley.

GRADING 2

TIME ALLOWANCE
5 hours.

DISTANCE

Excluding Height	15.8 km	(10 miles)
TOTAL HEIGHT GAINED	230 m	(755 ft)

PRINCIPAL HEIGHTS
None – highest point of 510 m (1673 ft) at MR 062929.

Allanaquoich to Clais Fhearnaig

Allow 2 hours

Begin on the track heading W from the parking place near Allanaquoich bridge. Pass in front of a white house with a red roof on your R and on to a sign on the R, 'Steep Slopes Please Take Care'. Bear R from here up a bank on which you realize the warning is perhaps over-cautious.

Proceed WNW between Scots pines and at the ruins of a cottage on your R, turn L to cross the footbridge above the Linn of Quoich. Here, the descending Quoich Water flows over flat slabs between high craggy banks in the loveliest of woodland settings. On the other side, turn R and continue WNW by the S side of Quoich Water. A gently rising path, on a bank between the pine and larch, brings you further from the water on your R. Bear L and walk out on open ground to a junction with a better track. Turn R and resume a course heading WNW into the Scots pines ahead. There is no ground layer of vegetation to this forest remnant, presumably the result of over-grazing, and regeneration seems unlikely.

Steady and rapid progress on the excellent undulating track through the trees soon finds you above a clearing on the R. This is a good spot to contemplate how various human practices have created very different landscapes. The natural forest of mixed age Scots pine on your L contrasts strikingly with the dense canopy and homogeneous regimentation of the plantation across the water, looking N. To the R of that, vast open heather slopes with burnt and bald patches depict a moorland scene managed purposefully for its grouse potential. In the more distant N looms the rounded top of Beinn a' Bhuird.

For a few hundred metres, the Water of Quoich finds a course that flows well to the R of the track. You meet up with it again near a footbridge on the

R which connects with a path on the N side of the water (see 'Escapes'). Here, the Scots pines are mixed with birch and there is a good, thick carpet of mature heather beneath, making a most attractive scene. The track comes very close to the water and on the opposite side an extensive sandy bank has been exposed by the erosive force of the river.

Ignore a path off to the L and stay on the track heading WNW following the water upstream. Old twisted and gnarled pines and the needle-stacked mounds of wood-ant colonies add much to both the aesthetic appeal and the wildlife interest of the glen. Your ascent is slow and almost unnoticed as you gradually swing R around the glen to come adjacent to a Scots pine plantation on your L. Walk on parallel to a line of deer fencing at its boundary, proceeding now NNW. Quoich Water is 150 m (165 yd) below, to your R. After passing a plantation access track at its top end, on the L, head N up to cross the Allt Clais Fhearnaig. Crude metal pipes channel the water under the track. After a further 10 m (10 yd), pursue a path off to the L.

Walking W, the path ascends the grassy slopes next to a fenced enclosure on the L. A sign on the L warns: 'Deer Stalking, August 1st to October 20th. Please Remain On Paths.' The path is not too worn due to the temporary nature of the enclosure. However, keep to a course on the R side of the fencing, passing a corrugated shed on your L. Then turn L, following the more distinct trace of a better defined path and making for an obvious narrow gap between the hill slopes ahead. To the SE, a distant Lochnagar can be seen if you glance over your L shoulder. Leaving the enclosure well behind, veer L a little and carry on WSW into Clais Fhearnaig, a long, narrow defile with steep and rocky banks on either side.

Clais Fhearnaig to Allanaquoich

Allow 3 hours

From where the allt of the same name flows out of the E end of Clais Fhearnaig, a simple dam of boulders has created an artificial ribbon of still water. Continue by the clear path above the N side of the lochan.

All is quiet in the shelter of Clais Fhearnaig, a peaceful haven where the pale, splayed root skeletons of long deceased pines protrude in a surreal way from shallow still waters. The ambience of the place will be appreciated by those in reflective mood, with time to linger. For me, it is in just such landscape that a need for escapist sanctuary is invariably fulfilled.

Beyond the W end of the lochan, there is a pool on your L. Shifting to the R, ford a burn before reaching the L side of a reedy pond at the bottom of a gully. When released from the confines of the defile, perhaps regretfully, you emerge on to the open moor.

Stay with the path and close to the embankment on your R, now at the highest point of the route at 510 m (1673 ft). Although not the best viewpoint, looking SW there are two plantations on the opposite side of Glen Lui.

Begin a downhill course towards the prominent meanders of Lui Water below. The gradient steepens on coming alongside the Allt a' Mhadaidh, in a gully on your R. Walk S from here and downstream of the allt, fording a small feeder burn flowing from the L along the way. Further down, pass the ruins of a hut on the opposite bank.

One of the best views on the route is at MR 058924, that NW along Glen Lui before having completely descended into it. Many of the Cairngorm mountains on the S side of the plateau are visible, including Ben Macdui and Derry Cairngorm and, to the WNW, Cairn Toul.

At the excellent Glen Lui track, turn L and walk SE by the E side of Lui Water. A line of parallel deer fencing is on the L. Your progress shifts SSE on approaching the near bank. Leave the track where it bends R over a bridge and then descends by the W side of the Water. Instead walk straight on, following a less well maintained track which soon veers L. Proceed uphill, resuming a course SSE. Pass a track to the L that continues uphill. Stay with the one that from hereon flanks the hillside forests of Doire Bhraghad, along roughly the 420 m (1378 ft)

16.1 *The Linn of Quoich from the bridge over Quoich Water.*

16.2 *The Cairngorm mountains from the track in Glen Lui.*

contour. The views back towards the Cairngorms deserve repeated pauses.

Progressively shifting to ESE, the higher slopes to your L are dominated by some fine stands of mature birch. Scots pine predominate across the slopes below, on your R. Approximately 1 km (⅔ mile) beyond the junction with the uphill track on the L, pass through a gap in deer fencing. On the skyline directly ahead, a transmission mast on Morven's distant summit confirms your course.

Further on, the forest is almost entirely a deciduous one until a crossroads of estate tracks is reached. Carry straight on and past an 'East Grampian Deer Management Group' sign on the L, again requesting you not to deviate from the tracks during stalking times. Beyond a black metal gate, obstructing access to vehicles, the track traverses a devastated area of pine stumps. Views across the Dee Valley bring new delights.

Turn L and walk E, along the road, passing the two cottages at Claybokie. Further on, a track on the R leads down through the trees to Mar Lodge but stay on the road above it. The owner does not welcome locals, visitors or wildlife.

Beyond the immediate grounds of the Lodge, pass a new Scots pine plantation on your R where the road bends NE. Turn L off the road and begin to walk up on the track opposite another one leading down to Cragan. Pass by the R side of a black gate and a fire warning sign. The track rises to give a more elevated view across Deeside, the valley and the confluence of Quoich Water with the River Dee. Above, on your L, the hillside bears the unfortunate scars of soil erosion from past clear-felling. At a junction of tracks on a hairpin, turn sharp R and descend to the bridge over Quoich Water where your motor-driven carriage awaits at Allanaquoich.

Alternative routes

ESCAPES

The best option for a very short walk is to begin the route as described, and after 2 km (1¼ miles) cross the footbridge over Quoich Water at MR 101922. Walk back down the path on the N side of the water to return to Allanaquoich. This still takes in the lovely Linn of Quoich, one of the finest aspects of the main route. Allow 1¼ hours.

For those who would rather not depart from the excellent tracks, then walk as far as you like along either glen and return the same way. If you wish for beautiful surroundings, Glen Quoich is the better option. For extensive views to the Cairngorm plateau, venture into Glen Lui. Such routes, avoiding the Clais Fhearnaig section, are Grade 1.

The Linn of Dee is a popular beauty spot and justifies a detour on the drive to Allanaquoich.

EXTENSIONS

Braemar is the obvious base for explorations on Deeside and on the southern Cairngorm mountains and glens. There are numerous opportunities to extend the route, especially to the N and W.

To the N, Glen Quoich divides 1 km (⅔ mile) beyond the crossing of the Allt Clais Fhearnaig. Dubh Ghleann is the W branch and for Munroists offers perhaps the finest approach to Beinn a' Bhuird. From Allanaquoich, to its summit and back, allow 8 hours.

On the Glen Lui side, Derry Lodge is a further 2.5 km (1½ miles) WNW of the point where the glen track is gained from Clais Fhearnaig. From here, walking routes to Ben Macdui and many of the other more southerly Cairngorm mountains are possible. The Lodge also lies at the S end of one of the finest and most famous of mountain passes, the Lairig Ghru. A long deep gash, it bisects the Cairngorms and links Strath Spey with Deeside. This marathon trek is not for those who have to return to a car. From Coylum bridge at the N end to Derry Lodge, allow 8 hours. To reach the road at the foot of Glen Lui, allow a further 2 hours.

Possibilities for extending the main route are endless and it would be easy to devise your own.

Route 17: CAIRN GORM

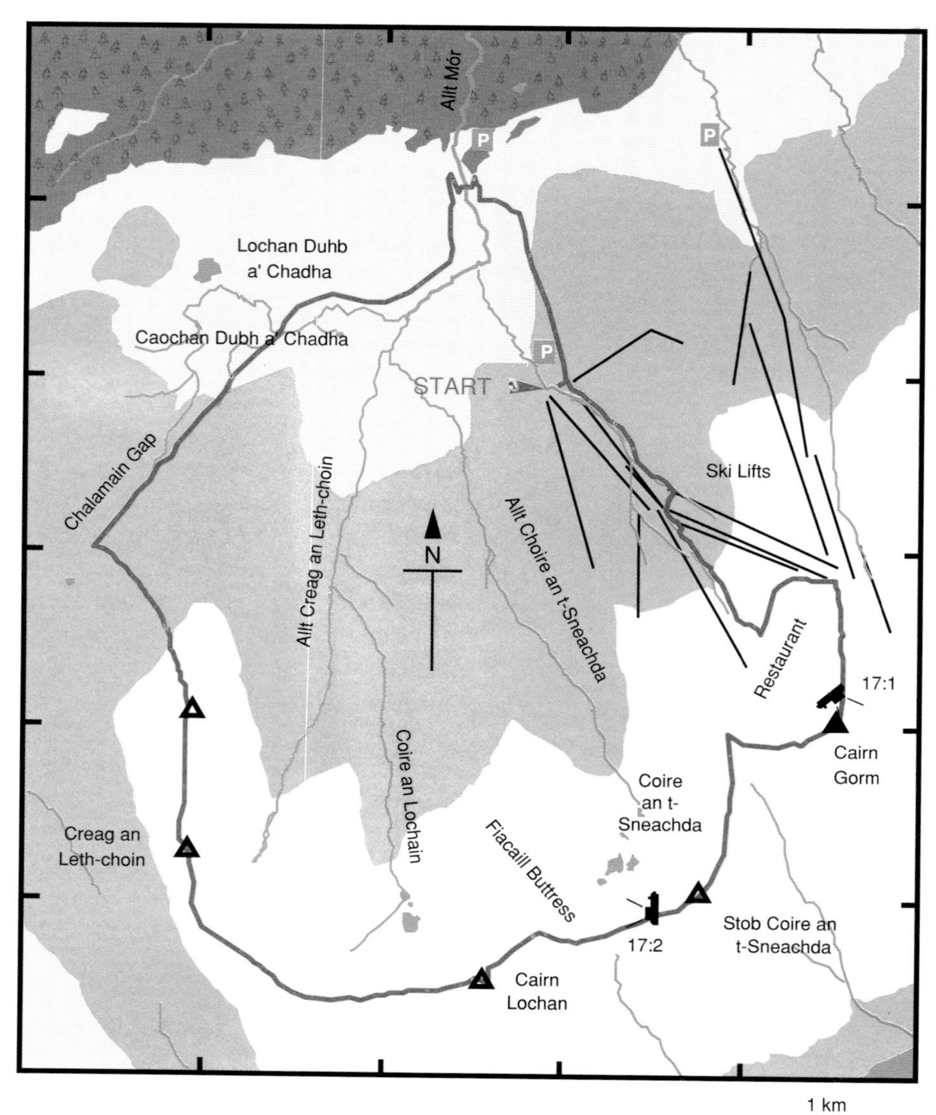

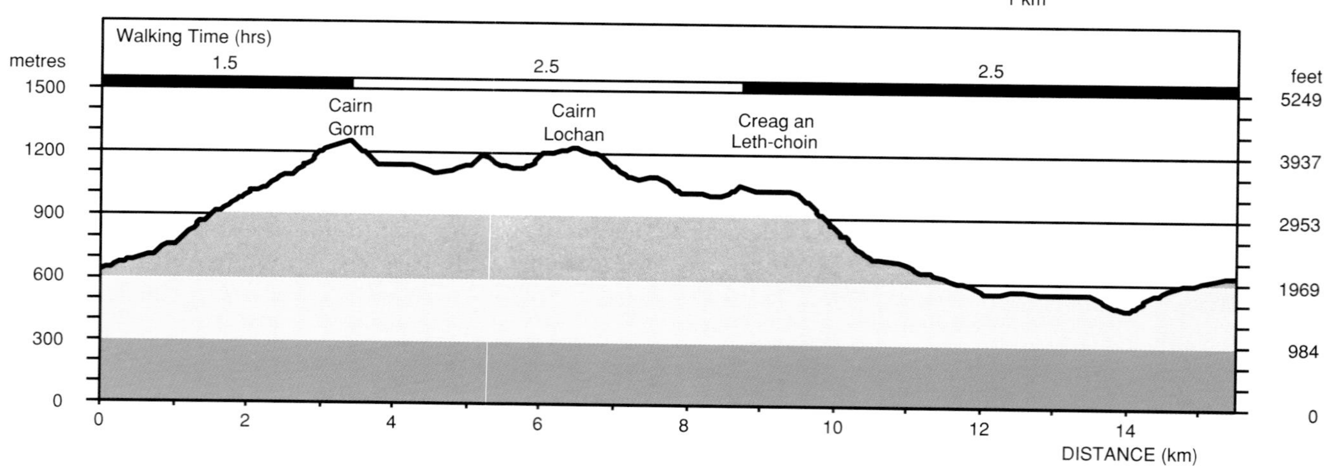

11

CAIRNGORMS

HIGH-LEVEL ROUTE

Route 17 · Cairn Gorm

STARTING LOCATION
The Coire Cas car park at the end of the Cairn Gorm ski road, 14.5 km (9 miles) from Aviemore.
OSLR 36 or OSOL 3/MR 990060.
A huge car park sited at the bottom of the ski tows and chairlifts near a WC and restaurant.
Accommodates approximately 200 cars.

ALTERNATIVE STARTING LOCATION
Parking by the Allt Mór, on the Cairn Gorm ski road at MR 985073.

PUBLIC TRANSPORT
Nearest railway station – Aviemore.
Regular buses, ten daily, from Inverness to Aviemore; four daily during ski-ing conditions, between Aviemore and ski slopes.

OVERVIEW/INTEREST
An easy ascent on one of Scotland's highest mountains.
Unique summit plateau of arctic terrain.
Superb summit panorama.
A walk above wild N-facing corries and the spectacular Lairig Ghru.
One of Britain's coldest environments, with significant wind-chill, even in summer – go well-clad.
Competence and skill with a map and compass are essential.
Physically demanding route.

FOOTPATHS
Good track and well-maintained path to summit.
Quite clear and mostly even over summit plateau.
Rugged on descent, from Lurcher's Crag to beyond Chalamain Gap.
Some free-ranging necessary.

GRADING 4

TIME ALLOWANCE
6½ hours.

DISTANCE

Excluding Height	15.5 km	(9½ miles)
TOTAL HEIGHT GAINED	1040 m	(3412 ft)

PRINCIPAL HEIGHTS

Cairn Gorm (Blue Cairn)	1245 m	(4086 ft)
Stob Coire an t-Sneachda (Peak of the Snow Corrie)	1176 m	(3858 ft)

Cairn Lochan (Cairn of the Lochan)
1215 m (3986 ft)
Creag an Leth-choin (Lurcher's Crag)
1053 m (3455 ft)

Coire Cas to summit of Cairn Gorm

Allow 1½ hours

Nowhere else in Britain is there such a large tract of arctic terrain than on the Cairngorm plateau. Here lies the highest land mass in Scotland. Together with the surrounding lower-level environs, the area is generally referred to as the Cairngorms. The plateau is also within the boundaries of Britain's largest nature reserve, the Cairngorms NNR. At any time of year, only those very well prepared should dare venture on to it.

Pass by on the L side of the restaurant, VC and chairlift buildings at the S end of the car park.

Pursue the track heading SE on the L side of the Allt a' Choire Chais. Simply follow uphill the obvious cables for the chairlift, which are above you on the R.

Beginning on a broken tarmac surface, the track continues agreeably underfoot and speedy, unhindered progress is possible. This is just as well, given the unsightly nature of the ski developments in Coire Cas. On your L pass a snow vehicle storage depot and then bear R in front of the middle chairlift station at White Lady Shieling.

17.1 *The weather and transmission station on the summit of Cairn Gorm in September.*

Pass under the chairlift cables and then turn L and head up on the track that continues SE, crossing the Allt a' Choire Chais by a bridge. To assist efforts to minimize erosion, heed the signs 'Please Stay Off All Verges'.

The gradient steepens, now about 100 m (110 yd) to the L of a ski tow. Bear L and then turn even sharper L at a hairpin bend to continue N. Curve round to the R and walk steeply uphill to reach the top of the chairlift and the Ptarmigan restaurant perched high on the mountainside.

A clear, well-marked and worn path continues S for the final 160 m (525 ft) of ascent to the summit of Cairn Gorm. Snow poles mark the route, should the path be covered. A radio relay and weather-recording station lies about 80 m (90 yd) E of a large summit cairn, a commanding vantage point from where the views are far-reaching. In the far distant NW, the Torridons, Kintail and the Knoydart hills can all be seen on a clear day. However, it is the more immediate aspect across the plateau, to its peaks and near corries, that most compels. Looking SW, the Fiacaill Buttress across Coire an t-Sneachda is a particularly impressive feature. Some of the peaks of the Cairngorms, and those nearby, include: SW, Braeriach; SSW, Ben Macdui; S, Derry Cairngorm; SE, Beinn Mheadhoin; ESE, Beinn a' Chaorainn; E, Ben Avon, A' Choinneach; ENE, Bynack More.

Cairn Gorm to Creag an Leth-choin (Lurcher's Crag)

Allow 2½ hours

Leave the summit by descending W over the rubbly granite terrain. There is no distinct path but simply head towards the top of the Fiacaill a' Choire Chais ridge, marked by a cairn at 1141 m (3743 ft). Turn L and walk S on a cairn-marked descent. Follow a path that is soon joined by one from the L which effectively cuts the corner. As you begin to ascend once more, bear R and keep to a course that stays close to the rim of Coire an t-Sneachda with its magnificent N-facing wall of crags and buttresses. On your R, there is some marvellous corrie scenery to enjoy, the crowds on the N side of Cairn Gorm now left far behind.

The flat terrain of the plateau to your L is a stunningly wild place. A unique variety of plants, of species normally associated with the arctic, can be found here, including rare grasses, heaths and mosses. Birds that find such a savage environment favourable for breeding include snow buntings and ptarmigan, the latter being common here. (I once saw five within an hour.) It is far less likely that you will glimpse a snowy owl, although they have been known to reside on the plateau.

On reaching the cairn at 1176 m (3858 ft), the summit of Stob Coire an t-Sneachda (not named on OS maps), you have gained a truly fine perch above the deep bowl of the corrie. Loose grey scree litters the corrie walls below the cliffs and lower down fills the gaps between a few desperate lochans. The view NE offers a re-appraisal of Cairn Gorm.

Continue along the rim of Coire an t-Sneachda. Descend, following a succession of cairns WSW to where, on your R, two narrow but conspicuous buttresses protrude above Central Gully. It is worth clambering out over their granite blocks to view the rugged profile of the Fiacaill Buttress, 500 m (⅓ mile) to the W. Return to the main path and head down to 1111 m (3645 ft), now above the shallow recesses of the Coire Domhain on your L and at the lowest point between two summits. From here, a path leads S across the plateau for Ben Macdui (see 'Extensions'). Instead, ascend the path up the slopes immediately W. A cairn marks the top of the Fiacaill Buttress and the ridge which demarcates Coire an t-Sneachda and Coire an Lochain. Bear L and walk SW by the rim of Coire an Lochain to a sizable cairn. It is a short distance SSW from here to the summit cairn of Cairn Lochan at 1215 m (3986 ft). As you make your way round, look to your R down the narrow and precipitous scree gully of The Vent. On no account attempt to descend it!

There is little of a discernible path on the W side of Cairn Lochan but endeavour to adhere to the slopes descending W. After about 800 m (½ mile), you reach an intersecting path which to the N heads down steeply into Coire an Lochain. Having come away some distance from the edge of the corrie, without deviating, cross the path and

17.2 *The Fiacaill Buttress, from the buttresses near the Central Gully on the rim of the Coire an t-Sneachda.*

proceed W over the broad grassy plateau of Miadan Creag an Leth-choin. Make the visible cairn at 1083 m (3553 ft) your immediate objective. At this point, re-orientate yourself to push on NW, making for the next cairn at 1010 m (3347 ft) and still on an unpathed course. You are now above the spectacularly deep and long running gash that bisects the Cairngorms, the Lairig Ghru, on your L. Looking S along it, the truly dramatic proportions of this enormous trench are revealed. On the other side and dominant among the West Cairngorm peaks is Braeriach, the third highest mountain in Britain at 1296 m (4251 ft).

From here, it is possible to follow a more discernible impression of a path N, up to Creag an Leth-choin (Lurcher's Crag) at 1053 m (3455 ft). It is a bit of a clamber among boulders to the summit, yet provides perhaps a still better vantage point for the Lairig Ghru. The natural pine forest of Rothiemurchus (see Route 18) carpets the ground to the NW.

Creag an Leth-choin (Lurcher's Crag) to Coire Cas car park

Allow 2½ hours

Walk out over the broad bouldery ridge, heading N from Lurcher's Crag to a noticeable cairn at the end. From here, carry on N down the rough though increasingly green slopes beyond, on a beeline for Loch Morlich in Glen More Forest. Although OS maps indicate a path on the slopes further W, there is little evidence of this and it is necessary to find your own way down over the rough moor. The slopes are nowhere too steep.

Lower down an obvious rocky defile is discernible and you should now be slowly bearing L. Make for a tiny lochan at its S side. On reaching it, pass to the L of it to gain a clear and obvious path. Turn R and walk NE traversing wet and peaty ground and into the confines of Chalamain Gap. To make further advances, it is necessary to boulder-hop your way across for about 250 m (275 yd). Returning to spongy and poorly drained ground on the other side, emerge from between the banks on to open moorland. Lochan Dubh a' Chadha is about 1.2 km (¾ mile) away to the N.

Continue downhill and NE and ford a burn after about 600 m (⅓ mile) from the Gap. The going underfoot becomes appreciably less demanding. Ford easily a further three burns, the last of them by stepping stones. Then walk up a steep and high bank above the Caochan Dubh a' Chadha, the burn on your R. Bear R and continue E for a while. Take up again a route NE when above the confluence of waters feeding the Allt Mór. Scots pine have been planted on either side of the path, presumably in the hope of extending the forest of Rothiemurchus in the years to come.

Resume downhill progress on veering N. Proceed to a sign 'Sugar Bowl Trail Ends Here' and then turn R at a hairpin bend to descend a path down a bank to a footbridge. Cross the Allt Mór, here at the tree line, and walk up the E bank. After about 150 m (165 yd), take an uphill path off to the R. At a cairn, bear L to the edge of a disused road, signed 'Reseeded Area, Keep Out/Main Path'. Head up on the path through the heather to join with the Cairn Gorm ski road. Turn R and walk S for 1 km (⅔ mile), returning to the car park at the end of the road.

Alternative routes

ESCAPES

In adverse weather, it is advisable to avoid altogether the summit plateau of Cairn Gorm. The lowest temperatures in Britain are frequently recorded here and it is surely at the top of the wind-chill league. It can snow any day of the year and it is difficult to imagine a more inhospitable or hazardous place to be in a winter blizzard. The Mountain Rescue Services are at their busiest on these mountains.

In a white-out, the only viable escape is N, back down through Coire Cas via the Ptarmigan restaurant. At certain times the chairlift can be used, up and down, between the restaurant and car park. However, venturing any way on the plateau W of Cairn Gorm is a serious undertaking and from the other summits descents are either steep or potentially difficult to navigate from, and in many cases both.

The 'there and back' option to Cairn Gorm via the Coire Cas track offers one of the quickest and easiest baggings of any Munro. Allow 2½ hours. The last chairlift is normally at 4.30 p.m. A siren sounds when the chairlift is stopping due to high winds.

EXTENSIONS

In good weather, the obvious extension is to venture across the plateau as far as Ben Macdui. At 1309 m (4294 ft) it is the second highest mountain in Scotland, though until the middle of the last century it was thought to be the highest. Only Ben Nevis is of greater stature.

From the Coire Domhain, walk SSW, later bearing S, to reach the summit after about 4.5 km (3 miles). Having bagged your second Munro of the day, return the same way to where the path divides after about 2 km (1¼ miles). From this point, take the L fork heading towards the W side of Cairn Lochan and then on to Lurcher's Crag. Allow an extra 3 hours.

Munroists wanting a very long day out might consider the peaks to the E of Cairn Gorm, specifically A' Choinneach and Bynack More. Such a route is best pursued by way of the eastern summits first, before continuing via The Saddle, finishing with Cairn Gorm and the Cairn Lochan section. Unless your only objective is Munros and you intend to descend via the Coire Cas ski lifts, you should start at a parking place further N on the Cairn Gorm ski road. Allow 11½ hours in total via a final descent from Lurcher's Crag.

An interesting scrambling route to the plateau is via the Fiacaill Buttress, on the W side of Coire an t-Sneachda, although this is really the preserve of those experienced on difficult terrain.

Route 18: LOCH AN EILEIN and ROTHIEMURCHUS

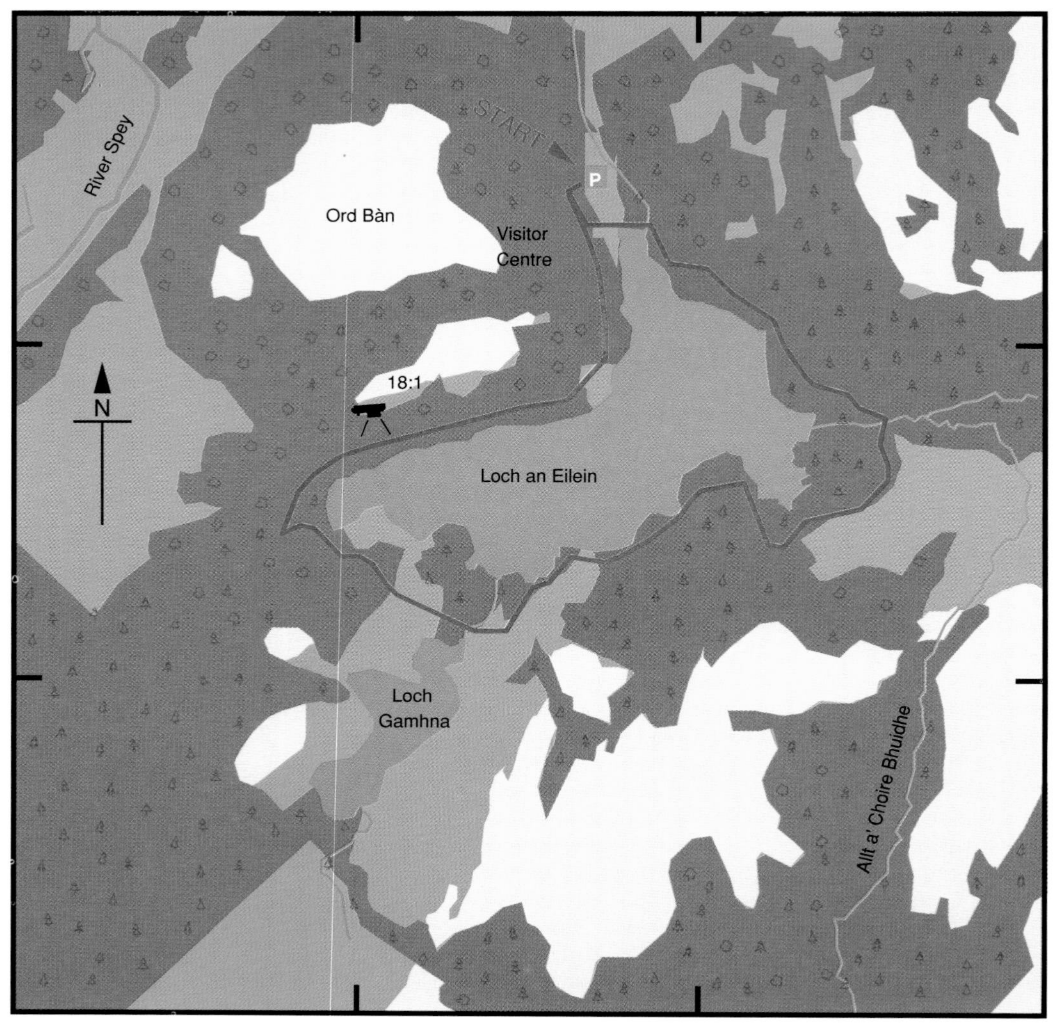

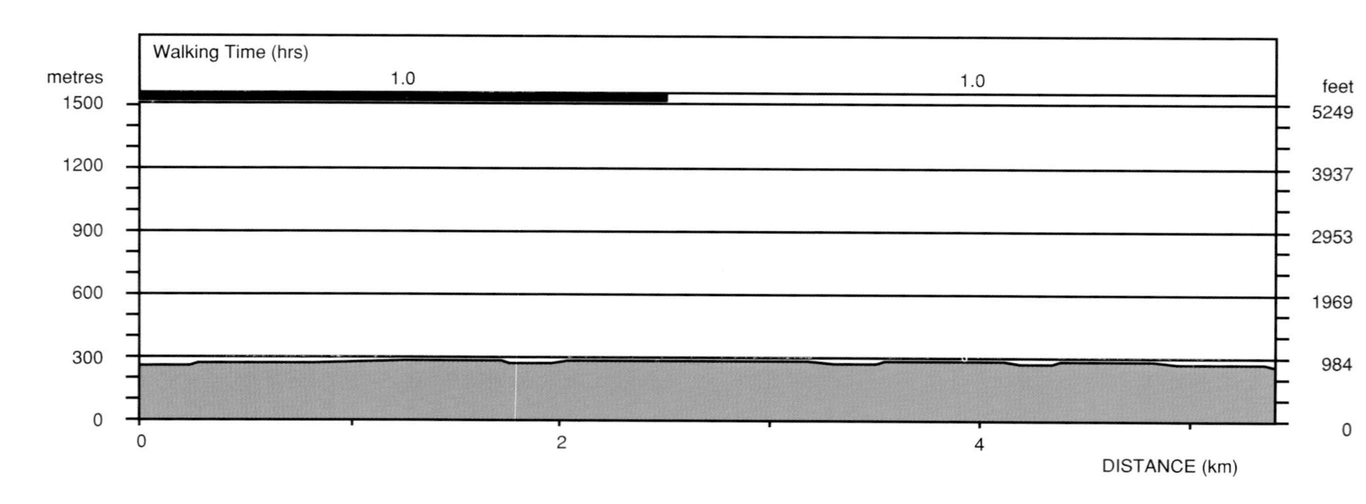

Route 18 · Loch an Eilein and Rothiemurchus

STARTING LOCATION
Car park adjacent to Loch an Eilein VC, on N shore of loch, 5 km (3 miles) S of Aviemore.
OSLR 36 or OSOL 3/MR 897085.
Accommodates more than 40 cars.

ALTERNATIVE STARTING LOCATION
None.

PUBLIC TRANSPORT
Nearest railway station – Aviemore.
Regular buses, ten daily, from Inverness to Aviemore.

OVERVIEW/INTEREST
Loch an Eilein (Loch of the Island).
Rothiemurchus (Plain of the Great Pine).
A straightforward loch-shore route on a nature trail.
Explores the finest remnant of naturally regenerating Caledonian pine forest.
Within the boundaries of Cairngorm NNR, Britain's largest National Nature Reserve – unique opportunities for observing wildlife.
Ruins of a fourteenth century castle on an island.

FOOTPATHS
A clear, broad, dry and level footpath for the entire circuit.

GRADING 1

TIME ALLOWANCE
2 hours.

DISTANCE

Excluding Height	5.4 km	(3½ miles)
TOTAL HEIGHT GAINED	50 m	(164 ft)

PRINCIPAL HEIGHTS
None.

The Visitors' Centre to Loch Gamhna

Allow 1 hour

Walk S from the car park, passing in front of the VC on your R. Follow the excellent lochside path S beneath lichen encrusted trees, here a mix of Scots pine with birch and larch. Loch an Eilein is on the western extremity of Scotland's largest remnant of Caledonian pine forest. The ground layer, predominantly of heather and juniper, is typical of that in much of Rothiemurchus Forest. The vast and impressive tableland constituting the Cairngorm mountains is seen across the loch at gaps between the trees looking SE.

Ignore the track to the R, after 200 m (220 yd), and continue S on the one closest to the loch-shore. At a clearing you come within 150 m (165 yd) of the loch's only island. The ruins of its fourteenth century castle are seen across the water on your L, looking E, set against a backdrop of heathery slopes beyond. Walk across the grass to the L of Loch an Eilein Cottage to reach a promontory. The outlook from here affords perhaps the best view across the loch. A memorial stone is dedicated to the memory of Major General Walter Brook Rice, who drowned while skating on the loch in December 1882.

Return to the main path, a few metres to the R, turn L and pass through a gate. Walk W through yet finer stands of trees while continuing on a route by the lochside. Scots pines are in abundance, displaying all the many and varied dimensions of an undisturbed ancient forest. Young saplings stretch to the light side-by-side with the fallen and half-rotten red timbers of huge trees, centuries old. Such a unique habitat is, not surprisingly, the home of some of Scotland's rarest birds and mammals. These species have enjoyed a long association with the Highlands and include: red squirrel and pine-marten. Among the bird species are: crested tit, Scottish crossbill, osprey and capercaillie.

At the W corner of the loch, where the path divides, close to a rack of fire beaters, take the L fork and walk SE. On the L, between the path and loch-shore, benches have been positioned for contemplative enjoyment of the place. Forested slopes extend to Kennapole Hill on your R. The

forest thereafter becomes more open with heather covered ground. Young trees are thriving here, continuing the process of forest regeneration. Proceed to a footbridge over the burn that connects the waters of little Loch Gamhna on your R to those of Loch an Eilein, now about 200 m (220 yd) away to the L. From here you have the option of a diversion on the path around Loch Gamhna before continuing along the shore of the larger loch.

Loch Gamhna to the Visitors' Centre

Allow 1 hour

Proceed W for 100 m (110 yd) and veer L. Continue on the path below Inshriach walking NE to meet the loch-shore again on your L. Pass by some very necessary fire brooms and some unnecessary pathside cairns.

Here, in the forest on the loch's southern side, the trees have a predominantly different character from those in the forest encountered previously: they are less mature specimens with straighter, closely spaced trunks.

Veer R, away from the loch-shore, and pass through increasingly more open heather moorland again. Maintain a generally NE bearing to the far SE corner of the loch and gradually bear NW. For those who wish to linger, less distinct paths leaving the main track on your L offer access to the lochside. For the main route, continue NW on the more obvious track by the E shore.

Where a sign on your R points E to 'Lairig Ghru', cross the Allt a' Choire Bhuidhe. A distinctive bench on your L incorporates a flat-cleaved boulder as a back rest and marks this junction of tracks. Continue through the forest NW, pass through a gate by a Nature Reserve Panel and proceed to Lorimer Cottage on your R. From here, gain the N corner of the loch after a further 300 m (330 yd). The prospect S across the loch to the vast Cairngorm plateau seems to imbue the sad castle ruins with a vulnerable remoteness. The car park is just a little further N.

18.1 *Old Scots pine in Rothiemurchus Forest, on the west side of Loch an Eilein.*

Alternative routes

ESCAPES

It seems inappropriate to want to curtail this, the most leisurely of routes. Perhaps though, like many visitors to Loch an Eilein, you wish merely to view the castle ruins from the loch-shore, in which case simply return to the car park from Loch an Eilein Cottage. If, however, you have walked as far as Loch Gamhna, you might just as well complete the circuit. This is well within the abilities of even the most lethargic.

EXTENSIONS

Rothiemurchus, and its magnificent Caledonian pine forest, extends as far E as Loch Morlich where it puts to shame the conifer plantations nearby. An extensive maze of tracks provides access to the forest and walking them is a joy.

The adventurous might wish to explore the open moors beyond the forest by heading S towards the great Cairngorm tableland. Consider the walk into Gleann Einich as far as Loch Einich. Allow an extra 6 hours.

Another option is along the best known of all Scottish foot-passes – the Lairig Ghru, walking as far as you like.

Those content with the ancient forest itself can nonetheless substantially extend their excursion. Take the track E from Loch an Eilein, MR 906077, as far as the Cairngorm Club Footbridge over the Allt na Beinne Moire. Then walk back 250 m (275 yd) to the junction of tracks, and head NNW on the L side of the allt to Coylum bridge. Complete the circuit by returning to the car park on minor roads, walking at first W and then S after Inverdruie. Allow an extra 2½ hours.

Route 19: THE FIVE SISTERS OF KINTAIL

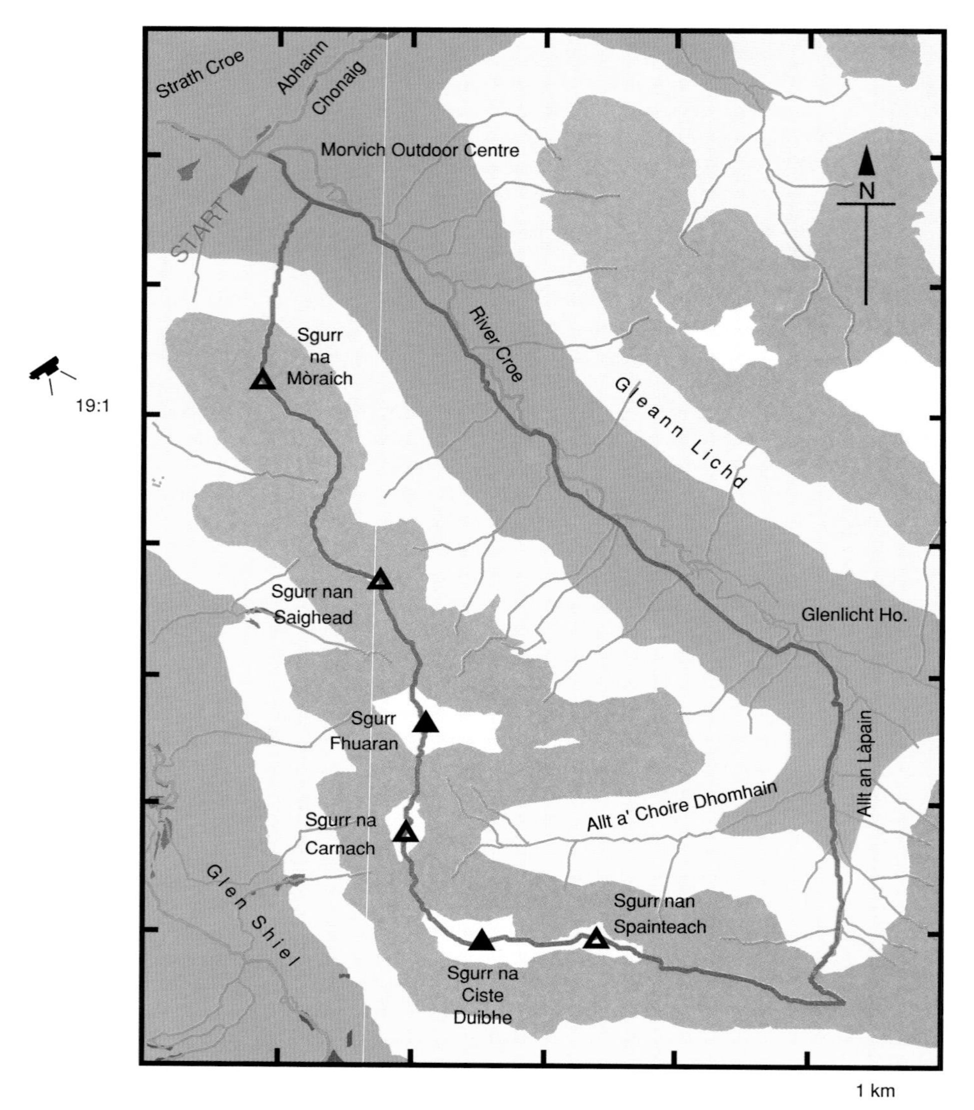

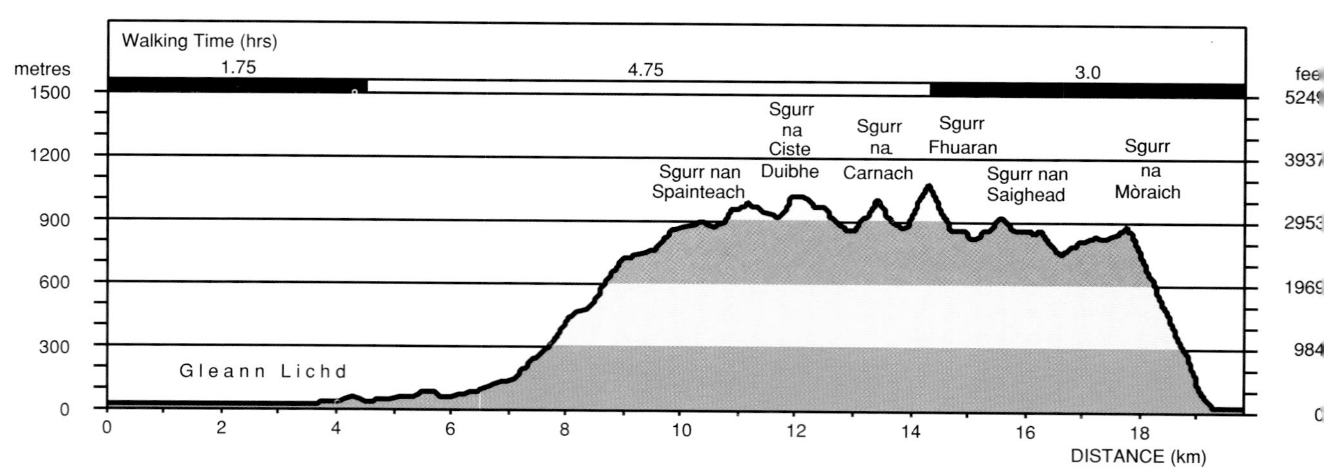

12

KINTAIL

HIGH-LEVEL ROUTE

Route 19 · The Five Sisters

STARTING LOCATION
Morvich Outdoor Centre in Strath Croe, 2.5 km (1½ miles) E of the A87(T) at the head of Loch Duich.
OSLR 33 or OSPF 205, 220 and 221/MR 967211.
Park on the verge on the minor no-through-road opposite, or just E of, the Outdoor Centre beside the River Croe.
Accommodates approximately 10 cars.

ALTERNATIVE STARTING LOCATION
Further parking at the NTS Kintail Countryside Centre.

PUBLIC TRANSPORT
Nearest railway station – Kyle of Lochalsh.
Regular buses to Sheil Bridge from Inverness and Kyle (except on Sunday).
Postbus, once daily, Kyle to Sheil Bridge (except on Sunday).

OVERVIEW/INTEREST
A classic West Highland ridge walk.
Opportunity to climb two Munros.
Magnificent views across Glen Shiel.
A roller-coaster route involving over 1500 m (5000 ft) of ascent.
Accurate compass work essential in mist.
Relatively undemanding terrain, free of scrambling.
Physically arduous due to total height gained.

FOOTPATHS
Excellent landrover track through Gleann Lichd.
Unpathed and steep ascent beside the Allt an Lapain.
Scramble-free ridge traverse on an obvious path.
Ends by free-ranging on a steep descent.

GRADING 6

TIME ALLOWANCE
9½ hours.

DISTANCE

Excluding Height	19.8 km	(12¼ miles)
TOTAL HEIGHT GAINED	1770 m	(5807 ft)

PRINCIPAL HEIGHTS
Sgurr nan Spainteach (Peak of the Spaniards)
990 m (3247 ft)
Sgurr na Ciste Duibhe (Peak of the Black Chest)
1027 m (3369 ft)
Sgurr na Carnach (Peak of the Stony Place)
1002 m (3287 ft)
Sgurr Fhuaran (Peak of the Spring)
1068 m (3503 ft)
Sgurr nan Saighead (Peak of the Arrows)
929 m (3047 ft)
Sgurr na Moraich (Peak of Morvich)
876 m (2873 ft)

Morvich to Glen Licht House *Allow 1¾ hours*

From Morvich Outdoor Centre, walk W along the road for about 50 m (55 yd) and then turn L on to the landrover track. Pass through a wooden gate to the L of a larger metal gate and cattle grid. Head off behind the Outdoor Centre, pursuing the excellent track SE into Gleann Lichd.

After about 400 m (¼ mile), ford easily a burn and approach two rusty corrugated sheds between the wooden fencing of sheep pens on the R. The track then comes alongside the River Croe where, on your L, alder trees line the bank. Follow the river upstream, continuing SE. On coming between the steep sides of Sgurr na Moraich on the R and Sgurr a' Choire Ghairbh on the L, the gleann narrows. Wildlife enthusiasts should note that otters are frequently seen patrolling these banks.

Where the track deviates from the riverside, pass between a gap in a dry-stone wall and then ford a burn. A little later cross another burn via a small bridge. Beyond a second gap in a wall, walk parallel to a dry-stone wall on your R and sheep fencing on your L. Ford a small burn and proceed between two further gaps in dry-stone walls, returning to the SW side of the river. Where the water has eroded a course between conspicuous sand banks, in spring and summer, look out for sand-martins darting in and out of nest holes. Migrants from Africa, these small birds are generally a rare sight in the north of Scotland.

Further on, river banks widen where the course of the water diverges either side of a small island. Two burns are easily forded just before the river twists sharply away to the L. Deposition has created a raised pebble beach. Cross a burn by a bridge constructed of railway sleepers and stones and then pass some ruined walls on your R, now incorporated into a sheep hold. On rejoining the course of the river, a dry-stone wall on your R heads off at 90° up towards a wooded gully below Sgurr nan Saighead.

Wetter ground soon comes between you and the river. Continue SE approximately 100 m (110 yd) from the near bank. Presumably to achieve better grip for vehicles, some wire fencing has been laid down in places to reinforce the surface of the track. At the point where the OSLR and OSPF maps show the track dividing into two separate paths, Glen Licht House can be seen to the SE 1.5 km (1 mile) distant. In truth, there is no real evidence of the two parallel routes indicated: the lower does not seem to exist. Simply continue along the deteriorating track (the more southerly representation on the map) 200 m (220 yd) to the R of the river and a little above it.

Walk through the remains of a dry-stone wall and then pass Glen Licht House on your L. A sign at the padlocked door commemorates an unfortunate pair: 'Haddon Woodburn Memorial Hut, open May 1956, in memory of Fred Haddon and Elliot Woodburn who lost their lives in a storm while climbing on Ben Nevis in May 1955 EUMC.' This is a sobering reminder that the Scottish hills should never be underestimated.

Glen Licht House to Sgurr Fhuaran

Allow 4¾ hours

Leave Glen Licht by the path heading SE. Ford a burn, pass a ruined croft and, when the path divides, take the R fork. (That heading L takes walkers over two footbridges and on through Fionngleann towards Glen Affric.)

Veer R and walk S on gently rising slopes just to the R of the N-flowing feeder to the River Croe, the Allt an Lapain. Follow the rough path over terrain which becomes more awkward underfoot, as steepness increases. You should be endeavouring to maintain a fairly direct route towards the low point on the skyline ridge ahead. Having encountered a succession of cascades and waterfalls, your progress is temporarily halted on reaching an intervening allt. At a point just to the R of the confluence of the Allt a' Choire Dhomhain with the Allt an Lapain, ford the former by boulder-hopping. When in spate, you might be forced to find a crossing point higher up.

Continue S, up steeper grassy slopes without deviating too far from the R side of the Allt an Lapain. You must pick your own route over the unpathed terrain though occasionally, alongside the allt, there may be traces of a rudimentary path. Any intervening burns are forded without problems.

The gradient relents on nearing the source of the Allt an Lapain. Veer slightly R and ford a burn flowing from the R. Proceed SSW and uphill on steeply rising slopes again, keeping to the R side of the more southerly feeder burn to the allt. On your L lie the almost unrecognizable remains of a hut. Beyond the top of the burn, bear sharply L and climb up to gain the ridge between Sàileag and Sgurr nan Spainteach. You should be at, or close to, the cairn in the Bealach an Lapain from where your endeavours are rewarded by a first view to the fine mountains on the S side of Glen Shiel. To your rear, the summit immediately N is that of Ben Attow (Beinn Fhada).

Turn R at the cairn and walk W along the narrow ridge path. Your first objective is the summit of Sgurr nan Spainteach, a simple ascent but likely to leave you panting for a while. Glance down to your R into the dramatic Coirein nan Spainteach. Depart from the summit cairn, descending W, and take care negotiating the path between boulders. The drop into the saddle requires careful footwork. Commence an ascent on a zigzagging path up on the moss-covered boulders of the E ridge of Sgurr na Ciste Duibhe. A large cairn, 3 m (10 ft) in diameter, marks the rugged summit plateau of the first sister. On having also captured your first Munro of the day, you can proudly bring water bottles together and toast your companions. Of course it would seem more fitting, though less wise, if they contained whisky!

Descend from the W side of the summit and veer NW following the path to where the ridge broadens out on wetter ground. Boulder-hop from here to reach an even lower part of the ridge at the Bealach na Craoibhe. Bear NNW for the next ascent, being aware of potentially hazardous loose boulders near the top. The diminutive summit platform of the second sister, Sgurr na Carnach, is topped by a modest cairn from where you can look down E into the impressive Coire Dhomhain. As is normal in N and E facing corries, snow can linger in its shadowed gullies well into summer. Proceed N, descending very steeply while continuing around the head of Coire Domhain. Ahead beckons Sgurr Fhuaran, the highest point on the ridge.

After dipping gently into the grassy saddle between the two sisters at the Bealach na Carnach, begin the gruelling climb that clocks up a further 200 m (650 ft) of height gained. Perched above what appears to be a huge pile of boulders capped by a small grassy summit platform, Sgurr Fhuaran is the other Munro of the ridge. It invites a long pause. The views from here (the big sister of the family) are the most far-reaching on the ridge. Your rewards are tremendous, extending NW as far as Skye on a clear day. High above Glen Shiel, the identifiable mountains of the area include: SW, the Saddle; SSW, Sgurr na Sgine; S, Sgurr Mhaoraich; SE, Aonach air Chrith; ESE, Sgurr a Bhealaich Dheirg; E, A' Chràlaig, Mullah Fraoch-choire; ENE, Beinn Fhada (Ben Attow); NE, Sgurr nan Ceathreamhnan; NNE, A' Ghlas-bheinn.

Sgurr Fhuaran to Morvich *Allow 3 hours*

Be warned that, in mist, descending Sgurr Fhuaran can be a disorientating affair. I once met a couple here who had walked up from Glen Shiel into a cloud. They promptly proceeded to descend the same way, believing themselves to be coming down the S ridge! After a compass reading, I was able to put them right. On this occasion, their route-finding error would have led only to to disappointment. However, such shortfalls in equipment revealed quite a worrying disregard for their own safety. On Scottish mountains, in bad weather, ignorance is no defence.

At first, head off NW from the substantial summit cairn, but soon descend N after skirting the L edge of Sgurr Fhuaran's precipitous North Face. There is in fact an alternative escape path which leaves the W side of the summit and connects with Glen Shiel. After about 400 m (¼ mile) bear L, keeping to the obvious ridge path. Proceed generally NNW, somewhat unexpectedly passing through a gap in a dry-stone wall at the Bealach Buidhe. Then, having re-ascended along the top of the enthralling East Cliffs, the insubstantial summit area of Sgurr nan Saighead is reached. Leave this, the fourth sister, by turning sharply L away from its cairn. Skirt the predominantly moss-covered ground on the narrow path at the top edge of the North East Face, walking as far round as Beinn Bhuidhe. The buttresses falling away to the R are especially impressive on this section – flat rock walls that have cleaved at 90° to each other. The effect is of a series of corners plunging vertically into the Coire na h-Uaighe.

Descend the rather insignificant top of Beinn Bhuidhe by walking NNE. After 500 m (⅓ mile) further around the rim of Coire na h-Uaighe, having begun the final re-ascent, the ridge broadens out and, on bearing NW, the gradient eases. Maintain this course across gently rising slopes for 1 km (⅔ mile). The final summit cairn on this marathon roller-coaster route caps a protruding outcrop on Sgurr na Moraich, the fifth and little sister. Its situation, at the northern terminus of the ridge, affords the finest view yet over Loch Duich to the WNW.

Free-range a very steep descent N, at first making a beeline for the large campsite in Strath Croe. Unfortunately, the relentless knee-jarring serves only to aggravate already tired legs. However, despite the lack of a path, you can proceed with confidence over grass that provides good grip. Having lost approximately 700 m (2300 ft) in height, veer R and traverse lower slopes to the NE. Regain the Gleann Lichd track just to the L of the rusty corrugated huts by the sheep pens. Turn L and backtrack NW for 400 m (¼ mile). Emerge at the no-through-road in Strath Croe from behind the Outdoor Centre. The start point is on the R.

Alternative routes

ESCAPES

By either omitting or returning from the fifth sister, Sgurr na Moraich, an easier if less direct descent can be made via the Coire na Criche, just N of Beinn Bhuidhe. Follow the Allt a' Chruinn down W, bearing NW on lower slopes, to emerge at the roadside at the SE shore of Loch Duich. Turn Left for Morvich, 1.5 km (1 mile) to the NE.

Should you tire sooner, then one option is to descend from the Bealach na Craoibhe to Achnangart in Glen Shiel. Walk downhill steeply W having bagged the Munro, Sgurr na Ciste Duibhe. Alternatively, consider the E-running spur from the highest top, Sgurr Fhuaran. Pursuing that ridge deposits you just SE of Glen Licht House. Another possibility from Sgurr Fhuaran is to make a careful descent of the slopes WNW of its summit which connect you with Glen Shiel. The last three escapes can also be used as ascent routes in order to curtail the main route. For those having to return to cars in Morvich, however, having gained the ridge it is probably best to complete the traverse.

The memorable view ESE from the Bealach Ratagain, accessible to all those with a car, should not be missed. From the A87(T) at Shiel Bridge, take the Glenelg road as far as the popular lay-by above Ratagan at MR 904198. The viewpoint prospect across the head of Loch Duich to the Five Sisters is a classic Highland scene. Such loveliness brings to mind the intriguing legend associated with these mountains. Supposedly, the Five Sisters are the five unclaimed daughters of a local farmer. Transformed by the local wizard into the peaks we see today, so as to preserve their beauty, they await the five brothers promised to them by a visiting family.

19.1 *The Five Sisters, across Loch Alsh from Auchtertyre.*

EXTENSIONS

The high boundaries of Glen Shiel are a Munroist's paradise. However, due to the rigours and physical demands of having to overcome more than 3000 m (10 000 ft) of ascent and descent, venturing beyond the Five Sisters ridge is not recommended.

Those staying in the area could benefit from further expeditions on the N side of Glen Shiel by tackling those mountains lying E of Sàileag. Together with the Five Sisters, these routes offer the walker a relatively complete picture of the area's varied topography.

Rising up on the S side is The Saddle, widely regarded as the finest mountain in Glen Shiel. Its infamous E ridge, the Forcan Ridge, provides one of the most sensational scrambles on the mainland. Alternatively, lying SE of the Saddle, a convenient chain of peaks allows mountain collectors the opportunity to tick off seven Munros in a single day.

All the suggested extensions are best pursued from starting locations in Glen Shiel.

Route 20: FALLS OF GLOMACH

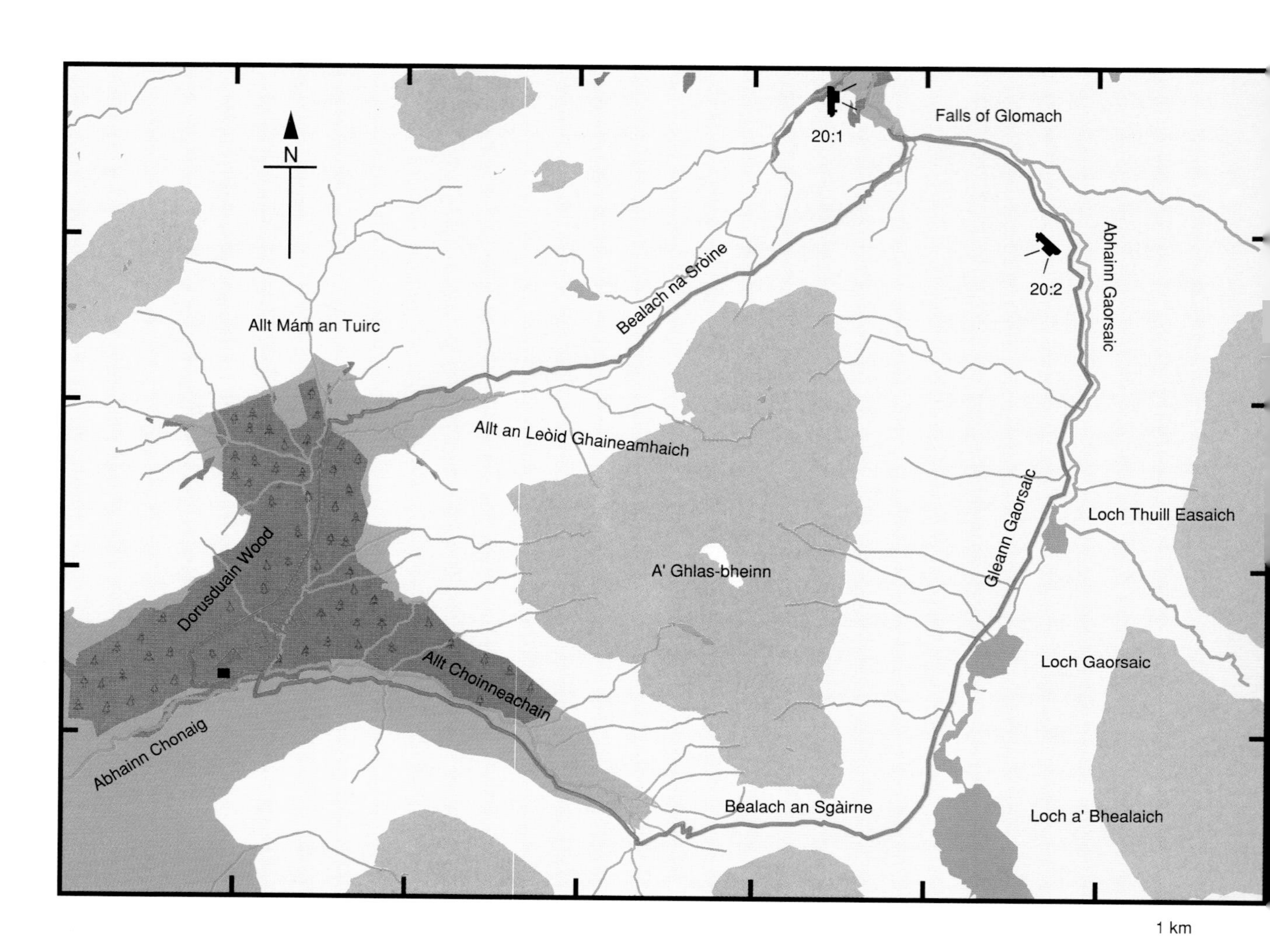

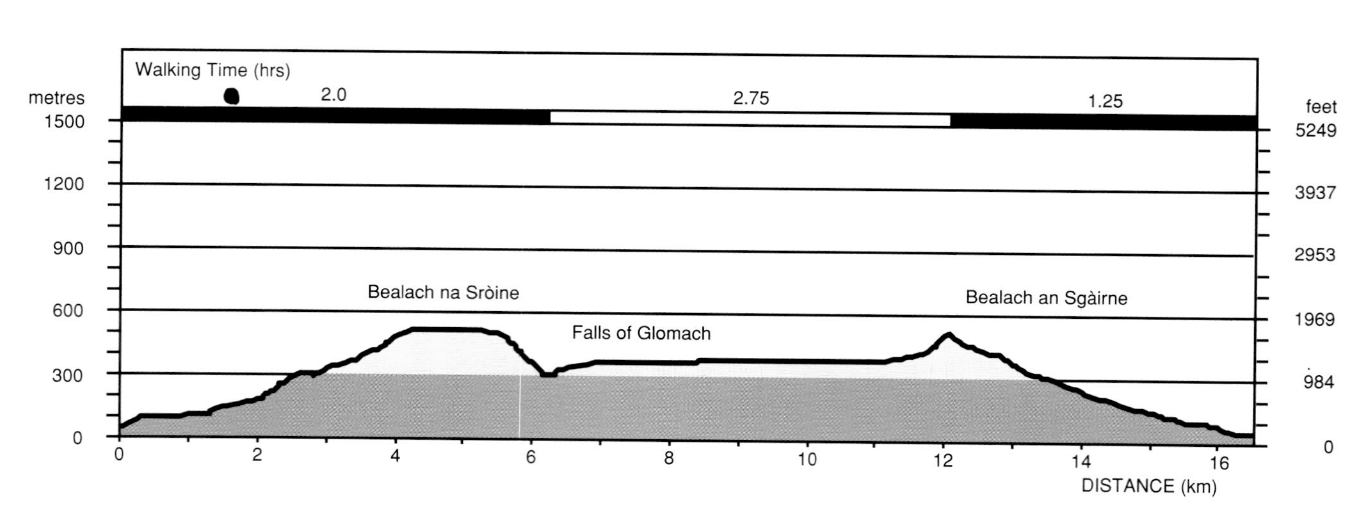

Route 20 · Falls of Glomach

STARTING LOCATION
Kintail Country Park, 2.5 km (1½ miles) ENE of Morvich, just off A87(T) at Loch Duich.
OSLR 33 or OSPF 205 and 206/MR 978223.
FC car park at E end of the minor road through Strath Croe, 400 m (¼ mile) W of Dorusduain House.
Accommodates approximately 20 cars.

ALTERNATIVE STARTING LOCATION
NTS Kintail Countryside Centre at Morvich. Allow at least an extra 1 hour from here.

PUBLIC TRANSPORT
Nearest railway station – Kyle of Lochalsh.
Regular buses to Sheil Bridge from Inverness and Kyle (except on Sunday).
Postbus, once daily, Kyle to Sheil Bridge (except on Sunday).

OVERVIEW/INTEREST
Visits the second highest waterfall in Britain.
Passes through an impressive bealach at the so-called Gates of Affric.
Golden eagle country.
Navigational problems unlikely.
Involves a significant traverse of an unpathed area across peat hags.
Physically quite demanding.

FOOTPATHS
Minimal waymarking.
Good forestry tracks at Dorusduain.
Cairned path approaching Falls of Glomach.
Awkward and often wet over unpathed section.
Eroded though well-maintained path descending Bealach an Sgàirne.

GRADING 3

TIME ALLOWANCE
6 hours.

DISTANCE

Excluding Height	16.5 km	(10¼ miles)
TOTAL HEIGHT GAINED	690 m	(2264 ft)

PRINCIPAL HEIGHTS

Bealach na Sròine	525 m	(1720 ft)

Bealach an Sgàirne (Pass of Rumbling)
514 m (1686 ft)

Dorusduain to Falls of Glomach

Allow 2 hours

Leave the car park and pursue the FC track, heading N into the forest, signposted 'Glomach Falls 4 miles, no cars please'. First, pass through a green metal gate and then begin on a gradual ascent between plantations of young conifers. Rapid progress can be made on the excellent track.

After 200 m (220 yd), turn sharp R where a sign directs you ENE to 'Glomach Falls'. The track continues gradually uphill as you then begin to follow the hill slopes round NE. There is a spacious and open feeling to the recently replanted forest area. (As in most plantation situations, however, the trees tend to block out the views on maturing; one expects a darker and more claustrophobic situation to return in later years.) Look to your rear SSE view, to the N end of the Five Sisters range.

Having progressed approximately 800 m (½ mile) from the car park, walk through a K-gate to bypass a much larger gate across the track between deer fencing. At a junction with another forestry track, joining from the R, a sign next to fire beaters points you in the direction of the falls. Soon after, the track divides where a gate between deer fencing on the L blocks that track. Continue via the R fork, walking down a little to cross a concrete bridge with iron railings over the Allt an Leòld Ghaineamhaich. Proceed N as the track veers L up on the E side of the allt and running parallel to it. Seen descending the crags to the WNW, a distant waterfall cascades from the slopes of Beinn Bhuidhe and Beinn Bhreac. It is worth scanning the skies above them as golden eagles are frequently sighted in the vicinity.

Having reached the far N end of the forest plantation, the track dissipates at a footbridge constructed from railway sleepers. Walk over the bridge to cross the Allt an Leòld Ghaineamhaich again and veer R. Begin to ascend steeply the opposite bank, initially beside a tributary to the allt on your L. A well-worn zigzagging footpath brings you quickly above the allt on your R. Proceed above its N side, following its course upstream. Stay on the path which varies in condition but progresses E up the L side of a steep-sided grassy gorge. Erosion has left a succession of pitted ravines scarring the mountain slopes opposite, to your R.

As height is gained, the severity of the gradient relents. Adjacent to a waterfall draining Meall Dubh on your R, veer L and proceed NE to emerge up on the Bealach na Sròine. Ford easily the upper reaches of a feeder burn to the Allt an Leòld Ghaineamhaich, then walk on to skirt the bottom of the NW-facing slopes of Meall Dubh. Higher up in the bealach, the path deteriorates, the going underfoot turning rougher and wetter. However, a succession of cairns guides you easily through. The summit of the bealach is reached at about 525 m (1720 ft) above sea-level, a point which affords fine views W to E across the mountains and wild moorlands of Inverinate and West Benula Forests.

Walk on gradually downhill, continuing NE to pass between the almost unrecognizable remains of a dry-stone wall. Beyond two further cairns, descend much more steeply towards the Allt a' Ghlomaich. At the bottom, having come down nearly 200 m (650 ft) since the top of the bealach, pass a red NTS sign on the L warning visitors of the danger of proceeding beyond the top of the Falls of Glomach, a little further on to your L. In order to view the falls at their most impressive, however, you should attempt to descend the well-worn but mostly safe path down the L side of its near-vertical gorge. Do not attempt to proceed beyond the end of the path. It brings you down about 30 m (30 yd) below the top of the falls, to a point where most visitors will plunder rucksacks for their cameras. The Falls of Glomach are spectacular and with more than a 110 m (360 ft) drop this is the second highest waterfall in Britain.

Falls of Glomach to Bealach an Sgàirne

Allow 2¾ hours

Return to the top of the falls and head off E following the Allt a' Ghlomaich upstream on its S side. Pursue if you can the vague traces of a path,

20.1 *The Falls of Glomach.*

little more than a sheep track, but more importantly maintain a course without deviating far from the allt on your L. Ford a burn which joins the allt from slopes on the R. The terrain soon becomes more awkward and inevitably progress is more sluggish.

Where the allt divides, after 1 km (⅔ mile) stay on the R side of the watercourse flowing from the S. This is the Abhainn Gaorsaic which, after veering R, should be followed upstream SSE. You are now entering Gleann Gaorsaic.

20.2 *The peat hags of Gleann Gaorsaic, looking SW to A' Ghlas-bheinn.*

Pick your own way through the gleann, the least demanding route being that alongside the abhainn. Gleann Gaorsaic divides the mountains of Sgurr nan Ceathreamhnan, Stuc Bheag and Sgurr Gaorsaic on your L with those of Meall Dubh and A' Ghlas-bheinn on your R.

Somewhat gruelling progress over seemingly endless peat hags brings you slowly S across the moor. Old and bleached root systems protrude from earthy banks like animal bones, a hint of a Highland landscape before sheep. These sad remains of the Caledonian forest of the past add some natural history interest to a landscape that is otherwise rather featureless. But there are com-

pensations and rewards for your persistence along the obstacle course. Rarely shifting from the 380 m (1250 ft) contour, the passage through Gleann Gaorsaic is without gradient. More significantly, for those seeking an antidote to the busy concerns of the twentieth century, there is a real sense of solitude and a unique ambience to be found. For the escapist, the lingerer and the dreamer, the place prompts a meditative response. What I would not wish on you is for your peace to be shattered, as mine was the last time I was here, by that menace of the Highlands: the military jet! Its eardrum-rupturing roars are made all the worse because they come upon you quite without warning.

In its upper reaches, the Abhainn Gaorsaic becomes more tranquil. Turbulent, tumbling waters give way to deeper, slow-moving peaty pools. Pass on the R side of the first of such pools and cross a burn via a ladder bridge. A subsequent burn is negotiated in the same way. Fording burns thereafter has mostly been made easier by rocks positioned as hopping-stones.

Diminutive Loch Thuill Easaich marks the confluence of the Abhainn Gaorsaic with the Allt Thuill Easaich. The waters of the latter drain off the mountain slopes opposite. Stay to the R of the loch-shore, picking up the faint trace of a path for a while. Walk on SSW, having veered to the R a little to bypass boggy ground near the waterside. At the end of the loch, pass to the L of some outcropping rocks. Gain drier ground on approaching the W side of Loch Gaorsaic. Follow the shoreline, passing a curious split boulder on your L, and on your R the roofless shell of a croft building. After about a further 200 m (220 yd), walk by a low rubbly wall no more than 3 m (10 ft) in extent.

Continue SSW and leave Loch Gaorsaic behind, making a beeline for a pile of boulders. Resume a free-ranging approach over the moor, similarly bereft (as on earlier ground) of any trails made by previous walkers.

Maintain a route as low in the gleann as the wet terrain will allow. This means bearing S to reach the NW corner of the last and largest of this series of lochs, Loch a' Bhealaich. Coming close to the loch, the summit of Ben Attow is identifiable on the skyline directly ahead. You will notice a small wooded island lying roughly 150 m (165 yd) from the shore – a green and prolific remnant of Highland safe from browsing mouths.

Strike off SW, uphill from the lochside towards an obvious bealach which breaches the imposing crags of mountains on your R. Ascend on a course of increasing steepness to ford a tiny burn in a gully, then gain a well-worn path just above it. The relative security of an obviously frequented route, as well as its more agreeable surface, comes as a welcome relief after the rigours of the previous few kilometres. Turn R and proceed WNW to a large cairn at the summit of the Bealach an Sgàirne, sometimes referred to as the Gates of Affric. The bealach is a superb vantage point for views E along Gleann Gniomhaidh and the upper reaches of Glen Affric as well as W down through the narrow defile of the bealach as far as Gleann Chòinneachain.

Bealach an Sgàirne to Dorusduain

Allow 1¼ hours

Descend W from the summit of the Bealach an Sgàirne, passing between the enclosing mountain walls of A' Ghlas-bheinn on your R and Meall a' Bhealaich on your L. Stay on the good path leading out through the middle of the bealach. On emerging at the upper reaches of Gleann Chòinneachain, stay on the slopes to the L. Looking out through the gleann NW, the Dorusduain plantations come into view below.

Where the path divides, take the R fork, thus continuing your descent rather than climbing uphill by the L fork which leads to Ben Attow. Take to zigzagging down on the path where the gradient becomes more severe. Erosion repair and maintenance is evident on this section. Ford the Allt a' Choire Chaoil at its confluence with the Allt Chòinneachain by straightforward boulder-hopping to the opposite bank. Bear R on the path and continue to descend Gleann Chòinneachain, passing between rusty fence posts and heading NW. Maintain a course downstream of the Allt Chòinneachain, staying above and to the L of it.

Dorusduain Forest lies directly ahead, on the N side of the gleann. Adjacent to the conifers at its E corner, evident windblown gaps between the trees have introduced an interesting unconformity to their otherwise regimental monotony.

The rowan- and birch-strewn gorge below marks the route of the Allt Chòinneachain, encountered at closer quarters. Gradually, the path curves W below the crags of Beinn Bhuidhe on your L where scattered deciduous scrub has taken hold. Somewhat confusingly, there is a second Beinn Bhuidhe lying 3 km (2 miles) NW on the other side of Strath Croe. It is to skies above this latter mountain that eyes should be fixed. When I was last here with a companion we had a wonderful time watching a pair of golden eagles, scouring the high slopes above Strath Croe until, as is so typical of these birds, they evaporated to a couple of high and distant specks on a rising thermal. The NTS claims such sightings in the area are reported frequently.

Beyond rusty fencing, come alongside the Allt Chòinneachain and its bankside birches. Loch Duich comes into view W looking down Strath Croe. Ford a small burn and walk on down across grass and bracken-covered slopes to a tiny cairn where the path divides. Turn R towards the wooded banks of the allt. By the bankside, turn sharp R at a hairpin bend and pursue a path to a sturdy wooden footbridge. A plaque informs you: 'Bridge constructed by 590 EOD squadron in June 1991 for the National Trust for Scotland.' Walk over the bridge where just to your R, in this beautiful woodland setting, is the confluence of the Allt Chòinneachain with the Allt an Leòld Ghaineamhaich. From their combined waters flows the Abhainn Chonaig.

From the N side of the abhainn, turn L on the path up the bank and through a K-gate between deer fencing. Traverse the marshy ground via the wooden planks as far as a junction with a forestry track. Turn L and follow the track W. Pass through a second K-gate, to the L of a deer fencing gate across the track, and proceed by the S edge of Dorusduain Forest on the L of its plantations. Your vehicle is on the R, 400 m (¼ mile) since bridging the Abhainn Chonaig.

Alternative routes

ESCAPES

The complete circuit is best curtailed by embarking on return routes from Dorusduain to either the Falls of Glomach or the Bealach an Sgàirne. In each case, returning the same way avoids the unpathed section through Gleann Gaorsaic and having to negotiate its endless succession of peat hags. For the energetic, both routes can be combined into a good day's walking. Allow 4 hours to the Falls of Glomach and back, and 3 hours for the Bealach an Sgàirne option.

EXTENSIONS

In *Wainwright in Scotland*, Britain's most famous walker describes Glen Affric as 'the loveliest of Scotland's valleys' and 'one of the finest walks in the Highlands for sustained interest'. If this is recommendation enough for you, then the marathon walk from Morvich, as far as Cannich at the E end of the glen, no doubt makes for a wonderful and very long day. When daylight hours are restrictive or you are simply not inclined to rush it, then break the journey either by camping or with an overnight stay in the remote bothy-like youth hostel at Allt Beithe. Begin via Gleann Chòinneachain, which leads on to Gleann Gniomhaidh. Alternatively, pursue the track through Gleann Lichd (see Route 19) to come around instead on the S side of Beinn Fhada (Ben Attow). Obviously, as with all one-way traverses, those with cars need to plan their way out of a logistical problem by arranging for transport from Cannich.

Munroists will no doubt wish to prolong their stay as there is a good concentration of mountains over 914 m (3000 ft) in the area. Those mountains closest to the main route are A' Ghlas-bheinn, Sgurr nan Ceathreamhnan and Beinn Fhada. They lie W, E and S of Gleann Gaorsaic, respectively. Other possibilities for extending the main route are few.

Warning: Heed the NTS sign and do not attempt to descend beyond the end of the path down the near-perpendicular gorge of the Falls of Glomach.

Route 21: BRUACH NA FRÌTHE

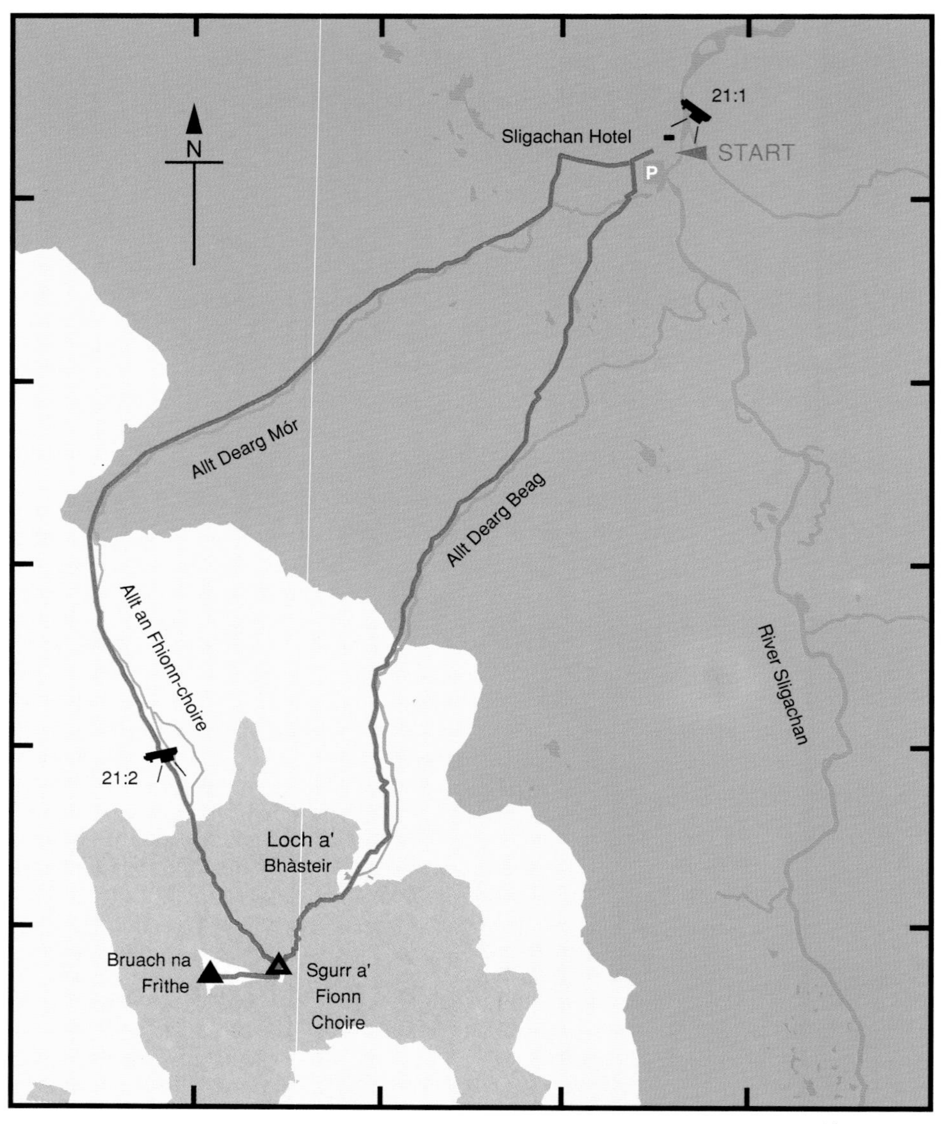

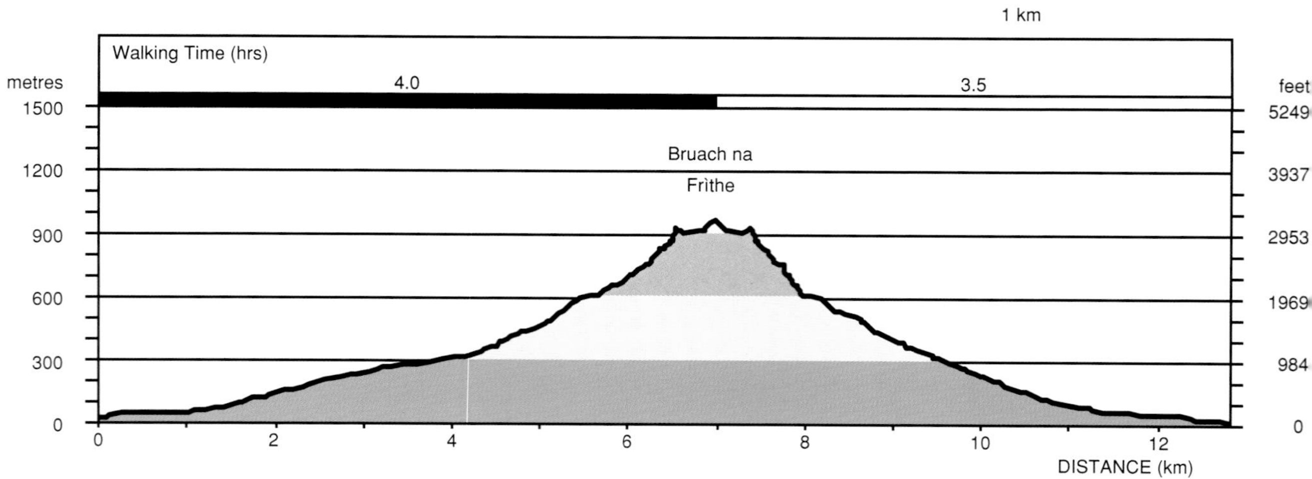

13

THE ISLE OF SKYE

HIGH-LEVEL ROUTE

Route 21 · Bruach na Frìthe

STARTING LOCATION
Rear of the Sligachan Hotel, 200 m (220 yd) SW of the junction with the A850.
OSLR 32 or OSOL 8/MR 485298.
Park along the disused stretch of road behind the hotel on the N side of the A863.
Accommodates approximately 15 cars – additional parking space in front of the hotel and at the viewpoint at MR 484297.

ALTERNATIVE STARTING LOCATION
Parking bay on S side of the A863, 700 m (⅓ mile) W of main starting location, by signpost 'Footpath to Glen Brittle'.
Accommodates approximately 6 cars.

PUBLIC TRANSPORT
Nearest railway station – Kyle of Lochalsh (for ferry).
Regular buses to Sligachan from Kyleakin and Portree.

OVERVIEW/INTEREST
Untypically easy ascent on the most demanding mountain range in Britain.
A spectacular skyline of summits amid incomparable mountain scenery.
Save for a clear day only.
The black gabbro rocks play havoc with the compass needle – unreliable readings are the norm!
Descent is via a steep, scree-ridden corrie.
Physically very demanding route.

FOOTPATHS
Minimal waymarking though sufficiently cairned.
Clear though eroded on ascent alongside the Allt Dearg Mór.
Unclear or non-existent in Fionn Choire.
Well-worn, if arduous, on the Cuillin ridge.
Steep and scree-ridden, often snow-covered, descending Coire a' Bhàsteir.
Peaty and frequently waterlogged approaching Sligachan Hotel.

GRADING 5

TIME ALLOWANCE
7½ hours.

DISTANCE
Excluding Height 12.8 km (8 miles)
TOTAL HEIGHT GAINED 1000 m (3281 ft)

PRINCIPAL HEIGHTS
Sgùrr a' Fionn Choire (Peak of the Fair Corrie)
935 m (3067 ft)
Bruach na Frìthe (Slope of the Forest)
958 m (3143 ft)

Sligachan Hotel to Bruach na Frìthe

Allow 4 hours

From Sligachan, the grandeur of Sgùrr nan Gillean, and the compact series of peaks at the N end of the Black Cuillin, is difficult to ignore. For so many, the view SSW from the hotel has proved the fatal lure to a lifetime obsession. In ever-increasing numbers, walkers and climbers continue to be drawn across the moors and up on to Britain's most demanding mountain range.

Leave the disused stretch of road behind the hotel by walking WSW beside the A863. Swing round W on approaching a line of timber fencing on the L side of the road. About 700 m (⅓ mile) from the hotel, turn L and strike-off across the moor on a track signposted 'Footpath to Glen Brittle'. Walk s, at first seemingly on a direct course for the Black Cuillin summits ahead. Having reached the Allt Dearg Mór on your L, veer R and cross an intervening burn via a convenient footbridge. Proceed SW towards a solitary house. Painted on a rock, 'PATH' diverts you to the R of, and away from, the driveway to Alltdearg House.

Beyond the house, the good track gives way to a footpath from where less straightforward progress can be expected. The path is clear to follow though prone to flooding in places after heavy rain. Continue by the R side of the Allt Dearg Mór on coming close alongside it again at a waterfall. Ford a small burn crossing the path from the R. A cairn indicates the route of the path when adjacent to a prominent waterfall.

Ascend gradually, maintaining a course upstream of the Allt Dearg Mór. Pass a second cairn on your R where the allt has cut a narrow channel between rocky banks. Subsequent cairns depict the route SW which deviates a little to the R of the allt for a while. On returning to the bankside, an extended NW aspect of the Black Cuillin is revealed. A series of lovely cascades and wee waterfalls between banks where stunted rowans cling on provide ideal foregrounds to an ever closer horizon of ridges and dark peaks.

At the Coire na Circe, veer L. Where the waters divide at the upper reaches of the allt, continue on the path beside the L-hand watercourse. Soon after, the footpath itself divides. Take the L fork and walk s. The R fork is a cairned route through the Bealach a' Mhàim to Glen Brittle, from where the mountain summits at the s end of the Cuillin Ridge are accessible.

Ford a burn flowing from the slopes above, on your R side, and pursue a path s following the Allt an Fhionn-choire upstream. The stony ground underfoot is increasingly of black gabbro, the hard, igneous, sole-removing rock that has shattered and eroded so spectacularly on the Black Cuillin. Small cairns plot a bankside course on the R side of the allt.

On reaching a steeper incline, bear SSE without deviating from the Allt an Fhionn-choire. The ascent through Fionn Choire is untypically green and grassy. Glance to your L from time to time for the improving view NE back across Loch Sligachan and to the distinctive bulk of Glamaig. This giant limpet of a mountain dominates the Red Cuillin, an unassuming line of pale, scree-ridden summits on the E side of Glen Sligachan. At the s end of

21.1 *The Cuillin Hills from the Old Sligachan Bridge over the River Sligachan.*

the glen, above Strath na Crèitheach, their red granites contrast strikingly with the black gabbros of their loftier neighbours. Both rock types meet on the slopes of one of Skye's finest mountains, Blà Bheinn.

Steepness increases still further until, at what appears to be a boulder-strewn plateau, a truly magnificent skyline encircles you. From here, in the upper reaches of the corrie, there is no real path to follow. However, making your own way SSE to the top of the corrie is a safe and straightforward affair. Walk on towards the lowest point on the ridge seen just to the L of an obvious serrated pinnacle and to the R of a sharp slanting blade, the Basteir Tooth. On resuming a steeper, more arduous ascent, stay well over to the L and on a beeline for the Bealach nan Lice.

Having gained the ridge, a halt is called for on

21.2 *Bruach na Frìthe from Fionn Choire.*

confrontation with the deep dark depths of Lota Corrie plunging down on the other side. Even more intimidating is the overwhelming array of sharp and shattered pinnacles. Turn R and proceed by clambering at first over Sgùrr a' Fionn Choire and then, continuing W, up the relatively easy slopes to Bruach na Frìthe at 958 m (3143 ft). The summit is unmistakable as it is the only height on the entire range marked by a triangulation pillar. From this Munro, the views are absolutely breathtaking, extending across many other Black Cuillin summits. Amid some of the most dramatic and exciting mountain scenery in Britain, the sights of knife-edged arêtes and towering precipices and the sensational rock architecture all around are unforgettable. Adrenalin runs fast. The unique exhibits of the Black Cuillin, seen anti-clockwise across the ridge from the WSW, includes the summits of the following: WSW, Sgùrr Thuilm; SW, Sgùrr a Mhadaidh, Sgùrr a' Ghreadaidh; SSW, Sgùrr Dearg (and the 'Inaccessible Pinnacle'); S, Sgùrr Thearlaich, Sgùrr Alasdair, Sgùrr Dubh an Da Bheinn, Sgùrr Dubh Mór, Gars-bheinn; E, Am Bàsteir, Sgùrr nan Gillean, Sgùrr a' Fionn Choire.

The prospect SSE affords fine seaward views out to Loch Scavaig and across the Strathaird peninsula. Two other distinct Skye summits visible beyond the Black Cuillin are: ESE, Blà Bheinn; NE, Glamaig.

Bruach na Frìthe to Sligachan Hotel

Allow 3½ hours

Turn E and backtrack along the ridge to the Bealach nan Lice. Beyond the bealach, bear NE to reach a N-pointing spur demarcating the W side of Coire a' Bhàsteir. Walking out to the summit of Sgùrr a' Bhàsteir is very worthwhile and not too time-consuming (see 'Extensions').

Begin a steep descent down the shifting scree slopes of the Coire a' Bhàsteir. Make a beeline NNE for the rocky defile, and the only viable exit from the corrie, just beyond tiny Loch a' Bhàsteir. Snow can persist in this corrie well into June. If the snow is extensive, an ice axe will be called for, or alternatively, an easier return can be made via Fionn Choire.

Where steepness relents at the bottom of the coirre, pass around Loch a' Bhàsteir, either on its

W or E side, to gain a cairn-marked path thereafter. Follow the cairns and begin to bear N, staying L of and well above the rocky gorge cut by the Allt Dearg Beag. To the NE, the view is dominated by the Red Cuillin and below, NNE, by the hotel and campsite at Sligachan. Look also to your rear to enjoy the receding skyline profiles of the Pinnacled Ridge, Sgùrr nan Gillean and Am Bàsteir. On descending the last of the scree from the corrie, the path emerges from the gorge closer to the Allt Dearg Beag. Proceed N, following the allt downstream on more gradual downhill progress over heather and grass.

Ford a burn and pursue the path as it sweeps away a little to the L. Follow the burn down to where it joins the Allt Dearg Beag after 500 m (1/3 mile). Come alongside the allt again and veer NNE after easily fording a subsequent burn. Keep to the path that maintains a route on the L side of the cascading allt, passing numerous waterfalls along the way. A footbridge on the R marks the junction with a path that intervenes from the other side of the allt, the one most often used by those pursuing an assault on Sgùrr nan Gillean.

Continue NNE across the moor in the direction of the Sligachan Hotel, now clearly recognizable. Depart from the course of the Allt Dearg Beag where it meanders NE to join with the River Sligachan. The going underfoot becomes increasingly peaty and the path more prone to being waterlogged. In the spring of 1994, a programme of maintenance was begun to improve drainage as well as general condition. This should ensure a more agreeable surface and therefore faster progress across the moor.

Cross the Allt Dearg Mór by a footbridge 400 m (1/4 mile) SSW of the hotel and also about the same distance W of the allt's confluence with the River Sligachan. Walk N to the A863 and then turn R. Follow the road for 200 m (220 yd) to the hotel.

Alternative routes

ESCAPES

Bruach na Frìthe is regarded as one of the easiest ascents on the Black Cuillin. It is undoubtedly the most readily baggable Munro of the range. Once on the main ridge, there are no quick escapes, although that back down Fionn Choire provides perhaps the least problematic descent route.

The gabbro rocks of the Black Cuillin are notorious for their compass-deflecting properties, which means unreliable readings. If you do get misted-out, descend via Fionn Choire remembering that running water from it ends at Sligachan.

EXTENSIONS

The ascent of Bruach na Frìthe by the north west ridge (which encloses Fionn Choire on its W side) provides a more sporting route that necessitates some straightforward scrambling. From Coire na Circe, continue on the Glen Brittle path into the Bealach a' Mhàim. Bear S from the bealach to gain the crest of the ridge all the way to the summit.

Before descending into the Coire a' Bhàsteir, wander out N on to Sgùrr a' Bhàsteir. A path just to the L allows for this worthwhile diversion, affording a fine prospect of the Pinnacle Ridge, Sgùrr nan Gillean, Am Bàsteir and the Basteir Tooth. Allow an extra 1 hour.

Possibilities for exploring elsewhere on the Black Cuillin are infinitely numerous. These mountains are positively addictive and can, in themselves, provide a lifetime of walking, scrambling and climbing opportunities. Beyond Bruach na Frìthe, however, there are few options for walkers to extend the ridge traverse without first descending and re-ascending further S. Sgùrr na Banachdich is considered the only other walkers' Munro on the range, ascended by the path from Glen Brittle. The capable and those prepared to become quadrupeds on some hard, airy scrambles can add many other Cuillin summits to their itineraries. Sgùrr Alasdair is the highest peak on the Black Cuillin, again accessible from Glen Brittle. Nearby, that infamous 'shark's fin' blade of rock, the 'Inaccessible Pinnacle', is the most difficult of all Munros and the one that involves a rock climb with considerable exposure. For a traverse of the entire ridge, which entails a number of rock climbs, experience with ropes is essential. It remains one of the greatest days possible on British hills.

Route 22: LOCH CORUISK

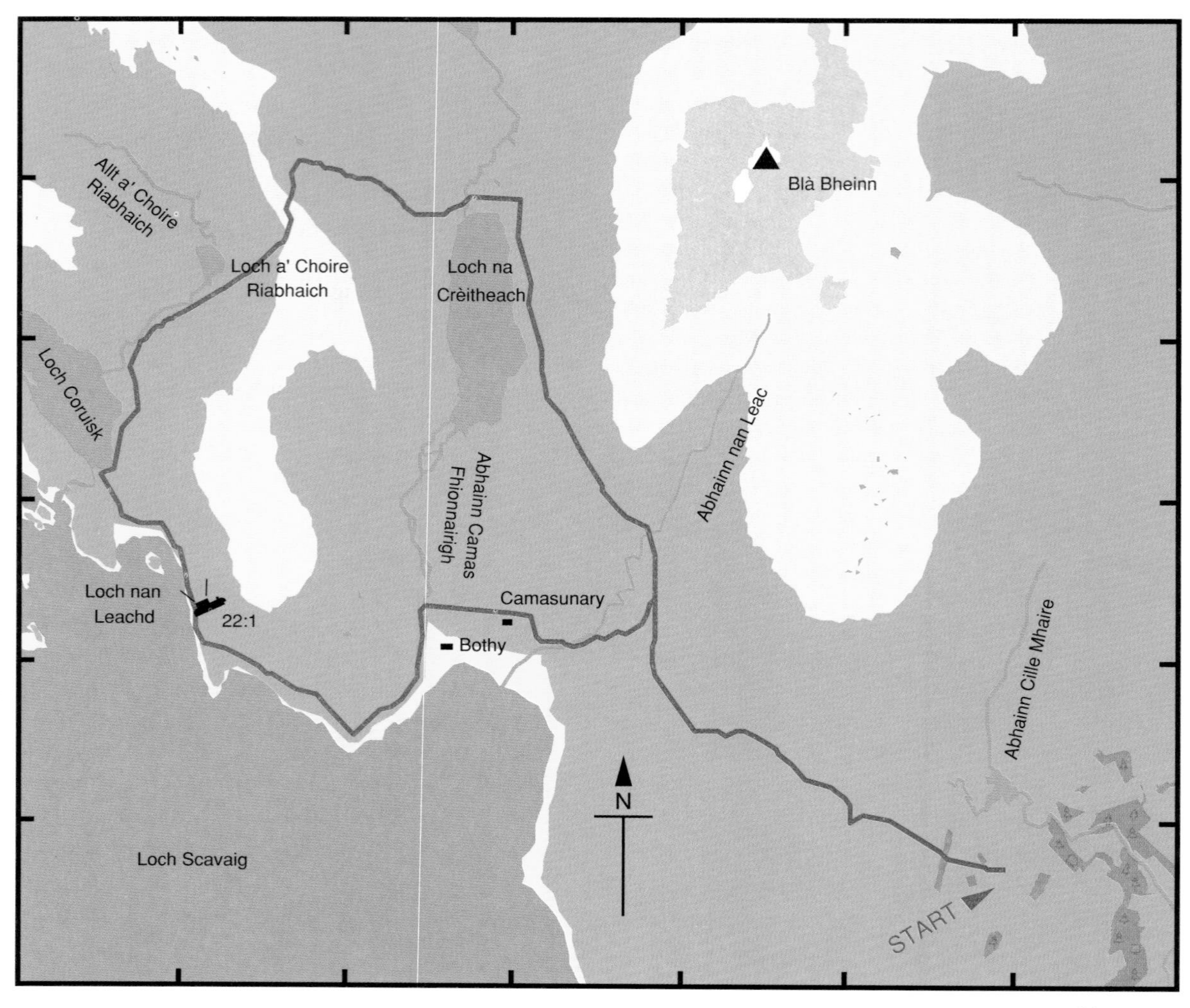

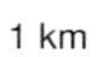

1 km

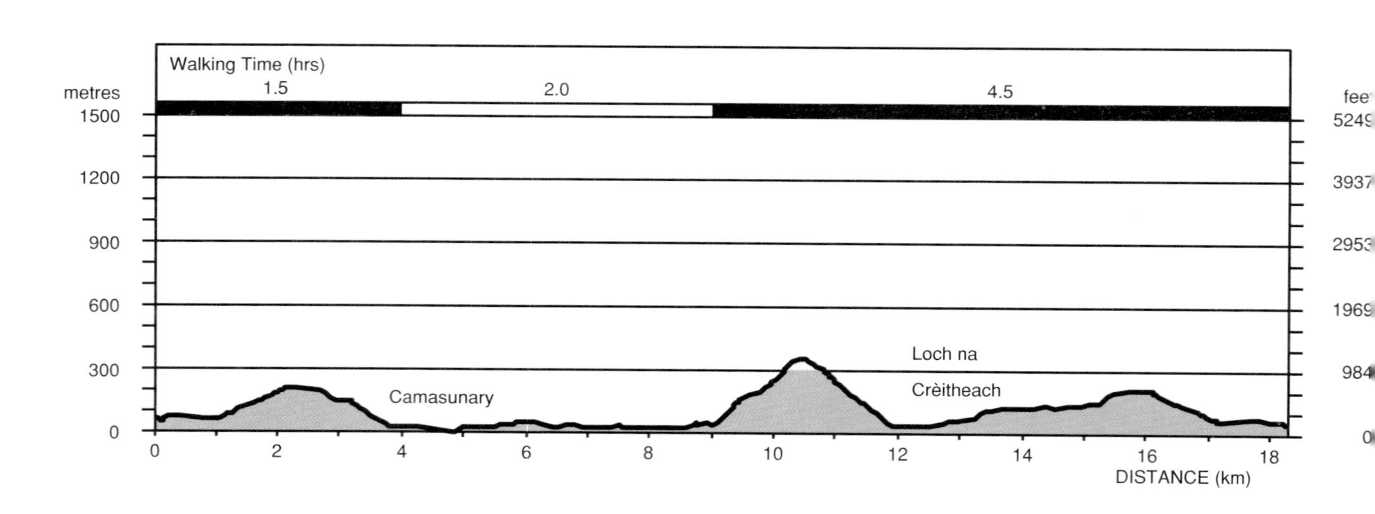

Route 22 · Loch Coruisk

STARTING LOCATION

Kilmarie, on the A881 Broadford–Elgol road, 5 km (3 miles) NE of Elgol.
OSLR 32 or OSOL 8/MR 545172.
Parking bay on the E side of the road opposite a metal gate and stile at the beginning of a landrover track.
Accommodates approximately 15 cars.

ALTERNATIVE STARTING LOCATION

Possible roadside parking nearby.

PUBLIC TRANSPORT

Nearest railway station – Kyle of Lochalsh (for ferry).
Regular buses to Broadford from Kyleakin and Portree.
Postbus, once daily, Broadford to Strathaird (except Sunday).

OVERVIEW/INTEREST

One of the most magnificent coastal walks in Britain.
Superb views to the Black Cuillin.
Visits arguably Scotland's 'wildest' loch.
Necessitates two straightforward wades in shallow water.
Involves negotiating 'The Bad Step'.
Compass work may be unreliable due to gabbro rocks.
Physically demanding.

FOOTPATHS

No waymarking though route-finding generally without problems.
Excellent landrover track to Camasunary.
Rugged coastal path to Loch Coruisk.
Rough and often wet elsewhere.

GRADING 4

TIME ALLOWANCE

8 hours.

DISTANCE

Excluding Height	18.2 km	(11¼ miles)
TOTAL HEIGHT GAINED	730 m	(2395 ft)
PRINCIPAL HEIGHTS		
Drum Hain ridge	312 m	(1024 ft)

Kilmarie to Camasunary

Allow 1½ hours

Cross the road and step over the stile to the L of a large metal gate. Walk WNW keeping to the obvious landrover track. Distant summits ahead hint at an enthralling mountain prospect to come.

After 250 m (275 yd) the track passes between conifer copses and there are some prominent ruins on your R. In the grassy depression immediately to the N, a small lochan formed by the Abhainn Cille Mhaire is visible. The path begins in a rather wet and disagreeable state but the going underfoot quickly improves. Soon after, pass through a gap between conifers and then ford a burn easily. Blà Bheinn, a Munro (see 'Extensions') is seen looking N protruding above the nearer Slat Bheinn. Ford a second burn and veer NW ascending a little more steeply while at the same time following the rowan-strewn banks of a burn on your L. Pass through a large metal gate and continue making steady progress up grassy slopes on the good track. There is a large cairn on the R. Blà Bheinn gains in stature but also the view, to your rear E, down to Loch Slapin and Loch Eishort, deserves passing attention.

After a cairn on your L, the route of the track, on which it is impossible to lose your way, is marked by a series of seemingly wasted ones. You then arrive at Am Màm, the highest point of the track, the end of which is a little further on at Camasunary. The early and easily won reward is a superlative view across a spectacularly beautiful coastline and to an incomparable profile of serrated peaks. From here, the Black Cuillin extends inland across nearly 60° of the compass, from W to NNW. Gars-bheinn rises abruptly from the sea at the S end of the mountain range with Sgùrr nan Gillean at its N end. Perfectionists may wish to climb a little higher on the slopes to your rear in order to gain an entirely unbroken panorama of the Black Cuillin. This effort brings into view the few remaining Cuillin peaks otherwise partially obscured by Sgùrr na Stri, the mountainous lump on the opposite side of Camasunary Bay. From just above the track, the main peaks in view, running L to R over a skyline ridge of more than 11 km (7 miles), are: W, Gars-bheinn, Sgùrr a' Choire Bhig, Sgùrr Nan Eag; WNW, Sgùrr Dubh Mór, Sgùrr Alasdair, Sgùrr Mhic Choinnich, Sgùrr Dearg (and the 'Inaccessible Pinnacle'), Sgùrr na Banachdich, Sgùrr Thormaid, Sgùrr a' Ghreadaidh; NW, Sgùrr a' Mhadaidh, Bidein Druim nan Ramh, Sgùrr na Bhairnich, Bruach na Frìthe, Sgùrr a' Fionn Choire; NNW, Am Bàsteir, Sgùrr nan Gillean.

Looking WSW, across Loch Scavaig and out to sea is the island of Soay. In clear conditions, on a seaward horizon further S, the distant island of Rhum is discernible. In the more immediate vicinity, below and W are seen the sands and vibrant green grasses of Camasunary Bay. Close to the beach and a few hundred metres apart, a remote croft house and a small bothy suggest the presence of other human beings in an otherwise untamed landscape.

Descend from Am Màm heading NNW towards Loch na Crèitheach, 3 km (2 miles) distant. Then bear N, more in line with Blà Bheinn, and cross a burn by a bridge made of railway sleepers. Where the track hairpins, turn sharp L and continue downhill over a second similarly constructed bridge. Veer R and proceed W where the gradient becomes less severe. The track surface deteriorates further down. When almost at sea-level, cross the wooden bridge over the Abhainn nan Leac and carry on across the surprisingly lush grasses of Camasunary. A sad and shameful site, and one impossible to ignore, is that which betrays a widespread human disregard for the environment and taints an otherwise quite lovely bay. Pollution on the beach here comes in many forms from discarded fishing nets, countless plastic containers, shredded ropes and rusty oil drums. With a little more care and forethought such situations are entirely avoidable; the realization that subsequent tides will deposit yet more only adds to the despair of lovers of wilderness.

Turn R towards the large white cottage and where the track divides take the L fork, passing the cottage itself on your L and some ruins on your R. A sign in white paint on an old wall with the words 'The route to Sligachan' points N. There is little trace of a track or path thereafter but simply cross the grass and head towards the white walls of a tiny building at the other end of the bay.

Camasunary Bothy is maintained by the Mountain Bothies Association, a charity which relies on volunteers. Their bothies are open to all for overnight stays and as a refuge, allowing access to the wild and lonely places. Large groups and long stays are discouraged. The Bothy code displayed at Camasunary can be taken as fairly typical of bothies throughout the Highlands, and is detailed in Appendix 3.

Camasunary Bothy is useful for longer expeditions in the area but you should be aware that, apart from respecting the code, there is a kind of unwritten constitution that you should leave the bothy in a slightly improved condition as a result of your visit. However, due to the risk of attracting undesirable fauna, do not leave food. The accommodation is always very basic and your own sleeping bag and food are essential. At Camasunary, there is a visitors' book.

Camasunary to Loch Coruisk *Allow 2 hours*

At the W end of Camasunary Bay, proceed to the near bank of the Abhainn Camas Fhionnairigh. Ford the abhainn by rolling up your trousers to wade across. Except at high tide, the water is easily negotiable and rarely more than knee-deep. At a point about 200 m (220 yd) NW of the bothy, there is evidence of some stepping-stones. On reaching the W bank, turn L and pursue the rugged coast path S. Some way downstream, near where the abhainn enters the sea, ford a burn draining the steep slopes on your R, using stepping-stones. On this section, occasional cairns depict the coastal route of a path that maintains a course

22.1 *Loch nan Leachd and the Black Cuillin skyline from the coast path near the Bad Step.*

well above sea-level. The sea is on your L all the way around.

About 500 m (⅓ mile) beyond where you were required to remove boots, curve round to the R and shift your bearing more to the SW. Continue in this direction as far as the headland at Rubha Bàn. Behind you there is a fine view back to Camasunary Bay and its mountain backdrop of Blà Bheinn. Turn R at Rubha Bàn, without deviating from the coast path, and walk NW. The closer proximity of the Black Cuillin is at once apparent, a more dramatic scenario slowly unfolding and a sense of being enclosed more acute. The path undulates. At about 40 m (130 ft) above sea level, ford a burn by swinging slightly to the R to come a little bit higher in the gully that it has cut. Walk on WNW, the going underfoot turning distinctly wet and peaty for a while. On approaching the headland of Rubha Buidhe, the path divides, the L fork taking you to the very end of the headland. Instead keep to the R of a craggy mound. Descend to come along the shoreline and bear R. Continue NNW below the steep slopes of Sgùrr na Stri on your R amid increasingly spectacular coastal scenery. The path directs you towards Loch nan Leachd and a grass-covered outcrop in the sea. When adjacent to this small island, you are confronted by 'The Bad Step'.

An apparently near vertical rock wall, this obstacle has long been attributed a reputation of notoriety, to my mind falsely so. Negotiating the Bad Step is really nothing more than an easy scramble. Stay low down on the rock face, taking care and making considered movements as you clamber along. There may well exist a bypass route to the R and higher up. One or two older guide books for the area describe such an alternative although no such path was apparent on my last visit.

Beyond the Bad Step, cross bouldery terrain followed by a rough grass and bracken section where a few scattered rowan struggle through. Behind the beach at Loch nan Leachd, bear L to regain the path after ascending a little. Proceed W but soon swing round NNW following a cairn-marked route through a gap between outcrops. Walk out to the S shore of Loch Coruisk, just to the R of where the Scavaig River drains it.

Loch Coruisk is arguably Scotland's wildest loch and it is easy to understand why. The experience of being shadowed by a surround of the Cuillin's highest peaks and a breathtaking skyline of pinnacles in this, the remotest of settings, is quite sensational. Its uniqueness in Britain brings to mind the feeling of a Norwegian fjord. One appreciates why Turner was so inspired for his painting here, lured not only by the unique drama of the place but no doubt also by the captivating quality of the light. If the galleries in Portree are anything to go by, it seems that many other artists have been similarly stirred.

Scenes as glorious as those at Loch Coruisk are the stuff of which long-lasting dreams are made but, to be fair, it should be pointed out that on Skye it is too often the stuff of nightmares! I first came here with a companion in June expecting at that time of year, naively perhaps, sunshine and warm days. We were blitzed at Loch Coruisk by near horizontal rain in a downpour which, mile after godforsaken mile, failed to relent. We were a pair of drowned rats on returning to Kilmarie, our spirits along with our clothes severely dampened. Despite believing ourselves to be hardened campers, the prospect of pegging out that night was just too depressing to contemplate. Instead, at the expense of forsaken pride, we readily accepted bed-and-breakfast at Elgol, intent on never returning without the irrefutable evidence of an established and securely anchored high pressure front.

Skye is unbeatable in sunshine but try not to be too taken in by the mediterranean clarity depicted in tourist board glossies, for it is diabolical in the rain. It is not without justification that the gaelic name for the Isle of Skye, Eilean a' cheo, translates as 'Island of Mist'.

Loch Coruisk to Kilmarie

Allow 4½ hours

Before departing, bird watchers will no doubt enjoy looking out for common and Arctic terns, not unusual sights at Loch Coruisk. From the S corner of the loch, turn R and walk N on the path by the E shore. On reaching the Allt a' Choire Riabhaich, veer R and proceed NE ascending rough, grassy slopes, leaving the loch behind. Stay on the path on the R side of the allt, following its course upstream and fording intervening burns where necessary. Traverse a series of flat, rocky, slab-like outcrops to where the gradient relents just above the S end of Loch a' Choire Riabhaich. Continue uphill, more steeply again and now on a more clearly marked path. As height is gained above the small loch, gradually swing N and commence a series of zigzags. Emerging on the ridge of Druim Hain, a group of cairns marks the highest point of the route. The just reward for your labours is a superb vantage point offering yet another perspective on the Black Cuillin. Looking N from here, the Red Cuillin is also in view across Glen Sligachan. Blà Bheinn lies immediately to the E, displaying the transition between the two very different rock types constituting the Red Cuillin and the Black Cuillin. Its pale granite platform appears visually conspicuous against the dark gabbro rocks on top – a detached mountain with a characteristically serrated Black Cuillin profile.

Descend the E side of the ridge, initially maintaining a bearing N. After about 300 m (330 yd), turn R to face Blà Bheinn and free-range downhill across heathery tussocks ESE. Make a beeline for the N end of Loch na Crèitheach below. The best route down is probably found by staying close to a small burn on your L. Simply follow it downstream all the way. On lower slopes, after easily fording a small burn, bear E and proceed over less steep though wetter ground as far as the Abhainn Camas Fhionnairigh. Crossed earlier at Camasunary, S of where it flows from the other end of the loch, the abhainn may again necessitate a short wade in shallow water unless there has been a good dry spell. Cross the cotton-grass and bog myrtle of the wet ground on the E side of the abhainn. Resume a bearing E to pick up the Strath na Crèitheach path. Further N the path connects with Glen Sligachan, but instead turn R and proceed S between the E shore of Loch na Crèitheach on your R and the slopes of Blà Bheinn on your L.

Progress is less demanding for a while on a more agreeable, well-worn surface. Where the path divides take the L fork on the higher route. Stay parallel to the loch-shore as far as the gap to the L of the rocky knoll of An t-Sròn. Ascend the slopes up to the top of the gap then veer L, passing through it SSE and on to a narrower defile. Follow a burn between steeper banks to emerge on bouldery terrain. On the R, a path from Camasunary connects as you skirt the far S end of Blà Bheinn.

At stepping-stones below a waterfall on the L, ford the Abhainn nan Leac, turn R and walk S. After 500 m (1/3 mile), rejoin the landrover track at the hairpin bend E of and above Camasunary at MR 524188. Return to Kilmarie by backtracking 3 km (2 miles) via Am Màm.

Alternative routes

ESCAPES

To reach the remote shores of Loch Coruisk, there are no options for curtailing the route. However, retreating from the loch by way of the outgoing route (via the coast path) offers the least difficult return. For emergencies and one-night stopovers, there is the Mountain Bothy at Camasunary.

A straightforward 'there and back' route as far as Camasunary is an easy and yet very rewarding 9 km (6 miles) in itself. While denied the mountain drama of Loch Coruisk, the magnificent view of the Black Cuillin from Am Màm is accessible to all but the least mobile. Allow 3 hours in total.

For non-walkers, the view of the Black Cuillin across Loch Scavaig from Elgol should not be missed. In season, there are boat trips once or twice daily from Elgol to the coast at Loch Coruisk.

EXTENSIONS

Opportunities for longer expeditions are numerous. Those described below are only suggestions and it would not be difficult to devise your own.

On arriving at Loch Coruisk, walkers with energy to spare might wish to walk right around the loch in order to prolong the continuing drama. If you intend later to return as described for the main route, then the circuit of the loch is best pursued in the clockwise direction. Begin by using the stepping-stones to cross the wide channel of the Scavaig River, which drains Loch Coruisk, and then proceed NW by the W shore. Follow the path to the N end of the loch and then ford the Coruisk River. Turn R and continue SE, following the E shore as far as the Allt a' Choire Riabhaich. Allow an extra 2½ hours.

Another possible addition to the route includes taking in the fine vantage point of Sgùrr Hain at 420 m (1378 ft). Proceed SSE to its summit up along the ridge from the cairns near Druim Hain, at MR 502214. The superfit, and those inspired enough to extend still further the views of the Cuillin, may wish to venture S as far as Sgùrr na Stri. Allow an extra 1 hour to take in Sgùrr Hain.

Munroists should note that scaling Blà Bheinn from the S is an untypically easy Cuillin ascent. It is also one of Skye's finest mountains. From Kilmarie, follow the landrover track beyond Am Màm as far as the hairpin above Camasunary. Strike off from the track on the path heading N to ford the Abhainn nan Leac by stepping-stones. Soon after, leave the path at the foot of the S ridge of Blà Bheinn and head directly up the ridge NNE. Of its two tops, the triangulation pillar lies at the one furthest N at 928 m (3044 ft) above sea-level. Return the same way or, alternatively, include it with the main route after a night's stopover at Camasunary Bothy. Allow an extra 6½ hours from Camasunary or Kilmarie.

For those not having to return to a car, consider pursuing the long walk through Glen Sligachan via the Strath na Crèitheach. The glen divides the dark gabbro rocks of the Black Cuillin on its W side from the granite of the Red Cuillin on the E side. The route can be traversed in either direction. From the S end, beginning at Camasunary or Kilmarie, walk N using the well-worn path to your eventual destination at Sligachan, easily manageable by most in a day.

Route 23: BEINN EIGHE

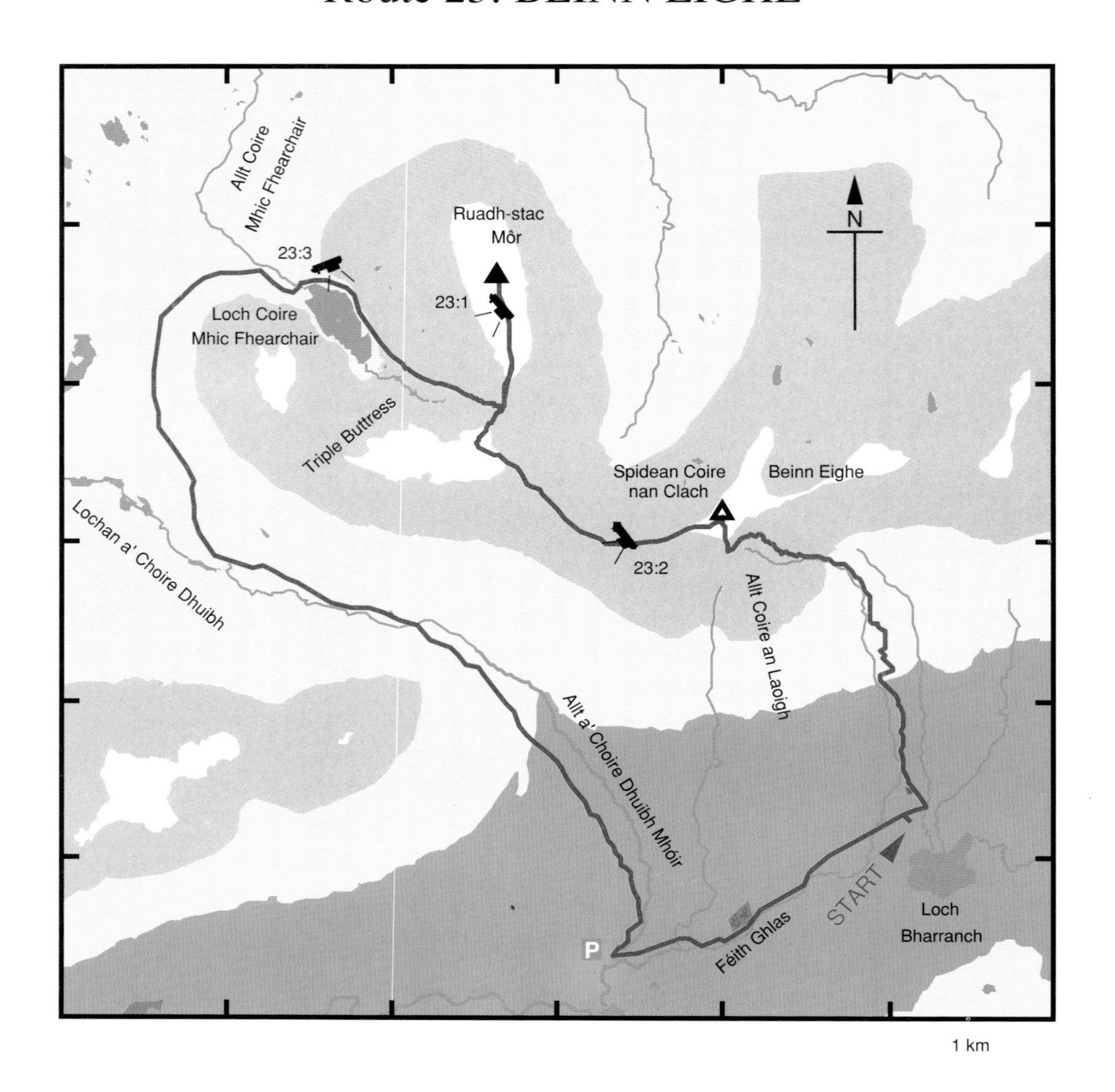

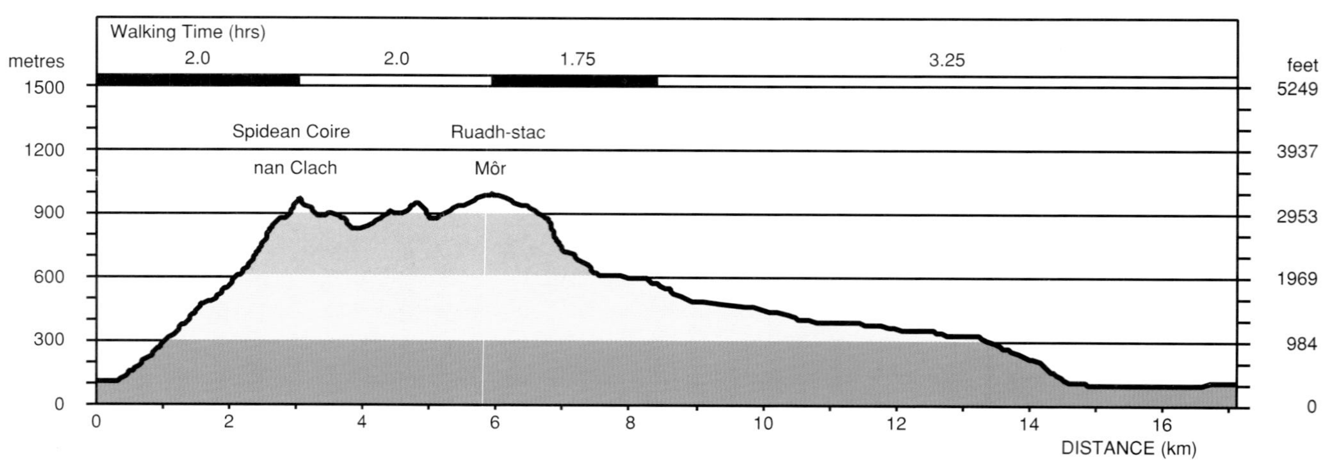

14

TORRIDON (EAST)

HIGH-LEVEL ROUTE

Route 23 · Beinn Eighe

STARTING LOCATION
Car park on the S side of the A896 Glen Torridon road, 8 km (5 miles) WSW of Kinlochewe.
OSLR 19 and 25 or OSOL 8/MR 976577.
Approaching from the E, car park entrance on L can easily be missed.
Accommodates approximately 15 cars.

ALTERNATIVE STARTING LOCATION
Car park on N side of road, 2 km (1¼ miles) further WSW, thus walking road section first.

PUBLIC TRANSPORT
Nearest railway station – Achnasheen.
Regular buses, three times a week, to Kinlochewe from Inverness and Achnasheen.
Postbus, once daily, Achnasheen to Coulin, Torridon and Alligin via Kinlochewe (except Sunday).

OVERVIEW/INTEREST
An awesome display of mountain architecture.
Fascinating geological features on some of the oldest rocks.
A high-level ridge with magnificent views from it in all directions.
Confidence and skill with map and compass essential in adverse weather.
Arduous and extremely demanding circuit.

FOOTPATHS
Route begins ascending on excellent stalkers' path.
Ascent and descent in steep corries without footpaths (ice axe essential when snow-filled).
Some easy scrambling necessary – not recommended for those without prior experience of high-level ridge walking.
Good, clear path descending Coire Dubh Mór although difficult terrain in places.

GRADING 6

TIME ALLOWANCE
9 hours.

DISTANCE
Excluding Height 17.1 km (10½ miles)

TOTAL HEIGHT GAINED 1150 m (3773 ft)

PRINCIPAL HEIGHTS
Beinn Eighe (File Mountain):
Spidean Coire nan Clach (Peak of the Stony Corrie) 972 m (3188 ft)
Ruadh-stac Mór (Big Red Stack)
1010 m (3313 ft).

Glen Torridon to Spidean Coire nan Clach

Allow 2 hours

On leaving the car park, turn R and walk ENE along the Glen Torridon road to a NNR sign on the L after 150 m (165 yd). Beinn Eighe was the first NNR to be established in Britain, declared as such in 1951, primarily to conserve the fragment of native Scots pine forest, Coille na Glas-leitire, further NE above the shores of Loch Maree.

Leave the road to gain the obvious path on the L, passing the NNR sign and, soon after, the Gairloch Conservation Unit panel. Walk N beside an enclosure of Scots pine on the L. In front, the great mountain expanse of Beinn Eighe, often described as a mountain range in miniature, confronts you as a long, scree-ridden, seemingly impenetrable wall.

Ford a small burn and begin ascending more steeply on the excellent stalkers' path. Following upstream the Allt Coire an Laoigh, continue N and to the R of it to where that other Torridon giant, Liathach, begins to emerge as the dominant feature to the W. After a wet start, the path becomes drier as altitude and steepness increase. While navigation is rarely a problem here, erosion is beginning to become one.

Having covered approximately 1 km (⅔ mile) while steadily gaining height, ascend much more steeply where the path begins to zigzag up from the 300 m (1000 ft) contour. From boulder-strewn heathery slopes, walk out to flatter ground at the point where the dotted line on the OS map (depicting the stalker's path) terminates at around the 475 m (1600 ft) contour. Pausing next to the allt, take time to marvel at a geological wonderland. To the S and SW the mountains of Ben Damph Forest exhibit typically sedimentary features with striking Torridonian sandstone layering and buckled strata in veins more than 800 million years old. Beinn Eighe's steep scree slopes to the NE, specifically those of Sgurr nan Fhir Duibhe, are topped by younger, pale grey quartzite exposures. The result is a covering in marked contrast with the Torridonian rocks beneath and bestows upon the mountain's eastern summits a permanent snow-covered appearance.

Ford the intervening watercourse to the R of the predominant stream and walk N towards the Coire an Laoigh. Climb more steeply again on entering the corrie, bearing W as you do so. Maintain the path next to the allt, keeping to its R side. Up into the corrie, steepness increases still further until, when immediately below its very steepest scree-covered slopes, the path comes to an abrupt end! Assess the situation yourself for the easiest way up. Snow can persist in this corrie's upper reaches until well into late spring and in such conditions an ice axe is essential. Without snow, the least treacherous route is best found on slopes to the R. Generally bearing NW, climb to a point where you are able to continue by contouring W. Thus, gain the ridge that is the connecting spur between Spidean Coire nan Clach and Stuc Coire an Laoigh. Bear R and ascend carefully N the steep path up shifting quartzite slopes, heading N as far as the triangulation pillar. The summit of Spidean Coire nan Clach is at 972 m (3188 ft) and is in effect the mountain's focal point, the others seemingly radiating from it. One appreciates the vast extent of Beinn Eighe's E-shaped mass when looking both E and W along its craggy ridges. The panorama to more distant horizons is magnificent in every direction but the summits identifiable in the vicinity include: N, An Teallach; NNE, Slioch; SSE, Sgurr Dubh, Beinn Liath Mhór; S, Sgorr Ruadh; SW, Beinn Damh; WSW, Liathach; W, Skye, Beinn Alligin.

The view NW is blocked by Ruadh-stac Mór, Beinn Eighe's highest peak and its only Munro.

Spidean Coire nan Clach to Ruadh-stac Mór

Allow 2 hours

From the triangulation pillar, begin an arduous descent over rugged terrain. Walk W from the Spidean on the narrow ridge path above the precipitous N-facing crags of Coire Ruadh-stac. From the ridge, looking out over the Coire Dubh Mór high above its diminutive watercourses, the huge dark buttress of Stuc a' Choire Dhuibh-Bhig rises high in commanding grandeur at mighty Liathach's eastern extremity. It is viewed at close range to the WSW, a proximity that is humbling and awesome: nature's own architecture carved from a stack of prehistoric sediment and possessing a presence quite unlike any other mountain feature.

Proceed, negotiating the quartzite boulders, to a low point on the ridge. Notice in the rocks at your feet the circular pimples of numerous fossil worm burrows. They are among the oldest traces of life known in Scotland. From here, head up on the narrow ridge path from where Skye is discernible out to sea. The island appears on the western horizon beyond the Abhainn Coire Mhic Nòbuil, between Liathach and Beinn Alligin. Walk NW over ground that begins on hard quartzite but, as height is gained, becomes suprisingly soft and wet underfoot. Continue for approximately 300 m (330 yd) up grass- and moss-covered slopes towards Còinneach Mhór. On reaching the cairn at MR 950602, turn R.

Leave the cairn and scramble down with great care the steep and narrow path NNE to the saddle in the ridge. Then walk N up along the easy ridge slopes leading to Ruadh-stac Mór. Approaching the summit you encounter a further quartzite topping, piled up as if fashioned into nature's very own cairn. Humans have, of course, added their own diminutive though more invasive one on top in recognition of a Munro and, at 1010 m (3313 ft), Beinn Eighe's highest summit.

Many of Torridon's most exhilarating highlights come into view. Particularly impressive is the famous Triple Buttress, seen looking SSW and forming a dramatic N-facing wall to the Coire Mhic Fhearchair. The pyramidal Spidean a' Choire Léith, the highest summit of Liathach, rises behind it. At the far W end of Beinn Eighe, Sàil Mhór provides a near vertical backdrop for the Loch Coire Mhic Fhearchair. Turn NW to where a labyrinth of lochans perforates the vast wilderness of Flowerdale Forest. Other mountains now in view on the horizon include: W, Beinn Dearg; WNW, Baosbheinn; NW, Beinn an Eòin; NNW, Beinn a' Chearcaill; NE, Meall a' Ghiubhais.

Ruadh-stac Mór to Loch Coire Mhic Fhearchair

Allow 1¾ hours

Proceed S from the summit cairn, returning downhill to the saddle in the ridge. After 1 km (⅔ mile) the Triple Buttress is viewed side-on as a layered feature to the W. Begin to come down the steep scree and rock gully on your R. Take it slowly and exercise extreme care while descending this so-called path. If snow-filled, then only those with an ice axe should succumb to the temptation of sliding down. Without such a tool, attempt a cautious scramble down across the rocks immediately to the R of the gully. On the rough ground where the gully deposits you, 200 m (600 ft) below, the considerabley less severe slopes near the Loch Coire Mhic Fhearchair come as an agreeable relief. Turn towards the loch and walk NW over an unrelenting terrain of outcropping rocks and rough grassy banks. There is no trace of a path until at the lochside. From the S end of the loch, bear NNW, pursuing if you can the rudimentary path by its E shore. The ground becomes

23.1 *The Triple Buttress of the Coire Mhic Fhearchair, with Liathach behind, from Ruadh-stac Mór.*

23.2 *Stuc a' Choire Dhuibh-Bhig (Liathach's easternmost pinnacle) from Beinn Eighe.*

wetter in places until reaching the N end of the loch. Walk close to the loch-shore, traversing enormous rock slabs as far as the waterfall at the top of the Allt Coire Mhic Fhearchair. The view SSE across the loch to the Triple Buttress is truly awe-inspiring, a memorable and exceptional corner of wilderness.

Loch Coire Mhic Fhearchair to Glen Torridon

Allow 3¼ hours

Cross the river just above the waterfall, using the easy stepping-stones, to gain the clear path below the cathedral-like buttresses of Sàil Mhór. Walk NW, beginning a descent that follows the route of Allt Coire Mhic Fhearchair on its L side. Begin to swing round W on the path that contours the base of Sàil Mhór at 470 m (1540 ft). Cross bouldery terrain that will test the sure-footing ability of your weary legs. When 1 km (⅔ mile) from the waterfall, the path veers S making a beeline for the precipitous N-facing buttresses of Liathach. There is a feeling of extreme remoteness here, exaggerated by a profound silence.

Keep close to the steep mountain slopes on your L and walk on towards Liathach. Pass at first above Loch nan Cabar on your R and soon after, a little further S down the path, Lochan a' Choire Dhuibh. The ground underfoot becomes distinctly peaty and more prone to boggy patches. Proceed to a junction of footpaths. The intervening one on the R takes a route W to the Coire Mhic Nòbuil.

Turn L and walk ESE to the top of Coire Dubh Mór. After 400 m (¼ mile), ford a burn (using stepping-stones) and regain the path that passes directly below Stuc a' Choire Dhuibh-Bhig. Where the path gets a little steeper, its condition improves. Bear SE to return downhill on the L of the Allt a' Choire Dhuibh Mhóir. This is the E end of a well-used footpath that is part of a route which arcs around the N side of Liathach (see Routes 25 and 26 on pages 147 and 153).

Approaching Glen Torridon, continue down to come close to the Allt Coire an Anmoich. The path swings SSW passing the car park on the L.

At the A896, turn L on to the road and cross the allt over the most incongruous of bridges, one displaying all the characteristics of late twentieth century motorway style! Continue by the road-side, walking ENE for 2 km (1¼ mile) to the car park on the R.

23.3 *Across Loch Coire Mhic Fhearchair to the Triple Buttress.*

Alternative routes

ESCAPES

Once on the main ridge there are no straightforward escapes. As is typical with Torridonian high-level routes, the exploration of Beinn Eighe's western-most summits and features is a serious undertaking. If the view from Spidean Coire nan Clach, or from the ridge soon after, is enough reward for you, then simply return by the ascent route. Be warned that a retreat down the steep slopes of the Coire an Laoigh, to regain the stalker's path, is never simple! However, due to familiarity, it remains the quickest and safest route to Glen Torridon.

The Coire Mhic Fhearchair is perhaps the most magnificent corrie in the Northern Highlands. Non-Munroists in Torridon Forest, and those with aspirations more modest than high-level ridge traverses, should access the corrie using the good path ascending the Coire Dubh Mór. Walk NW from the main Glen Torridon car park at MR 958568. The view of the Triple Buttress across Loch Coire Mhic Fhearchair, from where the path meets its N shore, is unforgettable. Return the same way and as described in the main route. Allow 6 hours.

EXTENSIONS

The complete route is equally achievable in reverse, but is no less demanding physically in the clockwise direction. Therefore, for strong walkers of capable abilities, further extensions are not recommended. Fearless scramblers might consider descending the Coire Mhic Fhearchair from further W along the ridge just below Sàil Mhór.

For mountaineers with excessive levels of energy, the full traverse of Beinn Eighe is a considerable but feasible undertaking and a long day. Beyond the Black Carls at the eastern end of the ridge, a path connects with the Glen Torridon road at Cromasaig 1.2 km (¾ mile) S of Kinlochewe.

Route 24: LOCH CLAIR and LOCH COULIN

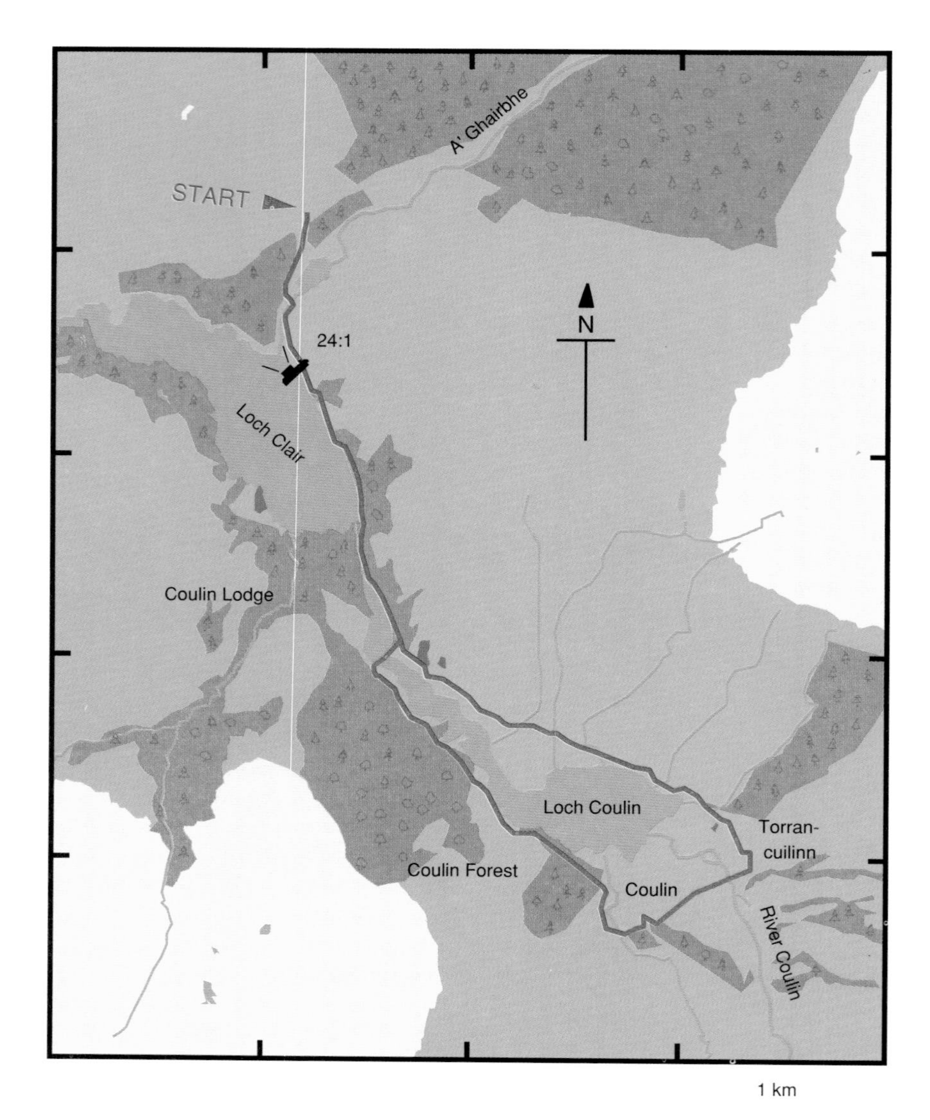

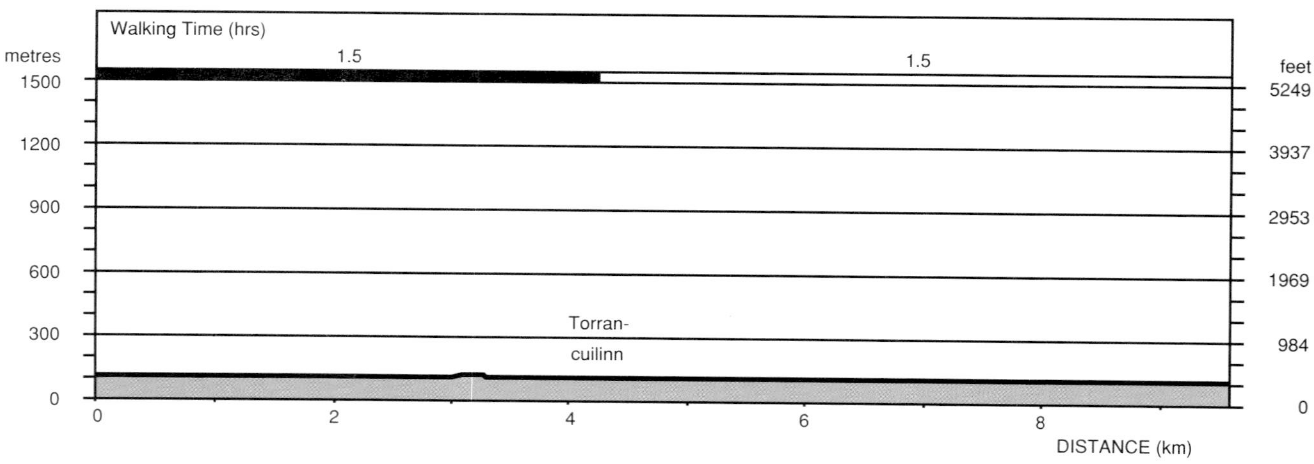

Route 24 · The Coulin Estate

STARTING LOCATION
On N side of A896 Glen Torridon road, opposite private road to the Coulin Estate, 5 km (3 miles) SSW from Kinlochewe.
OSLR 25 or OSOL 8 /MR 002582.
Roadside parking bay accommodates approximately 6 cars.

ALTERNATIVE STARTING LOCATION
At anywhere nearby in Glen Torridon, using the parking bays.

PUBLIC TRANSPORT
Nearest railway station – Achnasheen.
Regular buses, three times a week, to Kinlochewe from Inverness and Achnasheen.
Postbus, once daily, Kinlochewe to Torridon and Alligin (except Sunday).

OVERVIEW/INTEREST
Two beautiful lochs.
Fine views of Beinn Eighe and Liathach.
In a setting of Scots pine, rhododendrons and fungi-infested birch.
Easy and undemanding route.

FOOTPATHS
Minimal waymarking.
Metalled private road at N end of route.
Straightforward though sometimes waterlogged footpath on N side of Loch Coulin.
Clear, dry tracks elsewhere.

GRADING 1

TIME ALLOWANCE
3 hours.

DISTANCE

Excluding Height	9.6 km	(6 miles)
TOTAL HEIGHT GAINED	10 m	(33 ft)

PRINCIPAL HEIGHTS
None.

Glen Torridon to River Coulin

Allow 1½ hours

Leave the parking bay and walk over to the private estate road immediately opposite. Pass the sign at the top of the road, 'Coulin Estate, No cars, Footpath only'. From the junction, head S between forestry plantation enclosures. The mountain immediately obvious on the R, looking SW, is Sgurr Dubh.

After 500 m (⅓ mile), bear L over the wooden bridge to cross the A' Ghairbhe, here in its uppermost reaches where it drains Loch Clair. Bear R and continue S, on the L of the river, to where the road comes close by Loch Clair. Looking W across the loch, with Scots pine lining the opposite shore on the near horizon, you will appreciate why this is perhaps the most popular viewpoint for photographing Liathach. The SE slopes of Beinn Eighe fill the skyline to the NW.

Proceed bearing SSE next to the E shore of Loch Clair. Soon there are scattered birch trees on either side of the road, those by the lochside, R, exhibiting some interesting infestations of bracket fungi. Approaching the end of the loch, stands of Scots pine, together with the ubiquitous rhododendron that is really taking a hold here, cling to the steep slopes of Creag na Rianaich, on your L. The trees extend around the loch-shore on your R.

Walk on to reach the S end of the loch where the metalled surface ends. A bridge on the R, which crosses the watercourse connecting the two lochs, affords access to Coulin Lodge. However, walkers are discouraged from entering here. Instead, pass through a gate and continue S, thus bypassing the lodge to the E. Sustain a route on the tree-lined track. Follow the E shore of Loch Coulin to reach a long, narrow, wooden footbridge that crosses the water on your R. Beyond it, on the W side of the loch, an extensive birch

24.1 *Looking NW across Loch Clair to Beinn Eighe.*

woodland flourishes on the slopes of Leathad Mór.

The footbridge is to be your return route and so, instead, maintain your course on the good track. Walk SE for 150 m (165 yd) and then, immediately prior to a large boundary gate, take the footpath off to the R staying close to the lochside. At once the going is noticeably more demanding underfoot. Compensation comes on encountering open country where the feeling is wilder.

Continue SE over heathery ground. The clicking sound of stonechats is a likely accompaniment as you come between a line of deer fencing on your L and the loch on your R. At the corner of the fenced enclosure, go through a gate and head off on a more rudimentary path, one that can often stay wet after rain. Pursue a route roughly parallel to the deer fencing, now more distant on the L. Ascend on a very gradual incline just N of Torran Cuilinn, a rocky promontory affording a view of Loch Coulin as far as its waters extend eastwards. Make a beeline for the slopes of Cùl Leathaid and An Leathad, a few kilometres ahead SE, presenting to the skyline a long, running, mountainous wall. Proceed in this direction making also for the E corner of the loch. Pass around an obscurely placed metal gate where it mysteriously crosses the path, seemingly serving no purpose whatsoever! Walk between old ruined walls, ford a tiny burn and come close to the lochside again. At a post on the L, a red arrow points the way SE towards the green corrugated-roof house of 'Torran-cuillin' a few hundred metres distant.

Walk beyond the end of the loch, passing a track which intervenes from the L and provides access to a plantation. Gain a much better track on reaching the house and walk S in front of it. After 100 m (110 yd), bear R and proceed WSW to cross the River Coulin at a wooden bridge, built to take off-road vehicles.

River Coulin to Glen Torridon

Allow 1½ hours

After crossing the bridge, walk WSW on the excellent track. Make for the large and very solid looking house ahead with adjoining rusty barns. On your R, the view towards Beinn Eighe looking NW across Loch Coulin is one of the finest to be had of this mountain range in miniature.

Pass a ruined sheep wash, L, and then the large apparently neglected house on your R. For such a perfect situation, with views and solitude, it seems surprisingly vacant. Proceed over the bridge crossing the Allt na Feithe Buidhe and bear NW. Walk on the track at first to the L of the allt, but then alongside Loch Coulin again. Follow its S shore between more rhododendron scrub. Beinn Eighe continues to dominate the view ahead and, set amid Scots pine, Coulin Lodge is quaintly dwarfed by such a commanding backdrop.

Where the loch becomes much narrower at its N end, walk below the slopes of Leathad Mór between old and beautiful stands of birch. Here too, the trees are adorned with numerous growths of bracket fungi.

Walk on to the long and narrow footbridge, passed earlier on the other side of the loch. Having returned to the pine wood, a sign 'Lodge Only. No Access' deters further progress on the track. Turn R on to the footbridge and cross it to gain the E side of Loch Coulin once more. Leave the bridge by turning L on to the track and follow it N for 600 m (⅓ mile) to Loch Clair. Return to your car in Glen Torridon by continuing to retrace earlier footsteps, now back on the metalled estate road next to Loch Clair's E shore.

Alternative routes

ESCAPES

This is one of the shortest and easiest routes in the book and therefore curtailing it seems irrelevant. However, if the fine views of Liathach and Beinn Eighe from Loch Clair prove adequately inspiring then, having walked as far as Coulin Lodge, simply return to the Glen Torridon road by backtracking on the private estate road. Rucksacks and walking boots are for once rendered redundant; take only your camera.

EXTENSIONS

The circuit of Loch Coulin can just as easily be achieved in reverse. Beyond this, consider an exploration of the River Coulin. From the S side of Loch Coulin, pursue a track that heads S along the W side of the river.

Alternatively, take the path SW from near Coulin Lodge to explore the wild country of the Coire an Leth-uillt, below Sgurr Dubh. Some diplomacy with the owners of the estate may be advisable in this case. Return the same way.

The main route will in itself pleasantly fill an afternoon or morning. To fill the day, consider combining this route with the SNH woodland trail and/or the mountain trail on the Beinn Eighe NNR. Both trails commence in the forest at Coille na Glas-leitire, beside Loch Maree. The Scots pine forest on the reserve gives as good an example as any of what a primaeval forest was like in the Scottish Highlands. Start from the reserve car park by the lochside, 4 km (2½ miles) NW of Kinlochewe on the A832.

Allow an extra 3 hours for the mountain trail and 1 hour for the woodland trail.

Route 25: BEINN ALLIGIN

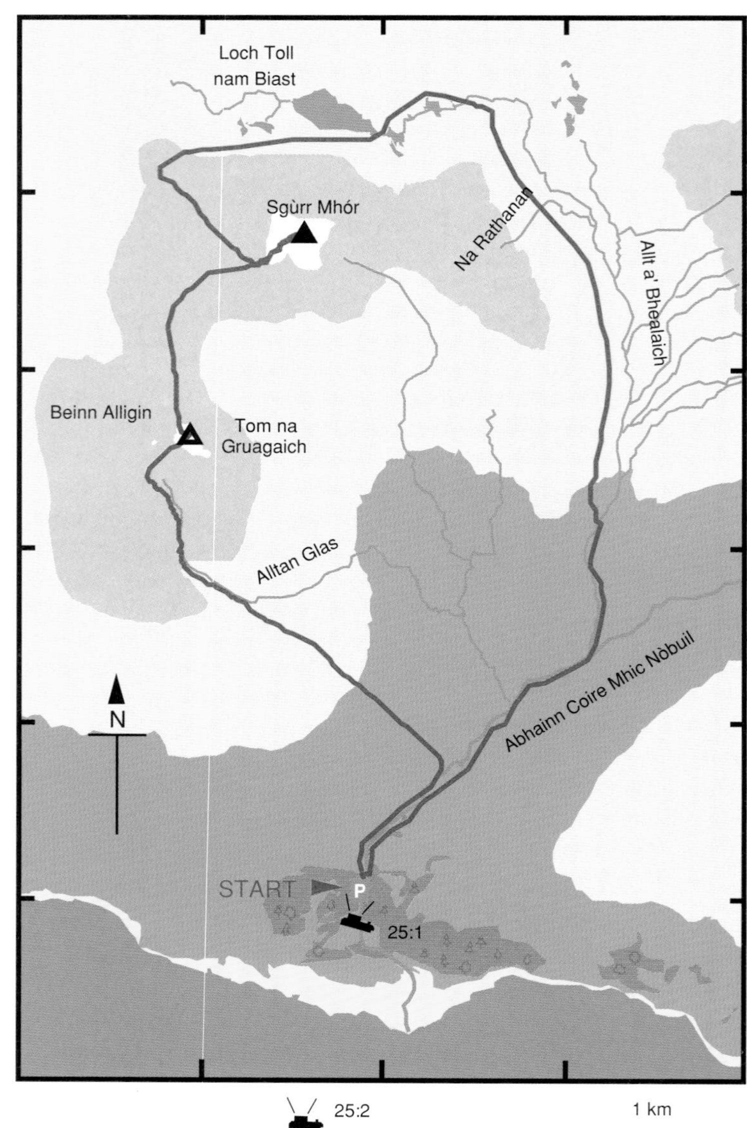

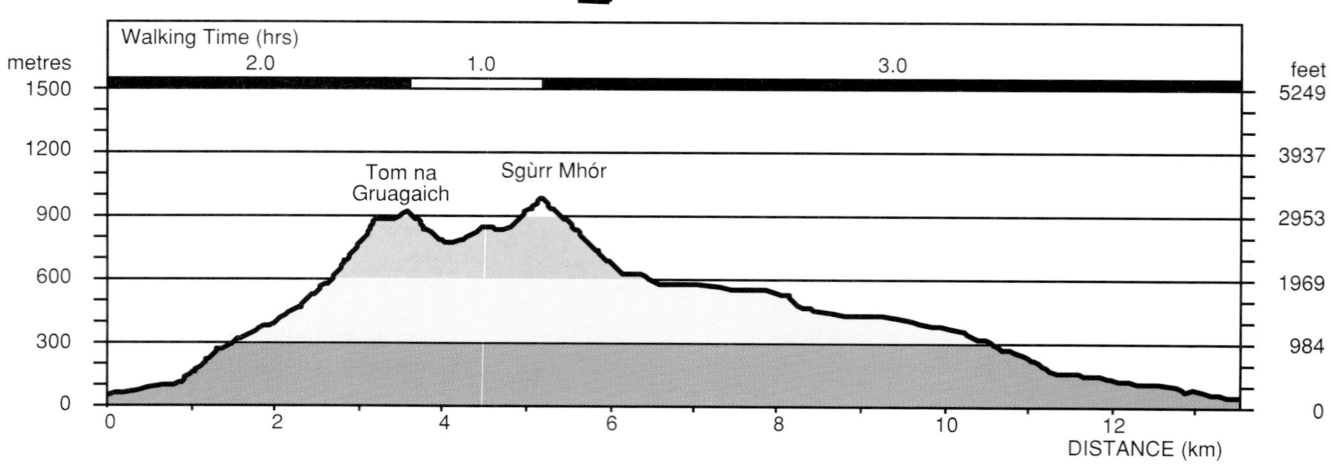

15

TORRIDON (WEST)

HIGH-LEVEL ROUTE

Route 25 · Beinn Alligin

STARTING LOCATION
Coire Mhic Nòbuil car park on Torridon to Diabaig road, 5 km (3 miles) WNW of junction with A896 in Glen Torridon.
OSLR 24 or OSOL 8/MR 868576.
Accommodates approximately 20 cars.

ALTERNATIVE STARTING LOCATION
None nearby.

PUBLIC TRANSPORT
Nearest railway station – Achnasheen.
Regular buses, three times a week, to Kinlochewe from Inverness and Achnasheen.
Postbus, once daily, Achnasheen to Coulin, Torridon and Alligin via Kinlochewe (except Sunday).

OVERVIEW/INTEREST
One of the more popular routes to a Torridon summit; an excellent first Munro in the area.
Stunning views both seaward and to the other mountains of the group.
Typical of high-level Torridon routes: ridge walk above plunging precipices, steep-sided corrie ascent, free-ranging across often difficult terrain, passes below towering rock buttresses.
Optional scrambling on the 'Horns'.
Physically very demanding.

FOOTPATHS
No waymarking.
Often muddy and wet at lower levels.
High-level ridge path requires care but no serious dangers.
Descent from Sgurr Mhor involves some free-ranging.
Two river crossings by footbridges.

GRADING 5

TIME ALLOWANCE
6 hours.

DISTANCE

Excluding Height	13.5 km	(8½ miles)
TOTAL HEIGHT GAINED	1120 m	(3675 ft)

PRINCIPAL HEIGHTS
Beinn Alligin (Jewelled Mountain):
Sgurr Mhór (Big Peak) 985 m (3231 ft)
Tom na Gruagaich (The Maiden's Knoll) 922 m (3024 ft).

Coire Mhic Nòbuil to Tom na Gruagaich

Allow 2 hours

Walk R from the car park to stand on the bridge over the Abhainn Coire Mhic Nòbuil. The superb view along the Coire Mhic Nòbuil to where Beinn Alligin rises behind it on the skyline, NNW, demands your passing attention before you commence your walk.

Head off on the path by the W side of the abhainn, which begins across the road opposite the car park. Proceed N but soon bear NE after the first waterfall. At MR 874583, a footbridge marked on the map has disappeared so it is no longer possible to start the route from the better path on the E side of the coire. Only disturbed ground either side of the river now marks its site 1 km (⅔ mile) from the road. From here turn to 90° and walk NW, persevering over muddy ground on a path that climbs gradually towards the Coir' nan Laogh.

Well-waxed boots and a pair of gaiters are not mere luxuries for walking in the Torridon hills,

but absolute essentials! However, normally the going gets progressively drier underfoot as height is gained. Such is the case on arriving at the bottom of the Coir' nan Laogh at the 430 m (1400 ft) contour. Follow the path to where it comes next to the gushing Alltan Glas and begin walking into the corrie, its steep sides closing as you ascend. Stay L of the allt all the way to its source near to the summit. After about 400 m (1300 ft) into the corrie, veer N where the contours pack more closely in its upper reaches. Take care as the rocks in places are loose and slippery on this steep path. Pauses from time to time to catch your breath might well be rewarded by the scurrying and clucking of a ptarmigan. Its plumage mirrors perfectly its surroundings and the season. I got quite close to one here on the snow field that has a reputation for lingering into the summer. The sight of this chamaeleon bird is normally a good indication that you are at high levels, as ptarmigans generally reside above 760 m (2500 ft).

The relentlessly steep climb out of the corrie seems never ending but eventually you gain the flat top at a broad moss-covered ridge. Turn R and walk NE across further moss. You soon reach the triangulation pillar on Tom na Gruagaich at 922 m (3024 ft). The views are far-ranging in all directions and quite simply breathtaking. On the seaward horizon is the Isle of Skye. Landward the panorama is a vast exhibition of primaeval Torridonian features in an unforgettable display. Mountains nearby include: E, Beinn Dearg, Beinn Eighe; ESE, Liathach; SE, Sgorr Ruadh; S to W, the southern Torridon group; N, Baosbheinn; NE, An Teallach; ENE, Slioch.

From Tom na Gruagaich on the ridge to Sgurr Mhór

Allow 1 hour

The red sandstones which form the Torridon mountains are some of the oldest rocks in Britain, having been laid down up to 1000 million years ago. Erosive forces have since sculptured a landscape of unique features. High-level walking in the area is characterized by long, often arduous ridge traverses but, that said, the ridge between Tom na Gruagaich and Sgurr Mhór, Beinn Alligin's more northerly peak, is well within the capabilities of most fit walkers.

From Tom, head N on the path which begins steeply and descend a series of almost tor-like sandstone outcrops. Be careful with your footwork here, this is definitely no place to twist an ankle. To your R, Beinn Alligin's E-facing precipices fall away almost vertically, or as some would claim, vertiginously!

Continue down until after 1 km (⅔ mile) the path rises as a small incline in the ridge is negotiated. Gentler slopes on your L, stretching out below and to the NW, give you an early impression of the return route downhill. However, continue into the saddle and begin to climb again when the path rises steeply and veers NE. Continue to Sgurr Mhór, a further 150 m (490 ft) above sea-level, a Munro and Beinn Alligin's highest peak at 985 m (3231 ft). The views are equally impressive from its summit cairn as they were from Tom na Gruagaich. Many of the same mountains are seen again, though of course, a little differently.

Horns normally come in pairs but those on Alligin are a trio. The famous Rathanan or Horns of Alligin extend E from Sgurr Mhór and traversing them involves scrambling over sandstone pinnacles before a descent to the Bealach a' Chomhla can be made. However, our route has bipeds rather than quadrupeds in mind! So, having savoured the views and captured precious memories in a cameraful of exposed film, try to tear yourself away, at least 2½ hours before sunset for safety.

Sgorr Mhór to Coire Mhic Nòbuil

Allow 3 hours

Turn back SW and come down the steep slopes from Sgurr Mhór to regain the saddle at the lowest point of the ridge. Leave the ridge by turning R on to the mountain's relatively gentle grass and moss-covered slopes. There are no paths depicting

25.1 *The Coire Mhic Nòbuil.*

a route but the descent NW generally is a straightforward ramble over terrain with few hazards. After 800 m (½ mile), at about the 620 m (2000 ft) contour, the ground flattens out, but progress is rendered a little more awkward by a boulder-strewn moorland. Proceed E, making a beeline for a group of obvious lochans and the wet desert beyond. Pick a route that has the immediate objective of skirting below the N-facing buttresses of the Horns. By staying close to them, it is possible to avoid the wettest of the ground further below and to your L. At the same time make towards the largest of the many watery expanses pitting the landscape, that of Loch Toll nam Biast.

Pass by the loch on its S side and continue E until you arrive next to the loch-shore at its SE corner. From here bear NE towards the two smaller lochans of Toll nam Biast, passing them both on their N sides. Beside the last of them, pursue (if you can) the very faint traces of a path, barely more than a vague depression of trampled grass and heather. Follow it if you have identified it, though it makes little difference. Beyond the lochans, bear E again for a few paces across the top of a waterfall at the head of the Bealach a' Chomhla, MR 874621. Striding over large sandstone slabs makes negotiating the shallow water an easy affair but it could be a very different story when in spate! In this case, walk downstream on the L side of the Allt a' Bhealaich to wherever it seems easier to hop across on more protrusive boulders.

From Càrn Doineig a much clearer, well-trodden path is gained. Walk SE, now immediately below the Horns on their E side. On entering the Bealach a' Chomhla, you again take to a more elevated route. This avoids the much wetter ground to the L and that closer to the Allt a' Bhealaich, the route of which is followed downstream.

Descend over some really wild country, an unforgiving moor scattered with huge boulders and pitted by peat bogs. After 1.2 km (¾ mile), the path swings S. The prospect is dominated by the dramatic and extensive W-facing precipices of Beinn Dearg. The mountain presents a solid unbreachable rock wall, a monster rising out of the wilderness on the other side of the bealach as Alligin's nearest neighbouring dinosaur.

Lower slopes soon reveal views sweeping out across Upper Loch Torridon. Emerging from the bealach, after 3 km (2 miles) along it, walk over the wooden footbridge, to cross again the Allt a' Bhealaich and continue S. After a further 800 m (½ mile) of progress along an improving path, cross another footbridge where the two rivers meet. Thus gain the E side of the Abhainn Coire Mhic Nòbuil. Marked on the map at MR 882588, this very solid wooden construction really does exist!

Turn R after the bridge and walk SW on the clear, generally dry if quite rough path to descend the Coire Mhic Nòbuil towards Upper Loch Torridon. After 1 km (⅔ mile), you pass again the site of the missing footbridge on your R though now on the other side of the coire and opposite the path that heads out towards the Coir' nan Laogh. The route continues along the Coire Mhic Nòbuil in the loveliest of settings, soon amid Scots pines and from where numerous deviations are possible for viewing the picturesque waterfalls of the abhainn. From here, Beinn Alligin is cast as a wild and idyllic backdrop returning into view and refusing to be ignored. Of the feature closer to hand, it seems 'Coire' is entirely the wrong word to describe what is more like a miniature gorge.

Emerging from the trees at the end of the path, turn R on to the Diabaig road and walk over the bridge to return to the car park, on your L.

Alternative routes

ESCAPES

The route can of course be undertaken in an anti-clockwise direction. However, be aware that, should the prospect of the ridge walk between Sgurr Mhór and Tom na Gruagaich seem too daunting to attempt, then an escape by retracing your steps from Sgurr Mhór would be considerably longer than by doing the same from Tom na Gruagaich.

For a lazier kind of day, consider a simple exploration of the wonderful mini-gorge that

25.2 *Beinn Alligin, looking* N *across Upper Loch Torridon from the Shieldaig road.*

constitutes the Coire Mhic Nòbuil described at the S end of the main route. Thus the path on its E side should be used, allowing you to follow the Abhainn Coire Mhic Nòbuil upstream as far as you wish. The path begins almost directly NE from the car park amid Scots pines and from which numerous detours can be made between the trees to view the river in the corrie'.

EXTENSIONS

If you enjoy scrambling then you will find the challenge of conquering Beinn Alligin's trio of horns, collectively named Rathanan, too inviting to ignore. Assess the difficulty for yourself at Sgurr Mhór from where they are seen clearly, extending E across Beinn Alligin's northern extremity. Their traverse can be achieved on a well-worn path that eventually descends to the Bealach a' Chomhla from the last of them. One thus returns satisfied in having completed an entire traverse of the mountain. Though with more difficulties, this option actually covers less ground than in the descent described for the main route and therefore requires no extra time allocation.

Those new to the Torridons will probably find Beinn Alligin pleasantly tiring but, if you still have the energy and inclination, then consider continuing upstream by the Abhainn Coire Mhic Nòbuil having descended the Bealach a' Chomhla. Rather than crossing the abhainn, turn L 100 m (110 yd) before reaching the footbridge and walk generally E. This ever popular low-level path allows for a close encounter with the craggy N-facing buttresses of mighty Liathach on your R all the way. The route traverses a remote wilderness, passing below some spectacular examples of mountain architecture. Descend the Coire Dubh Mór to emerge at the Glen Torridon road, but now 12 km (7½ miles) from your parked car.

It would be better to save this route for another day but if you are determined to finish off the day this way, then allow an extra 4 hours, not including the transport problem.

Route 26: UPPER LOCH TORRIDON

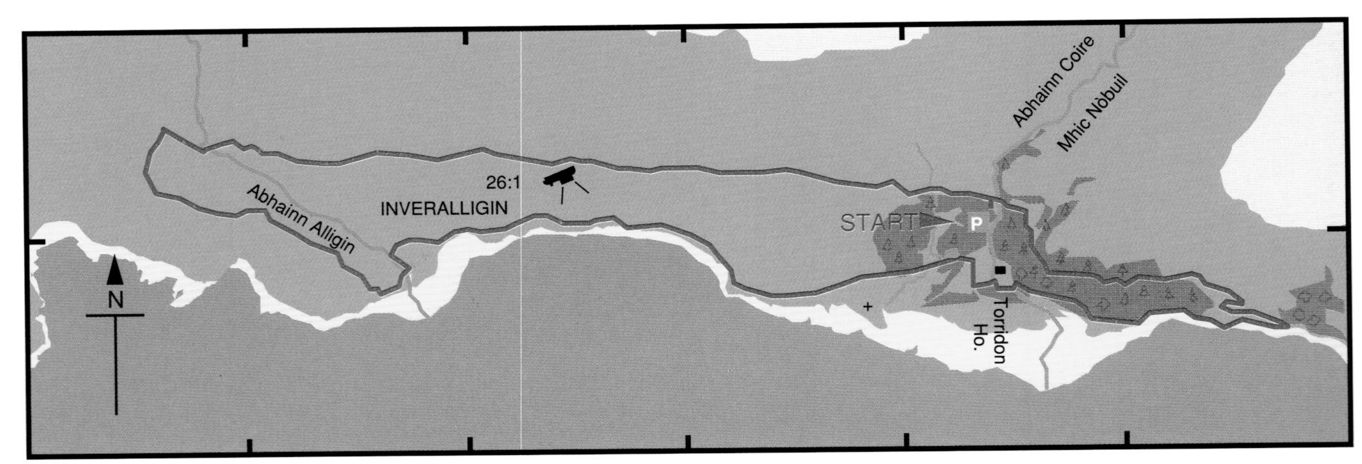

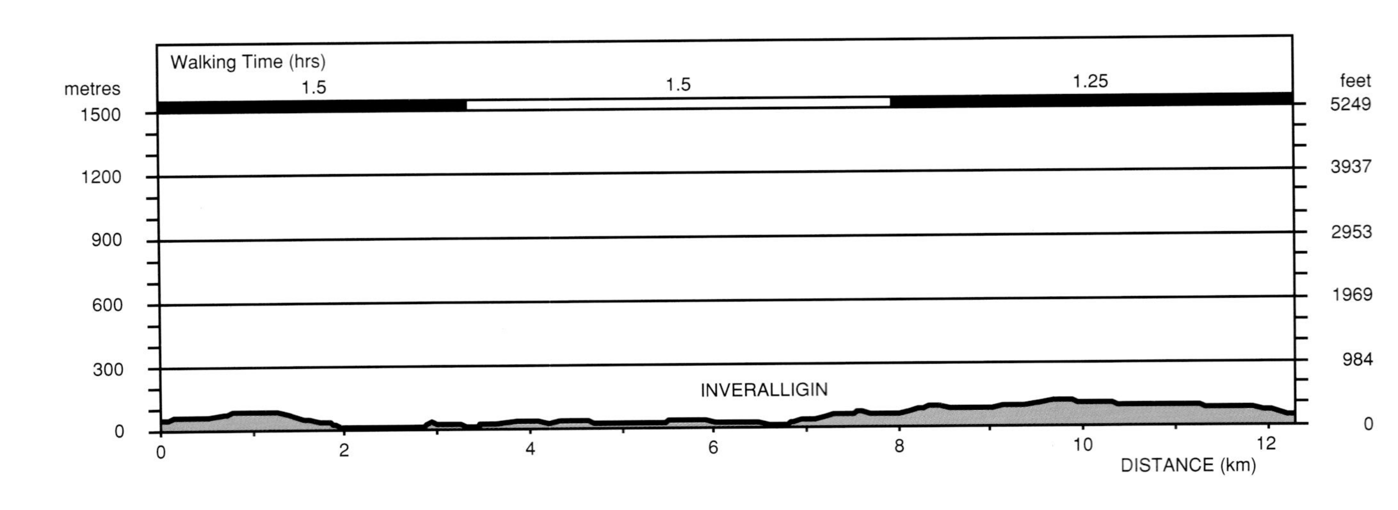

Route 26 · Upper Loch Torridon

STARTING LOCATION
Coire Mhic Nòbuil car park on Torridon to Diabaig road, 5 km (3 miles) WNW off junction with A896 in Glen Torridon.
OSLR 24 or OSOL 8/MR 868576.
Accommodates approximately 20 cars.

ALTERNATIVE STARTING LOCATION
Inveralligin or Alligin Shuas, on W side of route.

PUBLIC TRANSPORT
Nearest railway station – Achnasheen.
Regular buses, three times a week, to Kinlochewe from Inverness and Achnasheen.
Postbus, once daily, Achnasheen to Coulin, Torridon and Alligin via Kinlochewe (except Sunday).

OVERVIEW/INTEREST
Spectacular mountain and lochside views of unparalleled beauty.
Quaint lochside hamlets and a church of great charm.
Friendly sheep dogs!
Good opportunities for observing wildlife – red deer, otter, porpoise, seal, cormorant.
Generally straightforward and undemanding.

FOOTPATHS
Minimal waymarking.
Metalled single-track roads.
Good, clear and dry path and tracks elsewhere.

GRADING 2
TIME ALLOWANCE
4¼ hours.
DISTANCE

Excluding Height	12.3 km	(7½ miles)
TOTAL HEIGHT GAINED	240 m	(787 ft)

PRINCIPAL HEIGHTS
None.

Coire Mhic Nòbuil to Torridon Church

Allow 1½ hours

Turn R from the car park on the road to cross the bridge over the Abhainn Coire Mhic Nòbuil, stopping to savour the view upstream and N along the Coire's mini-gorge. Beinn Alligin's southernmost peak, Tom na Gruagaich, imposes on the skyline NNW as a mountainous backdrop.

Continue walking E, in a setting of Scots pines scattered across slopes on either side of the road. Views between the trees to Beinn Alligin NNW reveal its other summit, Sgurr Mhór, before the road bends S. After 400 m (¼ mile) turn E again, enjoying as you walk the views SE across Upper Loch Torridon. Close to where the road reaches its highest point, Fasag (Torridon village) is seen ESE, spreading out its line of cottages on the NE shore of Upper Loch Torridon. Mighty Liathach rises steeply above the village to its N and E. However, the peaks behind the village, at the head of the loch towards Glen Torridon, viewed from the W, form an alpine-like backdrop and skyline.

Descend by hairpin bends towards the loch to where birch trees now dominate the roadside. On reaching literally sea-level, turn sharp R on to the driveway for Torridon House which is signposted 'Public Footpath to Inveralligin'. Walk W, between the loch-shore L and a wall of rhododendron R, probably now feeling uplifted as you smell salt in the air. Upper Loch Torridon is a sea loch enclosed almost fjord-like with the main Torridon mountain group on its N side and with the southern group stretching W as far as Shieldaig.

Cormorants are numerous here, typically seen perched on rocks, their huge black wings spread out in the wind. The keen-eyed and patient might also be rewarded by sightings of seals, otters or porpoises. Sadly these magnificent marine mammals are still persecuted for their occasional raiding acts at fish farms for what is simply to them a well-stocked larder.

26.1 *Across Upper Loch Torridon to the Beinn Damh group, from the Diabaig road.*

About 800 m (½ mile) along the drive, the ubiquitous rhododendron gives way to an imposing red Torridonian sandstone outcrop, seen on the R, just before reaching a jetty by the shore L. Continue W on the track, the surface of which now becomes gravel, to pass a boathouse at the lochside, 100 m (110 yd) to your L and mysteriously named 'Ford's Folly'. Beyond it, the track comes near a large area of gorse scrub on the L, flowering with striking yellow blossoms in spring and adding the wonderfully sweet aroma of almonds to that of the invigorating sea air. The route follows a line of tall beech trees close to further sandstone outcrops and moss-covered rocks, a carpet that in April is speckled with white wood anemones. On a fine still day, the overriding feeling here is of tranquillity in the most beautiful surroundings. In such conditions, it is difficult to imagine anywhere else in the world you would rather be.

At a white gate, with the words 'Strictly Private' embossed on a plaque, turn L to cross an iron and timber bridge over the Abhainn Coire Mhic Nòbuil, here in its lowest reaches and just N of where it enters the loch. Pass below the gardens of Torridon House, heading W, continuing on the track which soon bears N. Beinn Alligin refuses to be ignored as it appears again impressively between the trees and straight ahead. Walk between two cottages before arriving at the estate's stables and kennels, now disused. Bear L here through an iron gate to where a small lochan on the R is banked by the encroaching evergreen, dark and dense rhododendron below a canopy of Scots pine – an example in the plant world of the indigenous being throttled by the alien.

Emerging on more open ground, walk W on the still good track now crossing typically rock-strewn Torridonian heather moorland. Before pursuing a path close to the lochside again, allow a few minutes for a brief detour from the route to Torridon church at MR 863572, not marked as such on OS maps and without a tower or spire. Take the obvious approach path R heading S away from the main route for 50 m (55 yd) to arrive at the church door. A big iron key is left in the door for visitors. Much of the old woodwork is being replaced and the interior is generally in a state of renovation. This work has been carried out with sensitivity and thankfully the place has retained all its peace and charm. There can be few churches in Britain in a setting of more enviable beauty or grandeur. The mountain prospect from the church door must be unique among places of worship. Lock the door and return to the track to commence the route W.

Torridon Church to Wester Alligin

Allow 1½ hours

From Torridon Church, turn L back at the track which becomes a coastal path, but remains clear and easily navigable. Coming closer to the lochside, bear N after an iron gate, towards Rechullin. Thus the route curves around the bay where the cottages of Inveralligin are seen dotted on gentle slopes above the loch-shore further W. Pass a quaint corrugated-roof fishing hut on your L to join the driveway of 'Rechullin' house. Here, a public footpath sign points back to Torridon.

The route becomes a metalled road again continuing, close to the lochside, but is no less pleasurable for that and vehicles are rare. Walk W passing more cottages and houses, towards the hamlet of Inveralligin. Here at the W end of the bay, you may well be welcomed by tail-wagging dogs. They are in fact very friendly, one having sniffed out in the grass my cherished sunglasses which I had begun to accept as lost. At Inveralligin, it seems sheep dogs are as common as sheep!

The hamlet, idyllically placed, has sadly suffered a little from a number of more modern, uglier developments. However, continue W to the very far end of the bay where the prettiness of the place is ultimately realized in a row of stone and slate-roofed fishing cottages behind a jetty. Walk on the single-track road between them, passing the jetty while making for the telephone box at a junction in the road. Turn L at the junction to where it is clearly signposted 'Inveralligin Field Centre', following the E side of the Abhainn Alligin. Continue along this tiny road to cross the abhainn by a bridge, R. Pass in front of a group of cottages on your R by diagonally crossing the grassy lawn in front of them to a path that hugs the shore and which at high tide is literally just a few feet from the sea. Walk WSW for a little way until immediately before the last cottage. Here, turn R, directed by a stone with the painted words 'Footpath to Diabaig', to follow a path NNW away from the lochside and up amid sandstone outcrops. Climbing above the crags, pursue a route on the path that roughly follows a line of elevated power cables NW across bouldery open country for about 600 m (1/3 mile). Then at Baclenbea, join a single-track metalled road above the cottages of Port a' Chaobaill. Walk W for a further 500 m (1/3 mile) to reach the E side of the lochside hamlet of Wester Alligin (Alligin Shuas) at a junction in the road.

Wester Alligin to Coire Mhic Nòbuil

Allow 1 1/4 hours

Turn R, walking uphill away from the cottages of the hamlet, to join the Diabaig road next to a pine and larch plantation on the R. Turn R again to head in a generally E direction along the road towards Torridon. Walking this pleasant unfrequented road takes a route, on average, 800 m (1/2 mile) further N of your earlier coastal route W and from which, in many places, you can look down R to discover its many beautiful features in reverse.

The S-facing slopes of Beinn Alligin (from Tom na Gruagaich) meet the roadside, L, and Liathach becomes increasingly dominant directly ahead E. The roadside here is well frequented by red deer, most often seen grazing these lower slopes in the relative half-light security of dusk. In summer, the mountains S across the loch glow a magnificent red when hit by the last rays of the day's sunshine.

The car park is on the R of the road, 5 km (3 miles) E of Wester Alligin.

Alternative routes

ESCAPES

The main route can be shortened by returning to the Diabaig road from various points along the lochside, and is still well worth doing. Reduce total distances to:

6 km (3 3/4 miles) by ascending path N of Torridon church to join Diabaig road 800 m (1/2 mile) W of car park;

10 km (6 1/4 miles) by ascending single-track road NE from Inveralligin to join Diabaig road 2.8 km (1 3/4 miles) W of car park;

11 km (7 miles) by ascending single-track road NW from Inveralligin to join Diabaig road 3.6 km (2 1/4 miles) W of car park.

EXTENSIONS

Another very rewarding low-level option in the area, or to maker a longer day of it, would be to explore the maze of footpaths on the S side of Upper Loch Torridon between the lochside and the A896 as far as Shieldaig. Walking here allows some classic views of Beinn Alligin and Liathach seen N across the loch.

A much easier addition, and one which avoids a drive in between, is to explore the spectacular Coire Mhic Nòbuil on the good path to the E of the abhainn. The path conveniently begins almost directly opposite the car park used for the main route and is described in more detail in 'Escapes' for Route 25.

Route 27: AN TEALLACH

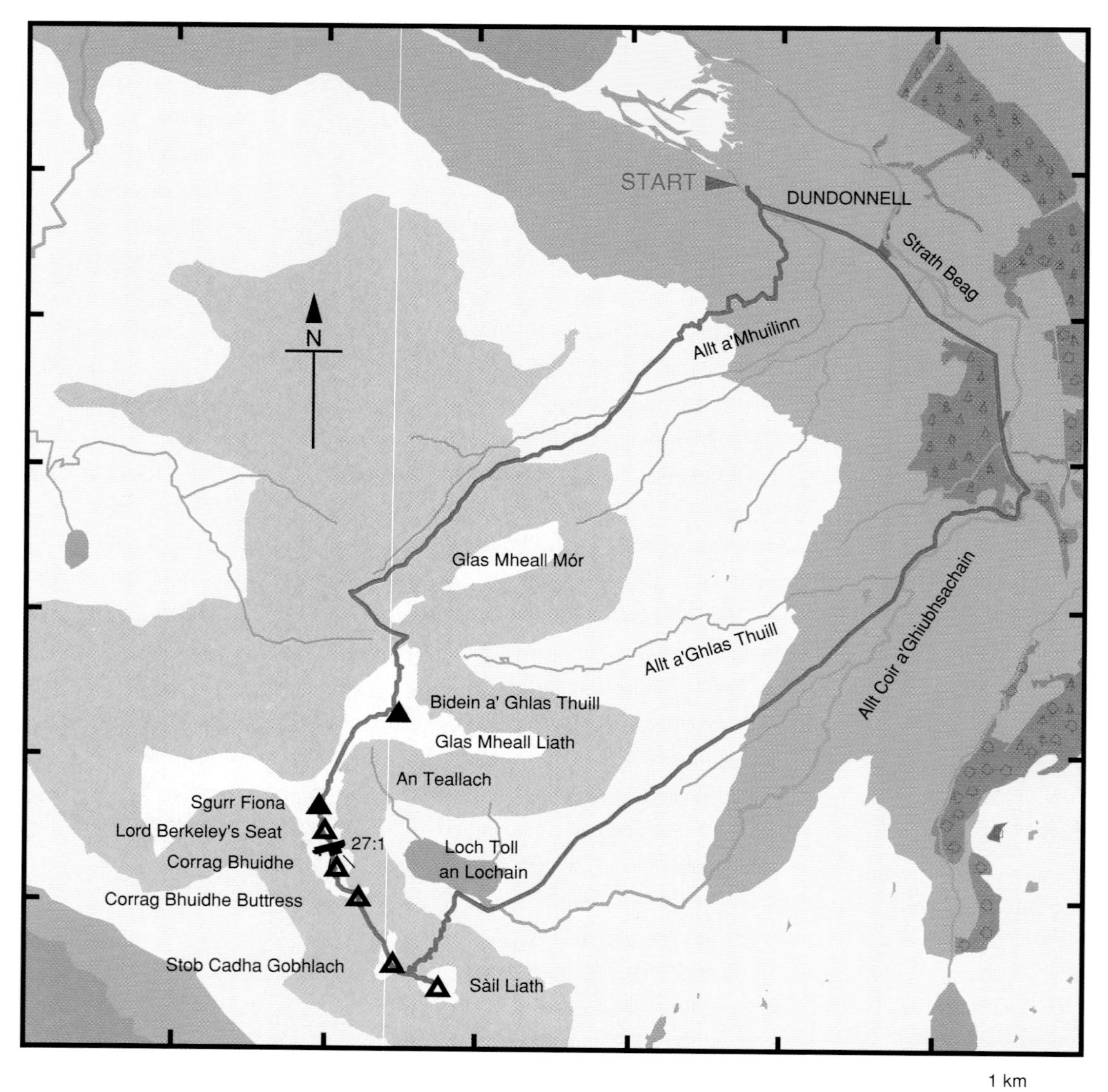

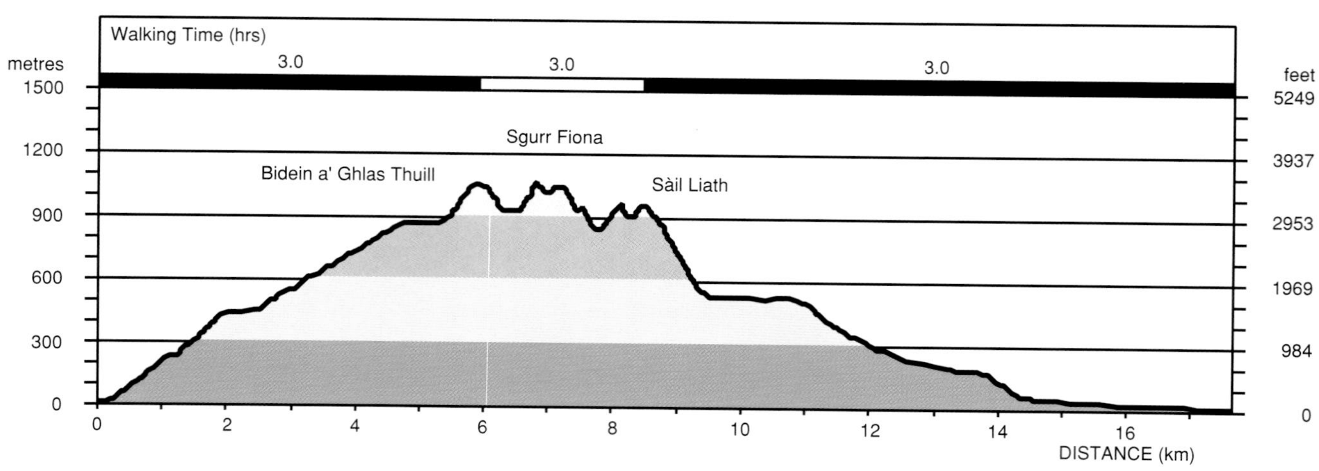

16

THE GREAT WILDERNESS

HIGH-LEVEL ROUTE

Route 27 · An Teallach

STARTING LOCATION
A832 at Dundonnell in lay-by on N side of road, 400 m (¼ mile) ESE of Dundonnell Hotel.
OSLR 19 or OSPF 120/MR 092879.
Accommodates approximately 10 cars. Further space available by Dundonnell Hotel.

ALTERNATIVE STARTING LOCATION
Parking bay near foot of Garbh Allt, close to junction of A832 with minor road to Dundonnell House. This alternative is recommended if only Loch Toll an Lochain is to be visited (see 'Escapes'); or An Teallach is gained via ascent of Glas Mheall Mór (see 'Extensions'); MR 113858.

PUBLIC TRANSPORT
Nearest railway station – Achnasheen.
Regular buses, three times a week, to Dundonnell from Gairloch and Inverness.

OVERVIEW/INTEREST
Enthralling ridge traverse on possibly one of Scotland's finest mountains.
A magnificent showpiece corrie, the Coire Toll an Lochain.
Spectacular examples of mountain architecture.
Descent in snow-filled gullies should be attempted only by those with experience in using an ice axe.
Best attempted on a fine day in summer.
All awkward and exposed scrambles can be bypassed.
Arduous and extremely demanding route.

FOOTPATHS
No waymarking.
Steep, though generally clear and dry on ascent path.
Rugged over ridge pinnacles.
Scrambles avoided via slightly lower-level and rough bypass path on W side.
Loose and very steep descent into Toll an Lochain.
Straightforward free-ranging to the Garbh Allt.
Finishes with a pleasant roadside stroll.

GRADING 6

TIME ALLOWANCE
9 hours.

DISTANCE

Excluding Height	17.7 km	(11 miles)
TOTAL HEIGHT GAINED	1420 m	(4659 ft)

PRINCIPAL HEIGHTS
An Teallach (The Forge):

Bidein a' Ghlas Thuill (Peak of the Green Hollow)	1062 m	(3484 ft)
Sgurr Fiona (Fair Peak)	1059 m	(3474 ft)
Lord Berkeley's seat	1047 m	(3434 ft)
Corrag Bhuidhe (Yellow Finger) 1036 m (3398 ft)		
Corrag Bhuidhe Buttress	929 m	(3047 ft)
Sàil Liath (Grey Heel)	954 m	(3129 ft)

Dundonnell to Bidein a' Ghlas Thuill

Allow 3 hours

Leave the lay-by by turning L on to the A832 and follow the road as far as the slate-roofed cottage on the L, after 150 m (165 yd). An old style red telephone box is a little further on the L. Strike off R, immediately before two cottages on the R, and proceed SE behind them. Soon after, veer S to follow the path uphill on slopes of increasing steepness. After a further few hundred metres, the path bears R and continues in a SW direction.

The path is eroded in places though generally clear and dry as it twists between numerous rugged outcrops on these lower slopes of Meall Garbh. To your rear an extending view seaward towards Little Loch Broom is revealed. Glas Mheall Mór, An Teallach's northernmost summit, appears on the SW skyline ahead of you. An Teallach is in fact a range of summits although, at this stage, few other features of the mountain are visible.

After a series of zigzags, the path divides. Take the R fork following small cairns generally SW up the slopes beyond. At roughly 430 m (1400 ft) altitude, the path divides again and a more well-worn cairned path bears R up towards Meall Garbh. Instead, continue SW on the less significantly cairned route over flat, outcropping slabs. These provide easy walking and compensate for the fact that there is no clear path for a while. Simply make a beeline for the unmistakable cone-shaped mound of Glas Mheall Mór. On approaching the Allt a' Mhuilinn on your L, a path becomes clearly discernible. Continue until it is necessary to ford the allt by boulder-hopping and gain its S side. Follow the route of the allt upstream, WSW, passing a number of tiny waterfalls. Strike off L when adjacent to the N-facing slopes of Glas Mheall Mór, coming in immediately below them. Continue your gradual ascent on the path heading WSW, now about 200 m (220 yd) L of the allt. The going underfoot becomes a little softer where the route begins to traverse grassy slopes.

Having reached the top of a broad grassy pass, cross a stony plateau and bear L. Proceed SW, a little more steeply, on the L side of, and closer to, the narrowing allt. Keep to the path below the barren slopes of the W side of Glas Mheall Mór which sweep down from the L. The skyline ahead becomes a sweeping crescent. A large cairn at its head is your immediate destination. On reaching it continue SW to pass two further cairns. The triangulation pillar on Bidein a' Ghlas Thuill can be seen looking S. The mountain's western spur, ending in Sgurr Ruadh, protrudes into the wilderness beyond Coire Mór an Teallaich.

From the third cairn, turn L and walk up a bouldery though easy gradient SE to gain the lowest point in the ridge between Glas Mheall Mór and Bidein a' Ghlas Thuill. The view looking down and E from the rim of Glas Tholl, the most northerly of An Teallach's two great corries, is a truly impressive taste of things to come. Turn R and head S, directly up steep, rubble-strewn sandstone slopes. There is an array of twisting paths to choose from though the more faint-hearted are advised to stay on those well over to the R. After nearly 200 m (700 ft) of ascent, all such routes lead to the triangulation pillar at the summit of Bidein a' Ghlas Thuill at 1062 m (3484 ft), An Teallach's highest summit.

Depending on your disposition, the view S to the other peaks of this mini-range will induce either intense excitement or apprehensive horror! The sharp, broken and serrated succession of pinnacles before you creates a skyline ridge quite unlike any other on the mainland. Legs may well turn to jelly at the sight of them, though I think few would dispute An Teallach's reputation as one of the finest of Scottish mountains.

The ridge ends with the less inspiring quartzite top of Sàil Liath, nearly 3 km (2 miles) away, beyond sheer buttresses plunging to Corrie Toll an Lochain 500 m (1650 ft) below. Of An Teallach itself, the principal tops in view are: S, Sgurr Fiona, Lord Berkeley's seat, Corrag Bhuidhe, Corrag Bhuidhe Buttress, Sàil Liath; E, Glas Mheall Liath; NE, Glas Mheall Mór.

It is the pinnacles and peaks listed to the S which are to be traversed. The more orthodox summits E and NE are optional spurs to the main ridge (see 'Extensions').

Beyond the ridge, there is a wonderful panorama of mountains to be savoured but this is described in more detail from Sgurr Fiona, the other Munro summit of An Teallach and from where more distant views are less obscured.

Bidein a' Ghlas Thuill to Sàil Liath

Allow 3 hours

Head off SW on the path downhill, leaving the triangulation pillar behind. Having lost about

27.1 *Corrag Bhuidhe pinnacle on An Teallach's serrated ridge.*

150 m (490 ft) in altitude, begin almost immediately a steep re-ascent. With such routes, when energy is seemingly wasted, a walker's morale is severely tested. You might wonder, as I did, why you never took up hang-gliding instead!

Beyond the top of a scree gully on your L, a viable descent route from the saddle to Loch Toll an Lochain (see 'Escapes') gradually veers S. Keep to the ascent path just to the R of the corrie rim. The climb relents on gaining the summit cairn on Sgurr Fiona at 1059 m (3474 ft). Sgurr Fiona is also a Munro peak, just 3 m (10 ft) lower than its neighbouring one, now behind you.

Sgurr Fiona is a superlative vantage point for views across a wilderness which boasts some of Britain's remotest mountains. A far-reaching horizon also extends seaward beyond Gruinard Bay and Loch Ewe to the W. Closer to hand, the dark waters of Loch Toll an Lochain are viewed below the precipitous cliffs ESE. However, the true prize is contemplation of the untamed wilderness to the S and SW. The mountain summits of the Fisherfield and Letterewe forests, seen beyond Loch na Sealga and the confluence of the Abhainn Strath na Sealga with the Abhainn Gleann na Muice, include: WSW, Beinn Dearg Bheag, Beinn a' Chaisgein Mór; SW, Beinn Dearg Mór, Ruadh-stac Mór, A' Mhaighdean (Scotland's remotest Munro); SSW, Slioch; S, Sgurr Bàn, Mullach Coire Mhic Fhearchair; SSE, A' Chailleach.

In clear conditions, Torridon summits are identifiable on a far horizon looking S.

The ridge from Sgurr Fiona introduces a new dimension to the route. A narrower, airy traverse begins over sandstone crags, typical of Torridonian ridges (being of the same sedimentary make-up). To make further progress, An Teallach demands a more adaptable approach from its guests.

Descend to a dip and then ascend on an easy scramble over sandstone terraces, keeping L and close to the corrie rim. From the tiny rock platform which is Lord Berkeley's seat, you have gained the reward of a vertiginous view to Loch Toll an Lochain. However, some may in fact consider this a punishment. Non-scramblers and those without a head for heights are advised to stay well to the R of the edge. There is a bypass path a little lower down on the W side of the ridge.

Leave Lord Berkeley's seat, the first of the pinnacles, by scrambling with relative ease S down along the ridge. Stay S on the path up the highest and most northerly of the Corrag Bhuidhe pinnacles. Again the scramble is an easy affair, though perhaps rendered more severe by the sense of exposure on the L. As elsewhere, minor difficulties are avoidable by the path on the R. Its airy summit platform affords a fine perspective N back to Bidein a' Ghlas Thuill and of Glas Mheall Liath protruding E from it. The summit of the latter is the end of a spur enclosing the N side of Corrie Toll an Lochain.

Magnificent views from Highland summits can normally be relied on in fine weather. An unexpected surprise was to have heard one day a cuckoo from Corrag Bhuidhe. In spring, these most vocal of birds seem to occupy just about every birch and rowan copse throughout the Highlands. However, such a discourse is rare on mountain summits. It was difficult to believe that the sound was emanating from a few scattered birches over 600 m (2000 ft) below and it was a sobering thought that the rigours of An Teallach really bear no comparison to unaided flight from Africa! Special places often become private places and for me An Teallach will be remembered as the Mountain of the Cuckoo.

Along Corrag Bhuidhe, progress becomes more awkward. Its three remaining pinnacles are enthralling airy scrambles, each to be scaled in turn by proceeding S. Exercise caution as you do so and if you doubt your abilities, bypass them on the R. Descending from the last of them is particularly tricky so do take your time here, exercising great care.

For the last of the day's scrambling, continue S to ascend with relative ease the Corrag Bhuidhe Buttress. However, leave the summit making an especially attentive descent. There have been fatalities here. The safest, if still exposed, scramble is found via the path out to the R. Further to your R, the Corrag Bhuidhe Buttress can be bypassed altogether, again using the bypass path on the W side of the ridge.

Proceed along the ridge, in a far less arduous fashion, to the small cairn on Stob Cadha Gobhlach. Footwork here demands less attention and at secure resting places eyes are free to feast on a continuing panorama. To the R, Loch na Sealga is seen at its best from the Stob, a large and remote finger of water pointing NW to the sea. Follow the path down and veer SE, keeping to the ridge path up the easy slopes of Sàil Liath. Its quartzite-capped summit adds a geological variation to the route and marks the southern extent of the ridge. Walk as far as the third cairn to reach Sàil Liath's highest point.

Sàil Liath to Dundonnell *Allow 3 hours*

Leave the summit by walking NW. Return to the dip from where the southernmost gully of Cadha Gobhlach heads into the Corrie Toll an Lochain. Turn R and descend carefully the steep scree gully NE. The gully may be snow-filled well into the summer and in such conditions an ice axe, and experience in knowing how to use it, is essential if a direct descent is intended. It may be possible to head down to the R of the snow-field, but pay particular attention to easily dislodged boulders that can potentially cause injury to companions lower down. The remaining option is a long and tiring return via the lower bypass path on the W side of the ridge and then to retrace footsteps at the N end of An Teallach. You should allow 5 hours for this, or 6 for the scrambling route back over the pinnacles.

As steepness relents, the gully deposits you on the S side of Loch Toll an Lochain. Turn R and walk SE, having gained an obvious path along its S shore. After 250 m (275 yd), at the E end of the loch, bear L and cross the allt over a basic bridge of boulders. The enthralling prospect is of being in a vast amphitheatre enclosed by formidable precipices and towering buttresses. One is left enraptured by a quite breathtaking skyline and an image of An Teallach equal to that from Bidein a' Ghlas Thuill. For me, having ventured elsewhere in Europe, such drama brings to mind an almost alpine-like scene with hints of the Picos de Europa in Northern Spain.

Leave the lochside, at first heading E but quickly bearing NE, aiming just below and to the R of Glas Mheall Liath. There is no clear path but this is more than compensated for by an agreeable surface of large flat sandstone pavements aiding steady downhill progress. Follow the route of the allt a few hundred metres to the W of it and keeping to the L side of the Coir' a' Ghiubhsachain. The E side is dominated by a long running escarpment which provides a useful reference. Make a beeline towards the crags at the N end of this escarpment, walking roughly parallel to it. In places, sporadic cairns guide you across. When below Glas Mheall Liath, ford a small burn and continue to the confluence of Allt Coir' a' Ghiubhsachain (on your R) and the Allt a' Corrie Ghlas Thuill (on your L). An attractive waterfall on the R is worth your passing attention: look out for dippers here. This brown, thrush-size bird is to water as lichen is to air – a reliable indicator of purity. Ford the smaller allt, flowing from the L, by stepping-stones. Bear R and pursue a definite path above the L side of what is now the Garbh Allt to where it flows through a small gorge. Bear E on descending slightly steeper slopes, from where a scattering of Scots pine are visible immediately N. Pause for the fine view to Strath Beag and the Dundonnell River below.

Swing out a little N of the Garbh Allt before passing between thinly spaced Scots pines and cairn-marked outcrops. The vegetation becomes denser where the path enters an area of prolific rhododendrons which here entirely dominate the ground layer. Proceed on the rooty path, which soon tunnels through the bushes and comes closer again to the tumbling waters of the Garbh Allt. At a gap on your R, steal a glance back to view a prominent waterfall before continuing E along the darker, leaf- and needle-thick path. On emerging at the next clearing, take the L fork where the path divides to skirt around the edges of the bushes until, on an increasingly muddy path, you come alongside the Garbh Allt again. Ford a tiny backwater to emerge at the roadside opposite Dundonnell House on the other side of the Dundonnell River. Although an A road (the A832), it is rarely busy.

Turn L towards Dundonnell to finish an especially satisfying day with a pleasantly rural roadside stroll through Strath Beag. Following the Dundonnell River downstream, the parking place is 3 km (2 miles) NW of Dundonnell House. The Hotel is at hand to offer refreshments.

Alternative routes

ESCAPES

The scaling of An Teallach's multi-pinnacled skyline requires a serious commitment. Once on the ridge, there are no quick or easy ways off. If at Sgurr Fiona, the prospect S seems too intimidating, retreat by the ascent route in relative safety.

To maintain a circular diversion, a steeper escape via the scree gully from the ridge between Bidein a' Ghlas Thuill and Sgurr Fiona is a possibility. Descend SE into Toll an Lochain and proceed to the E side of the loch to pick up the main descent route. However, all the awkward and exposed scrambles over the pinnacles S of Sgurr Fiona are conveniently avoidable via a bypass path. This lies a few metres lower on the W side of the ridge.

The traverse of An Teallach's dizzy precipices are the preserve of those with a head for heights. It is worth making the effort to visit the corrie of Toll an Lochain to experience the effect of the mountain's towering cliffs and its impressively serrated skyline surrounding the loch. The corrie is reached by the path striking off W from the road near Dundonnell House, MR 113858; in other words a reverse of the final section of the main route. Return the same way and allow 4½ hours in total.

EXTENSIONS

An alternative ascent route is possible by making a direct assault on Glas Mheall Mór. Begin on the path heading generally W from near Dundonnell House at MR 113858. At the confluence of the Allt a' Corrie Ghlas Thuill with the Allt Coir' a' Ghiubhsachain continue W and follow the former mentioned allt up into the corrie. Then veer R and climb the steep E-facing slopes to the summit of Glas Mheall Mór. From here, the other principal peaks of the range can be picked off in turn. Due to excessive steepness and an additional 90 m (300 ft) of height gained, allow an extra ½ hour for this.

Other than taking in the remaining ridge spurs of Glas Mheall Liath and Sgùrr Creag an Eich, extensions beyond An Teallach are not recommended.

Route 28: GRUINARD RIVER

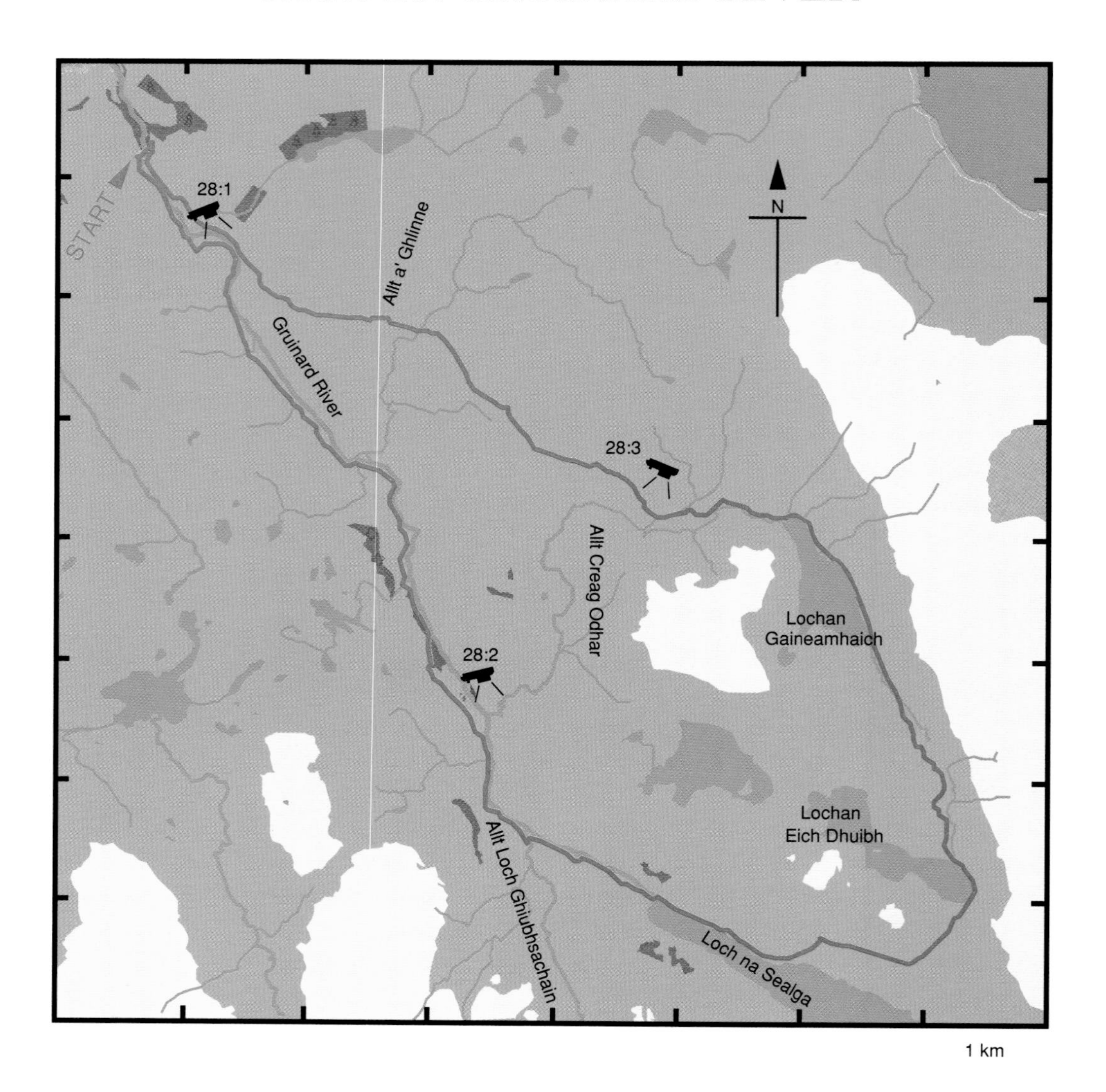

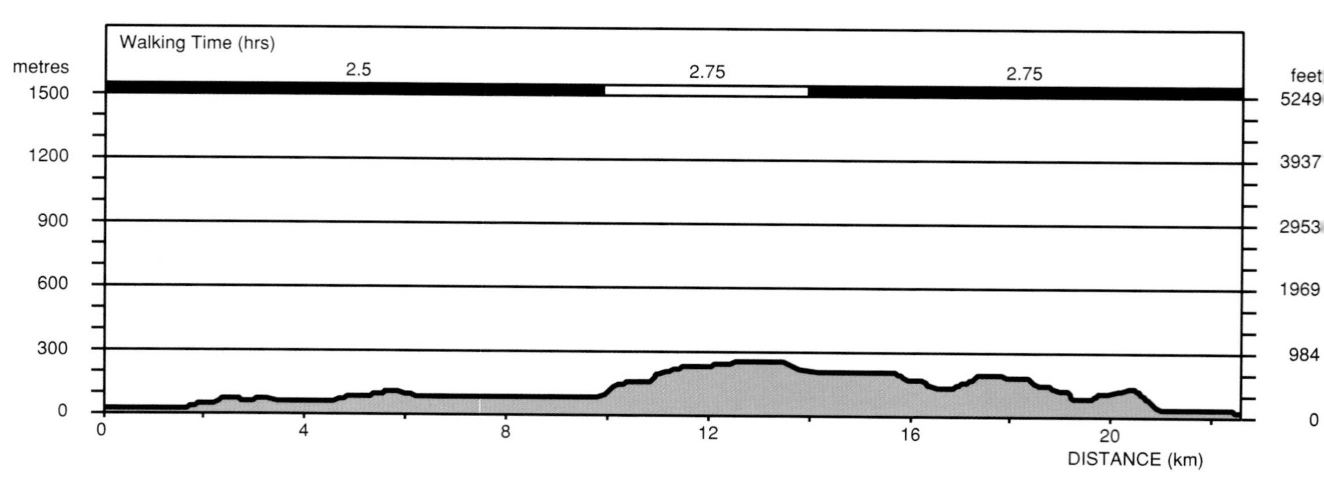

Route 28 · Gruinard River

STARTING LOCATION
A832 at Gruinard Bay by the bridge over the Gruinard River.
OSLR 19 or OSPF 110, 120 and 119/MR 962912.
Park on the W side of bridge using roadside verges, 1 km (2/3 mile) S of Gruinard House.
Accommodates approximately 12 cars.

ALTERNATIVE STARTING LOCATION
Additional verge parking nearby.

PUBLIC TRANSPORT
Nearest railway station – Achnasheen.
Regular buses, three times a week, to Laide and Badcaul from Gairloch and Inverness.

OVERVIEW/INTEREST
Explores the NW corner of Fisherfield Forest, part of Britain's largest uninhabited wilderness.
Crosses typically rugged Wester Ross terrain amid numerous Lewisian gneiss outcrops.
Gruinard Bay, site of the oldest rocks known in Europe.
A most likely area for seeing otters.
Superb mountain scenery surrounding Loch na Sealga.
Necessitates wading across a river up to thigh-high in depth (adding a small towel to the contents of your rucksack might be useful, or see 'Escapes'); the wade is suitable only for adults on a summer outing.
Physically demanding for a lower-level route.

FOOTPATHS
No waymarking.
Excellent track as far as Loch na Sealga.
Somewhat slower progress on more rugged footpaths elsewhere.

GRADING 4
TIME ALLOWANCE
8 hours.
DISTANCE

Excluding Height	22.5 km	(14 miles)
TOTAL HEIGHT GAINED	390 m	(1280 ft)

PRINCIPAL HEIGHTS
None – highest point of route at 260 m (853 ft), MR 026861.

Gruinard Bay to Loch na Sealga

Allow 2½ hours

Leave the road at the start of the track on the W side of the Gruinard River. Pass through a small wooden gate to the R of a much larger iron gate hosting a sign 'Fishing Prohibited'. Begin walking S, next to the river on your L and below a small copse of trees and two farm buildings on your R.

After 100 m (110 yd) or so, bear SE passing green timber huts and a white cottage on the opposite side of the river. Progress is straightforward and rapid on the excellent track. A tantalizing skyline of wild and remote peaks beckons in the distance. Maintain a route upstream of the Gruinard River, curving round to the L at a pronounced meander. A small plantation can be seen on slopes close by, to the NE. After a further few hundred metres, ford a burn, continuing SE, where more numerous outcrops on either side create a more enclosed situation.

Ascend gradually through something resembling a natural corridor, where the river flows straight and unswerving just below. Ford a shallow burn, after which a slightly steeper incline brings you next to crags a little higher. A narrow ribbon of birch scrub betrays a tiny gorge which intersects with the opposite bank. On coming further above the river, a more prominent birch wood cloaks the slopes to the R of the track ahead. Bear L and walk down E next to the river again, where subsequent meanders curve across flatter and boggier ground between widening banks. Ford a burn by stepping-stones and soon after pursue a course SSE, passing directly below the birch wood. From these trees, in spring and early summer, feelings of regenera-

28.1 *Distant Beinn Dearg Bheag, looking* SSE *along the lower reaches of the Gruinard River.*

tion and renewal are rendered more acute by the ubiquitous call of the cuckoo, and at the riverside by the restless performances of wagtails and dippers. Look out also for otters, NW Scotland being this mammal's stronghold in Britain. The Gruinard River is ideal otter territory.

Ford a burn on entering a woodland close to the bank and after 300 m (330 yd) pass through a wooden gate between deer fencing. This fencing has been erected by the Gruinard Estate and a sign on the gate describes their intentions to allow natural regeneration of this deciduous fragment. Indeed, the fence-line effect has created a visually striking juxtaposition in ground layer vegetation. Beneath the trees, you are immediately aware of many more plants in a ground layer left unbrowsed where grasses, mosses, ferns and wildflowers grow in profusion. Buttercup, primrose and Scottish bluebell (harebell) are just three examples. Rowan and birch saplings are taking a hold and the heather is far more developed on the protected side. Leave the enclosure after about 600 m (⅓ mile), via another wooden gate at the S end.

Walk on S, swinging away from the river a little, but then descend on resuming a course SE above the confluence of the Allt Creag Odhar with the Gruinard River. Pause to contemplate what is in my view the finest of mountain pairings, that of Beinn Dearg Bheag and Beinn Dearg Mór, the former broody and volcano-like on the immediate skyline SE. Craggy outcrops and sporadic lonely trees in a broad grassy valley, provide a fitting foreground to a mountain scene of untamed beauty.

Descend to meet the river again and follow the track S. Just before passing between two wooden posts, stepping-stones across a rudimentary dam enable you to negotiate a burn. On the R is a sign 'Letterewe Wilderness – Fisherfield Forest' which states that you are entering a 'precious wilderness'. Please respect requests that restrict camping and the lighting of fires. The message continues: 'No mountain bikes, no fishing, respect the flora and fauna, this is a Site of Special Scientific Interest (SSSI).'

After a sharp bend in the river, proceed SE. An Teallach begins to dominate the skyline ahead. Ruined walls are seen roughly 200 m (220 yd) to your R. Cross the Allt Loch Ghiubhsachain where the track bridges it just to the R of its confluence with the Gruinard River. Proceed on the same bearing to where the track terminates at the secluded W end of Loch na Sealga. The mountain scenery is superb, the loch overshadowed on its L side, ESE, by the SW-facing slopes of An Teallach and to the R, SSE, by Beinn Dearg Bheag and Beinn Dearg Mór. Loch na Sealga extends SE for 6.5 km (4 miles) into the remote Strath na Sealga.

Further progress is only possible by confronting, on your L, the Gruinard River. Roll up your trousers, or better still remove them completely, having assessed the river and found the shallowest crossing point. This is most likely to be a few metres to the L of the point where the river flows from the loch. If circumstances are not favourable, then for reasons of safety it is advisable not to proceed (see 'Escapes' for recommendations). Instead, return the same way by backtracking NW. However, in summer, most reasonably fit adult-only groups should have few problems wading across water rarely deeper than 0.9 m (3 ft). The current is gentle and the rocks on the river bed are not too slippery. Thus, gain the N side of the river.

28.2 *Beinn Dearg Bheag and Beinn Dearg Mór, looking SSE from the Gruinard River track.*

Loch na Sealga to Lochan Gaineamhaich

Allow 2¾ hours

Having dried off, congratulate yourself on successfully overcoming this route's one significant obstacle. The effect on feet can actually be quite invigorating, especially on a hot summer's day.

Proceed SE beside Loch na Sealga, following the path by its N shore. From here on progress is a little more arduous, traversing generally rougher, wetter terrain. The boldly marked footpath on OS maps is deceptively optimistic. However, navigational problems are mostly non-existent as the route described is easily followed.

After about 1 km (⅔ mile), pass a solitary, somewhat unexpected holly tree by the lochside on your R. Soon after, adjacent to where the loch begins to widen, swing L and begin to walk uphill ENE. These wet slopes provide ideal conditions for butterwort, a relatively rare insectivorous plant, though locally abundant. Glance to your rear for a new perspective on Beinn Dearg Bheag and Beinn Dearg Mór, now seen across the loch and both mountains revealing distinct, separate summits.

On higher slopes, bear R and walk ESE. Follow roughly the 160 m (500 ft) contour until the path turns to the L. Stride on upward, NE, heading away from the loch and towards a broad gap in the crags. The ground becomes increasingly bouldery underfoot.

Proceed to Loch an Eich Dhuibh, the obvious stretch of water on your L. Arriving here, directly below and to the W of Sgurr Ruadh (An Teallach's most westerly summit), signifies the easternmost point of the route. Take time to savour the stillness and the silence as well as the unique satisfaction of having ventured into Britain's last great wilderness.

Follow the path round to the L, by the E shore of Loch an Eich Dhuibh, walking NW for a while. Ford a burn by stepping-stones and strike off N away from the loch. Ascend to where the path divides and take the L fork heading NNW. At the 260 m (853 ft) contour, MR 026861, you have reached the highest point of the route. On commencing a gradual descent, ford a tiny burn and follow its course, staying just to the R of it, as far as the E shore of Lochan Gaineamhaich.

Lochan Gaineamhaich to Gruinard Bay

Allow 2¾ hours

Keep to the path beside the E bank of Lochan Gaineamhaich. After 1.2 km (¾ mile), bear L to skirt its N shore. Proceed W below the heathery slopes of Carn nam Buailtean on your L and following the Allt Creag Odhar downstream, also on your L. Pass a small cairn and then descend to the ruins of a settlement in a grassy depression. The crumbling walls are on the L side of a feeder burn just N of the allt. Using convenient stepping-stones, ford the burn and veer NW, passing further ruins on your R. On ascending again, glance to your L for fine views back over what seems a harsh wet domain, where solitary, wind-sculptured birch trees fight for survival between numerous outcropping rocks. It is a timeless landscape, where nature has been haphazard and untidy, and yet so typical a scene of wild and wonderful Wester Ross.

On descending, bear L and walk WNW. Pass through a wooden gate between low fencing and continue beyond yet more ruins on your R. The path takes to a series of undulations on traversing peat hags and heathery outcrops. Having swung a little more to the W, ford a burn easily at a metal sign with the letter 'B' on it. The Gruinard River and the track, pursued at the beginning of the route, emerge again in the immediate W. Proceed NW on beginning a steeper descent towards Gruinard Bay, the sea now in view between outcrops. The few buildings described where the walk began come into view again. Walk down bracken-covered slopes to gain a clearer, wider path on the E bank of the Gruinard River and head downstream.

When 200 m (220 yd) to the L of a small plantation, pass through a metal gate and walk on by the riverside well in front of a cottage on your R. Beyond three green wooden huts, keep to the L of a large house at Carn na h-Aire by walking to the N of it to emerge at the roadside on the A832. Turn L and cross the bridge over the Gruinard River where, looking N, it is seen tumbling seaward through a delightful oak wood. The start point is just beyond.

28.3 *Typical Wester Ross terrain, from the path near the Allt Creag Odhar.*

Alternative routes

ESCAPES

The complete circuit is recommended as a summer route and only for adults. Return from Loch na Sealga by walking NW back along the riverside track in any of the following circumstances:

- There are children in the group under 14 years old.
- The river is in spate or, at the crossing point, the water is anywhere deeper than 0.9 m (3 ft).
- You are walking the route between October and April when water temperatures can be dangerously low.
- There are fewer than 5½ hours until sunset.
- You are unsure of your own abilities in such river crossings as well as on negotiating the rough terrain thereafter.

Allow 5 hours in total for the 'there and back' option.

Beach lovers can indulge less active pursuits at Gruinard Bay, with its mile crescent of golden sand. Access to the beach is from the car park at the S end of the bay, MR 953899. Budding geologists should note that on the cliffs, where the road cuts through, rocks have been found that are the oldest known in all Europe.

EXTENSIONS

The main route is long and physically quite demanding. Adding distance and time to it are not recommended.

However, for the committed, there are numerous opportunities to explore the great wilderness beyond Loch na Sealga. Via the S shore of the loch, there is a bothy for overnight stays at Shenavall, located a further 8 km (5 miles) SE in Strath na Sealga. Anyone daring to penetrate deeper into this wildest of sanctuaries (over 450 km^2 (175 square miles) in extent) should be aware that such expeditions call for careful advanced planning. The rewards of peace and solitude, however, are beyond that found anywhere else in Britain. Solitary and silent among the mountains of Letterewe forest, Scotland's most remote Munros, A' Mhaighdean and Ruadh-stac Mór, are prizes only for the most dedicated of collectors.

Allow up to three days for the complete wilderness traverse, finishing at either Poolewe or Kinlochewe.

Route 29: SUILVEN

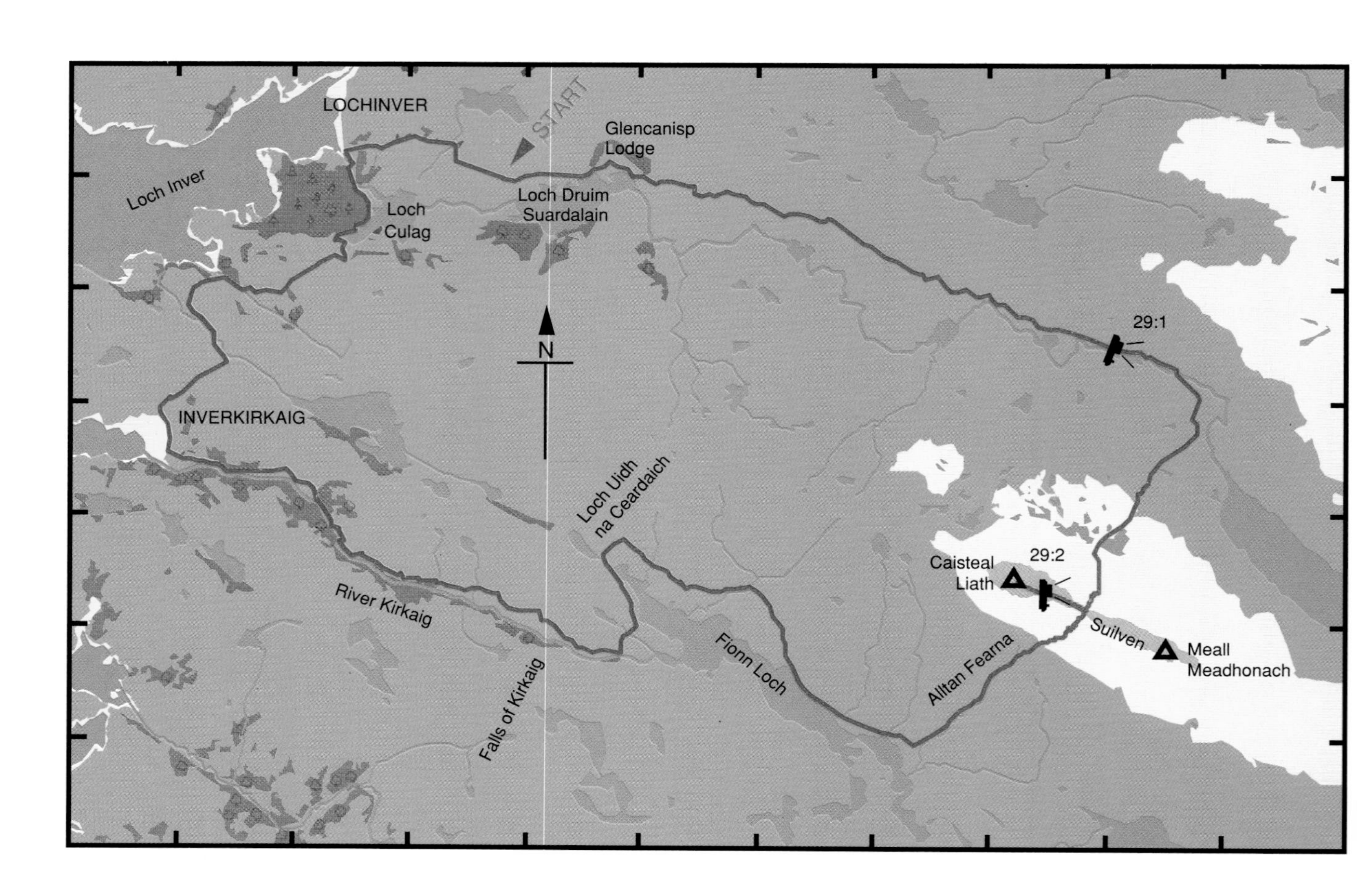

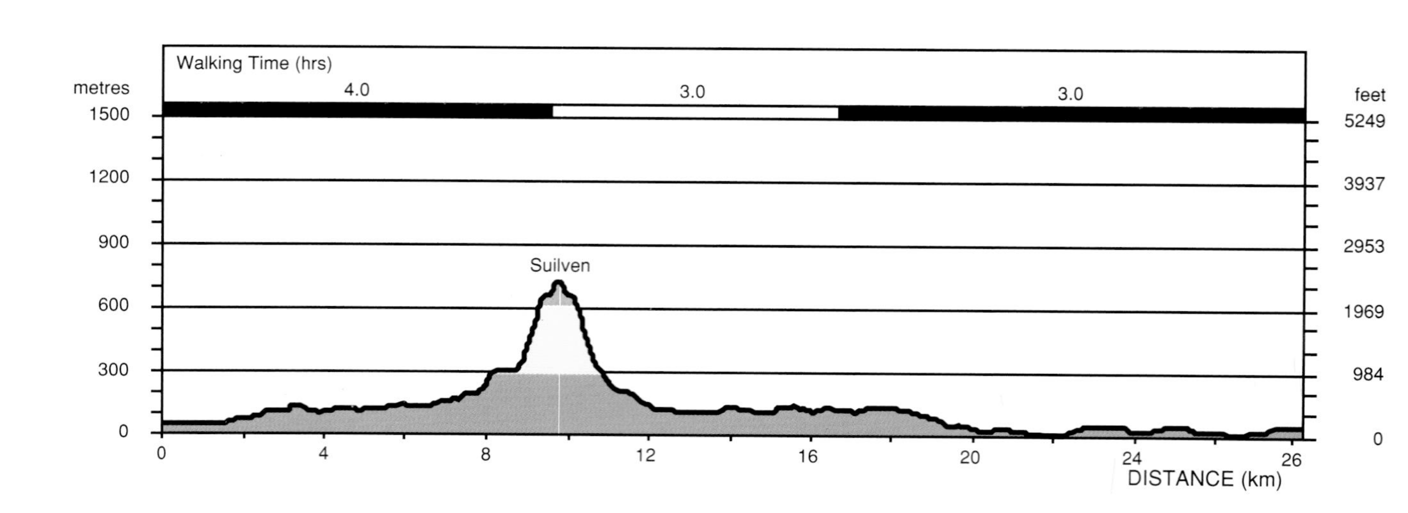

17

ASSYNT

HIGH-LEVEL ROUTE

Route 29 · Suilven

STARTING LOCATION
At end of minor road, 1.6 km (1 mile) E of Lochinver by Loch Druim Suardalain.
OSLR 15 or OSPF 82 and 92/MR 108220.
Parking bay on L before private road to Glencanisp Lodge.
Accommodates approximately 10 cars.

ALTERNATIVE STARTING LOCATION
At Lochinver or at Inverkirkaig.

PUBLIC TRANSPORT
Nearest railway station – Lairg.
Regular buses, once weekly, to Lochinver from Inverness.
Postbus, once daily, Lairg and Drumbeg to Lochinver (except Sunday).

OVERVIEW/INTEREST
Scotland's remarkable 'Sugar Loaf' mountain.
Stunning views seaward and across a strange lochan-studded hinterland to the other isolated mountains of Assynt and Coigach.
Optional exhilarating ridge scramble (see 'Extensions' for full ridge traverse).
Long but attractive approach and return over rugged terrain, recommended as a late spring or summer route, when daylight prevails.
Physically very demanding route.

FOOTPATHS
Minimal waymarking.
Well-trodden though dry on stalker's path in Glencanisp.
Wet and peaty below Suilven.
Good path from Falls of Kirkaig.
Potentially exposed scramble on a craggy ridge path.
Single-track metalled roads near Lochinver.

GRADING 5
TIME ALLOWANCE
10 hours.
DISTANCE

Excluding Height	27.1 km	(17 miles)
TOTAL HEIGHT GAINED	854 m	(2803 ft)

PRINCIPAL HEIGHTS
Suilven (Pillar Mountain):

Caisteal Liath (Grey Castle)	731 m	(2398 ft)

Lochinver to Caisteal Liath (Suilven)

Allow 4 hours

From the end of the minor road, head E on the private drive to Glencanisp Lodge. The weird and distant profile of Suilven's western buttress, a giant sandstone thimble rising boldly in isolation above the Sutherland moors, has a commanding presence. Seen looking SE and across the loch on your R, it is like no other mountain and is affectionately referred to as the Sugar Loaf.

Proceed on the driveway alongside Loch Druim Suardalain by its N shore to a tiny pier on the R after 1 km (⅔ mile). Bear L to cross a cattle grid between white fencing. Pass a footpath sign on your R and pursue the track round the back of Glencanisp Lodge near a row of stables and sheds. After a further 50 m (55 yd), pass through a green iron gate and continue ESE on the unmetalled track. Beyond larch trees on your R, and a grey corrugated shed on your L, the track narrows to a footpath. Adjacent to the far E end of the loch, pass through a second iron gate near a dry-stone wall on the L. A few hundred metres distant to your R, the Abhainn Bad na h-Achlaise meanders its way W to join with the loch. Continue on the path between dense thickets of gorse which in spring glow a vibrant yellow, providing a perfect colour contrast to the wild hyacinths* carpeting the ground beneath.

The gorse gives way to a more open terrain of gneiss outcrops and peaty hags, an untamed landscape that so typifies much of the NW Highlands. Walk on ESE, keeping to the well-trodden stalker's path and making a gradual ascent. Between heathery banks, come above the N shore of Loch na h-Airigh Fraoich on your R. Immediately ahead, Canisp dominates the eastern horizon, a quartzite-capped sandstone peak of more orthodox form, but like Suilven it rises from the moors in isolation. Progressively, the E end of Suilven's craggy ridge is revealed. This new skyline suggests a change of character in a mountain that defies early impressions of it.

In places, the path shows signs of erosion. Established as a stalker's route through Glen Canisp, it has yet to suffer the really serious deterioration seen on paths on the more accessible mountains further S. Suilven is never busy and wilderness lovers can be grateful that it does not figure on the Munroists' itinerary.

Undulating between countless outcrops, the path divides at Suileag. Take the R-hand fork and maintain your route ESE. Pass a dry-stone wall on your L and descend a little to where the path comes alongside the Abhainn na Clach Airigh, on your R. Cross a tiny burn via a footbridge of stone slabs. From above a reedy lochan on your R, Suilven (in side-on profile) deserves passing attention. Its skyline ridge, 1.6 km (1 mile) long, is a fine prospect and a perspective denied to non-walkers. Seen from the N, Suilven realizes the shape of a beached galleon and assumes a grandeur far in excess of its true height. It mesmerizes and draws you in like a magnet.

Coming beside the abhainn, follow its course

* Bluebells. (However, 'Scottish bluebells' are more widely known as harebells).

29.1 *Looking ESE from Lochan Buidhe to Canisp.*

upstream to Lochan Buidhe. Looking ESE, the lochan provides the perfect foreground to Canisp. After a further 400 m (1/4 mile), the track divides again. Take the R fork and walk over the obvious footbridge. From the S side of the abhainn, bear L and walk SE on a more appreciable incline. The path swings S to come above the abhainn, seen in a gorge on your L. A small cairn indicates a gully that heads down towards it. From this point, now 600 m (1/3 mile) since the footbridge, strike off R, leaving the better path for a less agreeable one heading SSW. Pursue a beeline for Suilven.

Climb a muddy bank to reach a peaty plateau above Loch na Gainimh on the L. Canisp takes command above its E shore. Proceed uphill on much steeper slopes between outcropping rocks as far as the level ground before Loch a' Choire

Dhuibh. Suilven is now confronted in close proximity and, from here, would seem to be an impregnable fortress.

However, veer off R and skirt around the W shore of the peaty loch. Use stepping-stones to cross a burn on its far side. Turn L to follow cairns leading to the bottom of a steep stone gully below the Bealach Mór.

Head S, directly up the mountain's N side, at first enjoying the firm footing of a boulder field. On gaining height, the path traverses shifting scree. A series of short, sharp zigzags aids progress up the steep slopes on a course to the L of the stone gully. The path crosses the scree to ascend higher slopes on the R side of the gully. At the top of the bealach, unremitting steepness eventually relents on gaining the intervening ridge path.

If the climb has not left you breathless, the view S, suddenly revealed, will. Persistence is rewarded by a wide and wondrous lochan-studded panorama that is as much of water as it is of land. On a not too distant horizon, the strange and isolated peaks of Coigach add to a sense of mystery about the place. Before you is nature at its least disciplined. The Inverpolly NNR, one of Britain's largest, has been established in recognition of this great diversity of habitats.

Having gained the ridge at its lowest point, turn R and pursue the path WNW. Quite unexpectedly, approach a dry-stone wall which straddles the ridge. Its surreal situation seems to defy logic! Walk through a gap in this folly and continue up on the path that passes around a blunt top. Dip down into a depression and then ascend steeply on a rough, worn path that requires a bit of a scramble. Emerge at the grassy table-top plateau of Caisteal Liath, Suilven's highest summit at 731 m (2398 ft).

For a 135° of the compass, a far-reaching seascape extends beyond a rugged coastline from the NNW to the SSW. Directly N lies a further profusion of lochans and a few other distinct profiles of the mountains of Assynt. On Suilven itself, the most arresting feature is the amazing spire of Meall Meadhonach at the E end of the ridge. Indeed, most of the significant peaks of Assynt and Coigach are identifiable. Turning clockwise over a

29.2 *Looking east along Suilven's ridge (below the summit of Caisteal Liath) to Meall Meadhonach (right) and Canisp (left, in the distance).*

landward horizon, they are: NNE, Quinag; E, Canisp, Ben More Assynt, Breabag; S, Cùl Mór, Cùl Beag; SSW, Ben Mór Coigach; SW, Stac Pollaidh.

Suilven to Falls of Kirkaig *Allow 3 hours*

Leave Caisteal Liath by retracing your route ESE to the saddle in the ridge at the Bealach Mór. Competent ridge walkers, intent on a more complete traverse and who wish to prolong the superb views, should continue ESE to Meall Meadhonach (see 'Extensions'). Non-scramblers should venture no further.

From the Bealach Mór, turn R and begin a steep descent by the stone gully on Suilven's S-facing slopes. Take care over the shifting scree of a path that leads sharply downhill SW, leaving the ridge behind you. Half-way down, the view to Cùl Mór warrants a halt, a vantage point from which the Coire Gorm resembles an enormous armchair. Listen carefully for the distinctive cooing sound emanating from below, betraying the presence of the red-throated diver. You are unlikely to identify just which lochan it is coming from.

Where a path heads off in a more W direction, maintain a route SW by taking the L-hand fork. Continue to where the gradient becomes a good deal less severe and cross the peaty ground towards an obvious outcrop, SW. Keep to a path little more than a sheep track, to pass the outcropping rocks on the L. Make a gradual descent on the R side of the Allt an Fearna pursuing a route between grassy banks as far as Fionn Loch. Close to the lochside, the ground underfoot becomes agreeably less boggy. A small cairn on the R marks a junction with a better, more established path. Turn R and walk NW beside the N shore of Fionn Loch.

After 250 m (275 yd), when close to the loch-shore, ford a small burn at a wall-like structure. Ford another burn soon after via the bouldery remains of a rudimentary bridge. After a sandy beach at the shoreside on your L, veer R away from the lochside. Proceed NNW on an easy incline to pass between craggy outcrops with a scattering of rowan scrub. Descend into Coire Mór and where the path divides take the L fork. The slopes of this shallow corrie surrounding you evoke feelings of being encircled by an enormous natural amphi-theatre. Bear L and pass between metal fence posts to cross a burn via a basic bridge constructed from stone slabs. Following the course of the burn downstream on its R side, walk W to come a little closer to the lochside again. After a while, the burn finds a route SW. Resume a NW bearing, pass a cairn on the L and take to undulating over peat hags. Note the ghostly rooty remnants of the ancient Caledonian pine forest that remain well preserved here. The loch is again visible on the L.

On reaching a cairn, just beyond the far W end of Fionn Loch, bear sharp L and walk SW. Gently swing round to come back towards the loch near the ruins of a dry-stone wall, and ford the burn that drains Loch Uidh na Ceardaich on your R. Proceed SE up a heathery bank to emerge directly above the western extremity of Fionn Loch. Where the path begins to veer R, it is worth pausing for the excellent view SE back out across this long ribbon of water.

Pass a small lochan on your R and join a path at a cairn beside the River Kirkaig. A scattering of trees above the bankside comes as a welcome relief, hinting at a return to a less severe environ-ment. Turn R at the cairn and walk W along the N side of the river. At a point above the Falls of Kirkaig, more substantial rowan and birch woods cloak the steep sides opposite.

Falls of Kirkaig to Lochinver *Allow 3 hours*

To view the fine waterfall, descend by a well-trodden diversion off to the L. From the main path, the sight of the deep and wooded gorge ahead is a delight. Feelings of vulnerability out on the wild moor seep slowly away when entering this idyllic riverside setting.

Leave the falls bearing WNW on a more eroded though well-maintained footpath. This part of the route beside the River Kirkaig is particularly popular among sightseers whose destination is the waterfall (see 'Escapes'). Proceed above the slopes on the R side of the gorge. The river is a steep 70 m (230 ft) below on your L.

The path winds its way over the heather before beginning to descend through gorse scrub. Closer to the river, the gorse gives way to a carpet of bracken and a scattering of birch trees where creatures are seen to stir. Red deer are frequent browsers at the woodland edge. In spring, one is greeted by a sudden crescendo of birdsong, the most reassuring of tonics after the silent moors.

The sound of water, as well as that of birds, is increasingly audible as you come down next to the river again. Continue along its N side to follow a line of fencing on your L. Veer NW, pass through a metal gate and, in a birch and alder wood, a much larger iron gate between deer fencing. Follow the line of the fencing on your L as far as an intervening track. A sign points back to 'Falls and Suilven'. Turn L on to the track heading W, passing between Scots pine and, unexpectedly on your R, the remotest bookshop in Britain (or so the tourist board would claim). Walk through a K-gate to bypass the large iron gate at the bottom of the track. Emerge at the roadside next to the bridge over the river, on your L. A sign on the R points back to 'Akins Bookshop'.

The River Kirkaig has long provided a convenient boundary between Sutherland and Ross and Cromarty, although both counties are now absorbed in the new Highland Region. Continue W on the road by the river, passing a small car park on your L. On arriving at Loch Kirkaig, after 1 km (⅔ mile), turn sharp R at the sandy beach by the little coastal community of Inverkirkaig. Walk N on the road that sweeps gently around the bay and in front of the croft cottages on your R.

Bear NE on the coast road that leaves the hamlet, walking gently uphill for 800 m (½ mile) before turning a sharp L. Follow the road around to Strathan and its enchanted wooded bay of Bàgh an t-Strathain. Ignore a road on the L to 'Lochinver Holiday Lodges' and instead descend NE to Loch Culag. The road hugs its W shore before you pick up a pedestrian path on the R side of the road next to the Culag River. Approaching Lochinver, turn R at the junction with the A837 and walk through the village to regain the minor road on the R that heads E towards Glencanisp Lodge. Retrace your earlier 1.6 km (1 mile) drive out to the parking place by Loch Druim Suardalain.

Alternative routes

ESCAPES

For those without wings, there is only one viable way off the mountain and that is, as described, via the Bealach Mór. Suilven is remote and therefore scaling it is a serious undertaking. There are no shortcuts and once on its ridge the nearest road or habitation is at least 8 km (5 miles) and 3 hours away. The swiftest retreat is to return by retracing footsteps back along the stalker's path in Glen Canisp.

For a much shorter route in a more tranquil setting, the riverside walk to view the Falls of Kirkaig is highly recommended. The River Kirkaig and its beautifully wooded gorges are included as part of the main route but the less energetic should begin at Inverkirkaig and pursue the good path ESE for 3 km (2 miles) to reach the falls. Park at the car park next to the bridge over the river at MR 086193. Return the same way. Allow 2 hours.

EXTENSIONS

Even before the hard work begins up Suilven's steep N-facing slopes, a long walk out over rough terrain is necessary to reach the base of the mountain. The ascent, descent and return place still further demands on stamina. For this reason, only a short extension, with the reward of a satisfying full traverse of Suilven's narrow ridge, is recommended. However, to gain the spire-like summit of Meall Meadhonach, at the E end of the ridge, some moderate scrambling is necessary.

From the top of the Bealach Mór, continue ESE along the narrow ridge path to reach, with relative ease, a level top. Descend steeply on the other side to a confined bealach.

Scrambling up the rocky terraces of the buttress beyond calls for some nerve in an exposed situation. Those intimidated by the prospect can bypass most of the awkward sections by a less demanding scramble to the R. The tiny summit platform of Meall Meadhonach 723 m (2373 ft), is marked by a small cairn. From here, looking SE, you have a clear impression of a wide and flat expanse towards Glen Oykel. Extraneous to the mountain itself is the insignificant top of Meall Bheag seen below. To the S, Cùl Mór dominates and offers a fine, unobscured view into its impressive N-facing bowl, the Coire Gorm. The seaward horizon is partially blocked by the huge dome of Caisteal Liath. The other mountains of West Assynt and Coigach, those described from the higher peak, remain clearly visible.

Return with great care on the scramble down, eventually to regain the saddle at the top of the Bealach Mór. Turn L on to the steep stone gully on the mountain's S side and continue as per the main route. Allow an extra hour.

Those considering the route in an anti-clockwise direction would do best to start from the car park at Inverkirkaig at MR 086193. This avoids a much longer walk out to reach Suilven. Also, be aware that an ascent from the mountain's S side to gain the ridge involves marginally more effort than ascending the N-facing scree gully as described.

Route 30: POINT OF STOER

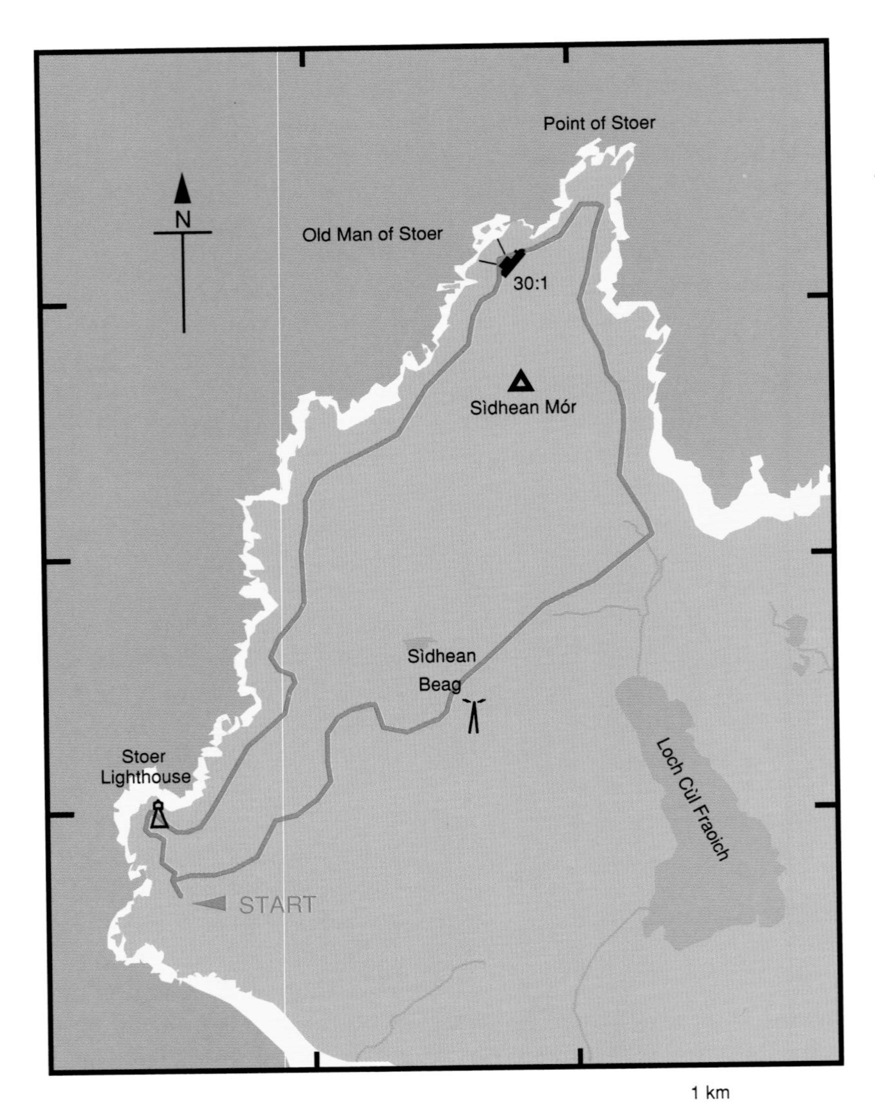

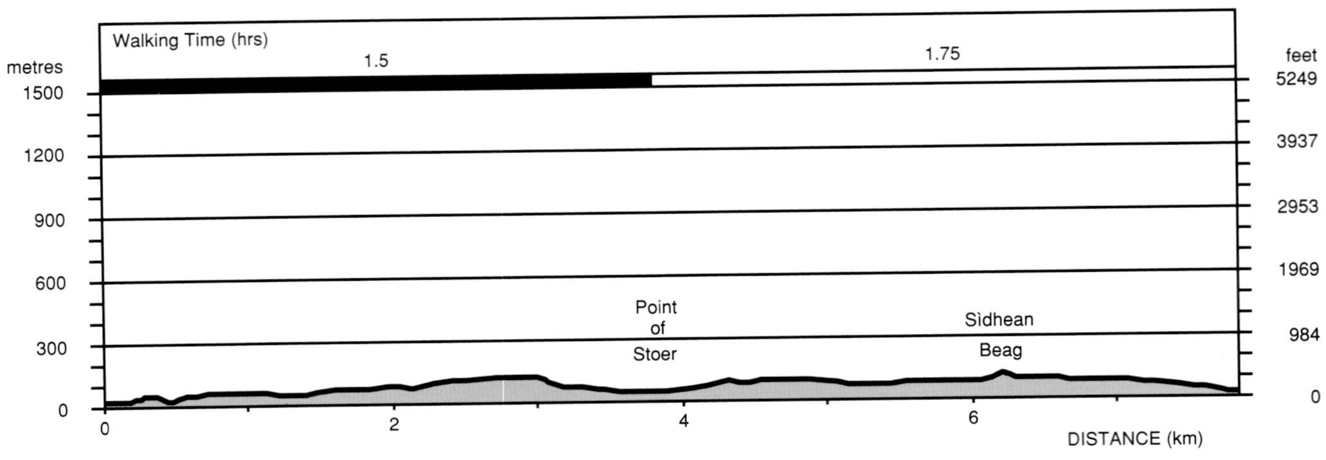

Route 30 · Point of Stoer

STARTING LOCATION
Stoer Lighthouse at end of minor road at W extremity of Ru Stoer peninsula.
OSLR 15 or OSPF 72/MR 005327.
Parking bay below lighthouse.
Accommodates up to 20 cars.

ALTERNATIVE STARTING LOCATION
Additional parking space possible on roadside nearby.

PUBLIC TRANSPORT
Nearest railway station – Lairg.
Regular buses, once weekly, to Lochinver from Inverness.
Postbus, once daily, Drumbeg to Culkein via Lochinver (except Sunday).

OVERVIEW/INTEREST
Spectacular sea stack – an 'Old Man' 65 m (200 ft) tall.
An exhilarating coastal walk above cliffs over 100 m (300 ft) high.
In contrast, return is via a bleak and windswept moor.
Affords opportunities to view a variety of sea bird species.
A treat for seal watchers.
Straightforward and undemanding route.

FOOTPATHS
No waymarking.
Clifftop coast path that becomes more rudimentary beyond the Point of Stoer.
Some free-ranging over wild moorland thereafter.
Final descent is via an excellent gravel track.

GRADING 2

TIME ALLOWANCE
3¼ hours.

DISTANCE

Excluding Height	7.8 km	(5 miles)
TOTAL HEIGHT GAINED	240 m	(787 ft)

PRINCIPAL HEIGHTS
None.

Stoer Lighthouse to the Point of Stoer

Allow 1½ hours

From the parking bay, turn R and walk uphill N for 200 m (220 yd) to reach the lighthouse. To your rear, a distant skyline from E to S is dominated by the mountains of Coigach and Assynt.

In a clockwise direction, walk around the white walls of the lighthouse as far as its E side. Then strike off SE down grassy slopes and into a depression, keeping on the L side of a stone wall. Ascend the opposite bank to gain the beginnings of a clifftop path above a small cove with a stony beach.

Proceed NNE, following a rugged coastline of headlands, coves and caves. Make an immediate beeline for the headland at Geodh' nan Uan. The path is distinct, if narrow, and the ground here generally remains dry. Pass over sandstone outcrops and peat mosses traversing land that is well grazed by sheep. Look down to your L from time to time: the sea surrounding the Ru Stoer peninsula is a favourite feeding ground for seals. On the near horizon to the E, you cannot fail to notice a prominent transmission mast on Sidean Beag. This will prove a useful reference point on the return leg. Approximately 1 km (⅔ mile) from the lighthouse, ford a burn by first coming down a steep embankment and then heading a few metres inland to meet it. Clamber up the other side. At the top, veer L to return to the cliff edge. Continue NNE as far as the headland.

Leave Geodh' nan Uan behind you by walking N from it. Stride over a second burn and proceed towards the next headland at Cìrean Geardail. Lichen-encrusted outcropping rocks are encountered on the way, evidence of the purity of air. As expected of a peninsular jutting out into the western seaboard, it is salt spray that blows here, not exhaust fumes!

Behind you and to the SSW, the location of the lighthouse does not conform to expectations. It is situated 3 km (2 miles) short of the extremity of the peninsula.

On coming more immediately above the sea again, bear R and walk NE from Cìrean Geardail. Looking out across a wall of dramatic cliffs, it is the solitary and distant pillar of rock that most captures the imagination.

To your R the triangulation pillar on Sidhean Mór is just discernible. The coast path remains clearly marked from here as far as the cliffs at their highest point. When you begin to come downhill, swing L a little, bearing NNE. Descend more than 60 m (200 ft) in height to a clifftop vantage point immediately adjacent to the top of the great sea stack.

30.1 *The Old Man of Stoer from the cliff path.*

The purple-tinged column of rock that is the Old Man of Stoer rises quite spectacularly nearly 65 m (200 ft) above the waves. Permanent ropes and tackle dangle from its summit, accessible only to the most experienced of climbers – it was first climbed in 1966, having been until then the exclusive preserve of creatures with wings. In spring and summer its ledges are the nesting platforms for kittiwakes.

From the Old Man, proceed a further few hundred metres NE to the peninsula's northern most extremity: the Point of Stoer.

The Point of Stoer to Stoer Lighthouse

Allow 1¾ hours

The Point of Stoer is a sharp and rugged headland. The erosion of sedimentary strata has created a cliff face of ledges and rocky platforms that are the nesting sites for various species of sea birds. Keen-eyed walkers are likely to see cormorants, fulmars, skuas, guillemots, gannets, kittiwakes, black-backed and herring gulls, among others.

Walk out on the headland as far as a fence which prevents you, as well as the sheep, from venturing any further. It seems to have been erected for reasons of safety. The Point of Stoer really is a point, the headland tapering to a narrow top above an unforgiving sea. The unintentional fence-line effect on the flora is striking and a good example of the difference sheep can make to a landscape. On the ungrazed and untrampled ground, flowers and grasses can grow to profusion. This few square metres of nature reserve lies undisturbed, in stark contrast to the naked land S of the fence where mouths relentlessly prune.

Close to the water line, a cave has been carved, seen when looking down the cliff face from the L-hand edge of the fence. Leave the Point of Stoer from the R-hand side of the fence by making an almost complete turn around. Then strike off S maintaining a route above the E-facing cliffs towards Geodha an Leth-roinn. The coast path fades to a more rudimentary one, as most visitors do not venture any further than the Point.

The ground becomes softer and more peaty underfoot. Progress and navigation remain straightforward enough, the sea always immediately to your L. From the clifftop, there is more than enough interest to warrant further pauses.

The view SE and E, to Aldany Island and beyond, is across a far-reaching coastline. A succession of islands, cliffs and coves as well as further erosive features await the adventurous. Closer to hand you encounter many more nest sites and of course always the seals, a special reward for those with binoculars.

At the cliffs of Geodha an Leth-roinn, pay passing attention to the geologically interesting and impressive rock strata. For botanists, the scattered flower heads of orchids are a treat, as you bear SSE on a slow but sure ascent. Where the path splits and deviates to the L, stay on the higher course to the R. The occasional glance back to the Point of Stoer affords new perspectives of it, now seen from the E side of Sidhean Mór.

Having gained some height, follow the line of a cliff edge fence on your L. Continue S towards a gravelly beach in a bay 1 km (⅔ mile) away. Leave the line of fencing at a 90° corner, from where it then follows the E-running coastline on your L. Instead, head off overland, making straight for the obvious transmission masts on the skyline. Plot your own course SW away from the sea and prepare for a taste of a very different landscape. The return is via the bleak moors of Ru Stoer.

Make your way over demanding heathery tussocks and peat hags. In places, the moor is bog-ridden but generally without hazards. Avoid this route in mist, however, when your only useful reference points, the two transmission masts, are likely to be obscured. In these conditions, head back along the coast.

After a few hundred metres of free-range walking, pass above the N end of Loch Cùl Fraioch on your L. Endeavour to maintain a course SW, aiming a little to the R of the masts. Cross over a rough track leading down to the loch on the L. Proceed to the L side of a small lochan beyond. For a short distance, head up the steep heathery banks of the hillock that supports the masts. Arrive on top at a large cairn about 10 m (10 yd) to the R of the largest of the masts. Persistence is rewarded by seaward views over at least 225° of the compass. The prospect is rather featureless but such voids do have their own appeal.

Leave the cairn and the transmission masts by walking down SSW to gain the obvious access track. An excellent gravel surface allows for an undemanding final 1.6 km (1 mile) and a very gradual descent SW. Near the end of the track pass a couple of stone and brick ruins on the R. On gaining the metalled minor road, return to the parking bay on the L.

Alternative routes

ESCAPES

The complete circuit is, in itself, a relatively short and straightforward undertaking. However, to return from the Point of Stoer, as most do, by backtracking along the coast path in a SSW direction reduces route-finding problems to a minimum. This alternative is recommended in mist. Since the Point of Stoer is about half-way along the main route, such an option has only a marginal effect on reducing total walking time.

EXTENSIONS

The Ru Stoer peninsula is part of a rather bleak and barren coastal strip and, as such, extensions overland are not recommended. Excursions that prolong the coastal scenery, however, are certainly rewarding, particularly when undertaken on the N side of the peninsula.

After reaching the Point of Stoer, as described in the main route, continue above the shoreline as far as Clashnessie Bay, a further 9 km (6 miles) SE. The rigours of such a journey are more than compensated for by successive encounters with a variety of coastal features including caves, sandy bays and a natural arch. This option, for those who do not have to return to a car, requires arranged transport from the village of Clashnessie. The really energetic might consider the possibility of a complete coastal circuit of the Ru Stoer peninsula via the B869.

Route 31: BEN HOPE

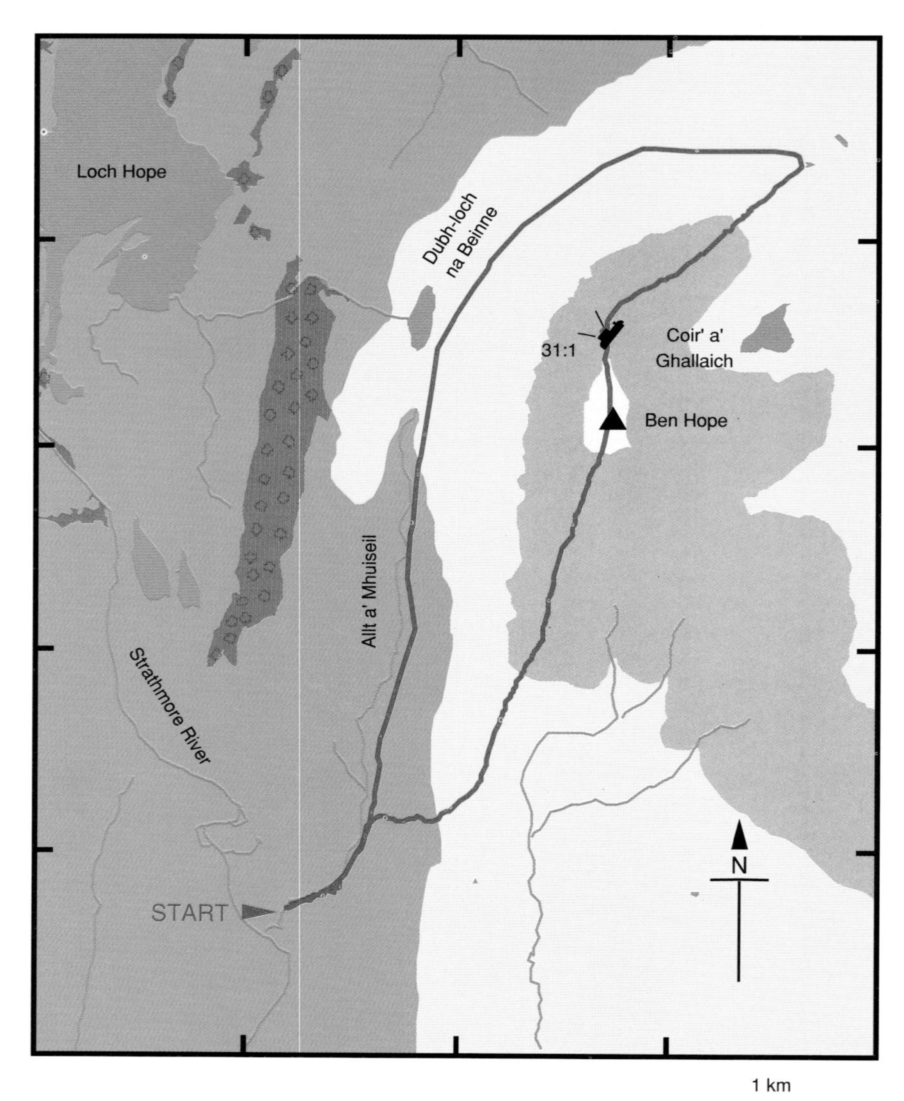

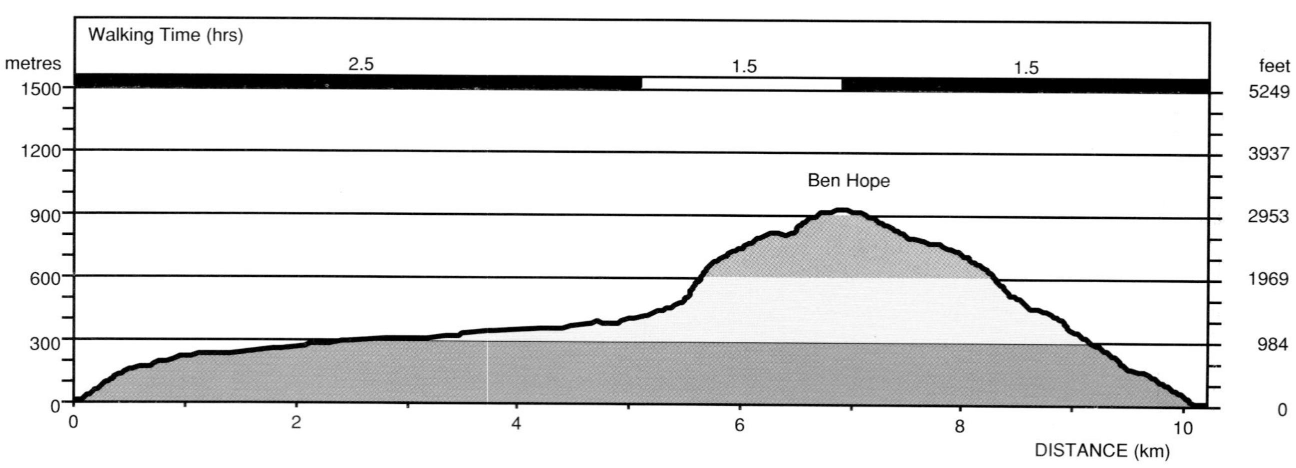

18

FAR NORTH

HIGH-LEVEL ROUTE

Route 31 · Ben Hope

STARTING LOCATION
On the minor road (the Road of Desolation) between Loch Hope and Dùn Dornaigil Broch.
OSLR 9 or OSPF 54 and 63/MR 462477.
Accommodates approximately 6 cars at roadside.

ALTERNATIVE STARTING LOCATION
Additional roadside parking possible nearby.

PUBLIC TRANSPORT
Nearest railway station – Lairg.
Postbus, once daily, Lairg and Durness to Hope (except Saturday and Sunday).

OVERVIEW/INTEREST
A rewarding ascent on Scotland's most northerly Munro.
Overlooks Strath More and the Road of Desolation.
An isolated mountain dominating a wide and wild landscape.
Physically very demanding route (if scrambling unavoidable due to persistence of snow in gully).

FOOTPATHS
Minimal waymarking.
Generally clear and dry although badly eroded in places.
Some free-ranging over open moor necessary.

GRADING 5 (4 if scrambling avoidable)

TIME ALLOWANCE
5½ hours.

DISTANCE

Excluding Height	10.2 km	(6¼ miles)
TOTAL HEIGHT GAINED	945 m	(3100 ft)

PRINCIPAL HEIGHTS
Ben Hope (Mountain of the Bay)
927 m (3041 ft)

Strath More to Loch na Seilg

Allow 2½ hours

From the road near a large cow shed, walk ENE obeying the sign 'Ben Hope, this way up'. Pass through an area of gorse scrub on the well-worn path. Begin uphill on the steep slopes to the R of a stream with gorge-like banks strewn with rowan and birch. A series of waterfalls are encountered as you gain height quickly beside them. The views back down along Strath More become progressively far-reaching, its river aiming N and seaward in snaking, silvery meanders.

Continue upwards on the often badly eroded path. On veering NE, ford a tiny burn. Where the path bears E up the steep slopes towards a breach in the cliffs, leave it and instead head off N. Follow a rudimentary path for a while and then begin free-ranging across the heather moor. Maintain a route along the Allt a' Mhuiseil on its E side, with the likelihood of stonechats to keep you company. At times it may be possible to follow something resembling a sheep track but the ground is mostly dry and the ascent gradual. Proceed N below Ben Hope's rugged escarpment-like buttresses on your R. Rising in isolation, the feature affords the mountain its distinctive wedge shape when seen from the S.

After about half an hour across rough country, gain a clearer path which intercepts your progress

31.1 *Loch Hope and Loch Eriboll from the approach to the summit of Ben Hope.*

from the L. Follow it to come closer to the escarpment of cliffs. Here the allt on your L is now close to its source. After a few hundred metres resume the free-ranging approach and continue N. The ground becomes noticeably wetter. Springtime walkers on such hills will realize that these are ideal conditions for butterwort, their bright green star-shaped arrangement of sticky leaves spreading out to trap insects. An unassuming carnivore of the nutrient-starved Highlands, it flowers a beautiful but deadly purple in May.

Pass an area of peat hags on your L at the source of the allt. Walk on to the R of the obvious loch, Dubh-Loch na Beinne, ahead and pass it about 100 m (110 yd) from its E shore. Proceed below the Ben's rocky W-facing buttresses on your R, following the escarpment round to the E. After a further 1 km (2/3 mile), the panorama N widens to reveal a vast and featureless expanse to the R of Loch Hope and extending as far as the sea. On a windless day, the silence here is absolute.

At the northern extremity of the escarpment, climb a little more steeply to a point from where a lochan is seen below on your L. Beyond it, looking E, is the far larger Loch na Seilg. Begin an assault on the exposed N-facing slopes of Ben Hope by first orientating yourself SW to face them.

Loch na Seilg to Summit of Ben Hope

Allow 1½ hours

Walk SW across the wet ground towards the steep bouldery slopes of Carn a' Ghallaich. From here, choose your own route by boulder-hopping but with great care. The rock surfaces offer good grip but many are loose and this is no place to twist an ankle! As height is gained it is soon obvious that you are ascending the N side of a corrie, the Coir' a' Ghaillaich, the dark waters of its lochan seen below and to your L. Continue in your own way to the point where, on less steep ground, an obvious ridge is gained.

Proceed SW on the ridge path directly above and between Ben Hope's NW-facing precipitous cliffs on your R and the NE-facing corrie on your L. Distant views from here extend N to a seaward horizon. To the E, the compelling skyline ridge of Ben Loyal, a beautiful mountain affectionately referred to as the Queen of the Scottish Highlands, rises majestically from a flat moorland.

Pass a cairn where a steep path in a rock gully on your R offers an alternative ascent to the ridge. It is a more abrupt one, seemingly defying the mountain's sheer NW-facing wall of crags. The summit cairn beckons, now close at hand on the skyline in the S. Before the reward of further views, however, your nerve will be tested if there is snow on the mountain.

Arriving at a seemingly vertical rock wall, turn L and walk below it for 30 m (30 yd) to a gully. Climb sharply up through it to come above the difficulties. This is the only apparent weakness in the cliff and the one feasible route that does not demand the prolonged use of all fours. The gully is treacherous when snow-filled and should not be attempted in such conditions. Snow can persist here until early summer, and a short airy scramble then becomes unavoidable in order to reach the summit. Pick a route up rock steps on the far R-hand side, in other words, ascending on the NW corner of the rock wall. Climb almost vertically on good steady footholds, the real anxiety being caused by extreme exposure. It may be best not to look behind: the level ground is nearly 500 m (1600 ft) below! Depending on your disposition, the task will induce either intense excitement or fearful apprehension. The faint-hearted should turn back and perhaps try again another day (see 'Escapes'). Following a 15 m (15 yd) scramble, you gain easier rocks on a far less severe gradient, the worst of difficulties now overcome. Bear S and walk to the obvious triangulation pillar and cairn, marking the spacious summit at 927 m (3041 ft). The view N beyond Loch Hope and Loch Eriboll is to a watery horizon stretching along the coast NW as far as Cape Wrath and the North Minch. High above Strath More, landward views convey the remoteness and isolation of Ben Hope rather than suggesting it is part of a community of Sutherland mountains. However, other mountains that are prominent from the summit include, clockwise: E, Ben Loyal; SSW, Ben More Assynt; SW, Quinag; WSW, Arkle; W, Foinaven.

Summit of Ben Hope to Strath More

Allow 1½ hours

Walk S for 100 m (110 yd) across the summit plateau to a smaller cairn. The broad back of a ridge extends to your SE and above an E-facing corrie. Leave by an obvious path that is the more direct route to the summit, descending in a straightforward manner. The path is badly eroded, loose and scree-like in places. Cross an area of rock slabs where the descent becomes steeper, while gradually bearing SSW. Numerous cairns mark the way on top and close to the edge of the mountain's sheer W-facing buttresses, encountered earlier from below. Exercise great caution in mist and do not deviate from the path. Beyond further scree, the upper reaches of the Allt na Caillich appear ahead, intervening from slopes on the L.

On slopes which relent, having descended 2 km (1¼ miles) from the summit, veer R and ford a tiny burn. Head off on the eroded path W, much more steeply again and through a breach in the cliffs. Descend to the L of the burn; the corrugated roof of the cow shed is soon visible below by the Strathmore River. After a further 800 m (½ mile), the junction in paths is reached close to where the burn joins the bigger stream. Turn L and walk generally SW to Strath More, returning downhill and in reverse of initial footsteps.

Alternative routes

ESCAPES

If Munro-bagging is your objective, or if your legs turn to jelly at the prospect of a potentially exposed scramble, then ascend by the clearly marked, more orthodox main path – in other words, a reverse of that described in the descent. By pursuing this established route to its summit, one also has the advantage of a security factor. Compared with an ascent from the N side, however, it is undoubtedly bereft of interest and excitement. Route duration is reduced by 2 hours.

An escape from Loch na Seilg is possible by crossing the open ground to the N. Then, on gaining the Moine Path, descend SW to the Strath More road beside Loch Hope.

EXTENSIONS

Having come down from the summit as far as the breach in the cliffs, and before bearing R on the main path through it, continue instead above the crags of Leitir Mhuiseil. Thus continue S on a path a few hundred metres to the R of Allt na Caillich. Ford the allt above a waterfall and descend to the road at Alltnacaillich. Dùn Dornaigil Broch, an ancient monument, is 600 m (⅓ mile) S along the road. From the broch, follow the road N along Strath More for 3 km (2 miles) to return to your car. Allow an extra 1½ hours.

Route 32: SANDWOOD BAY

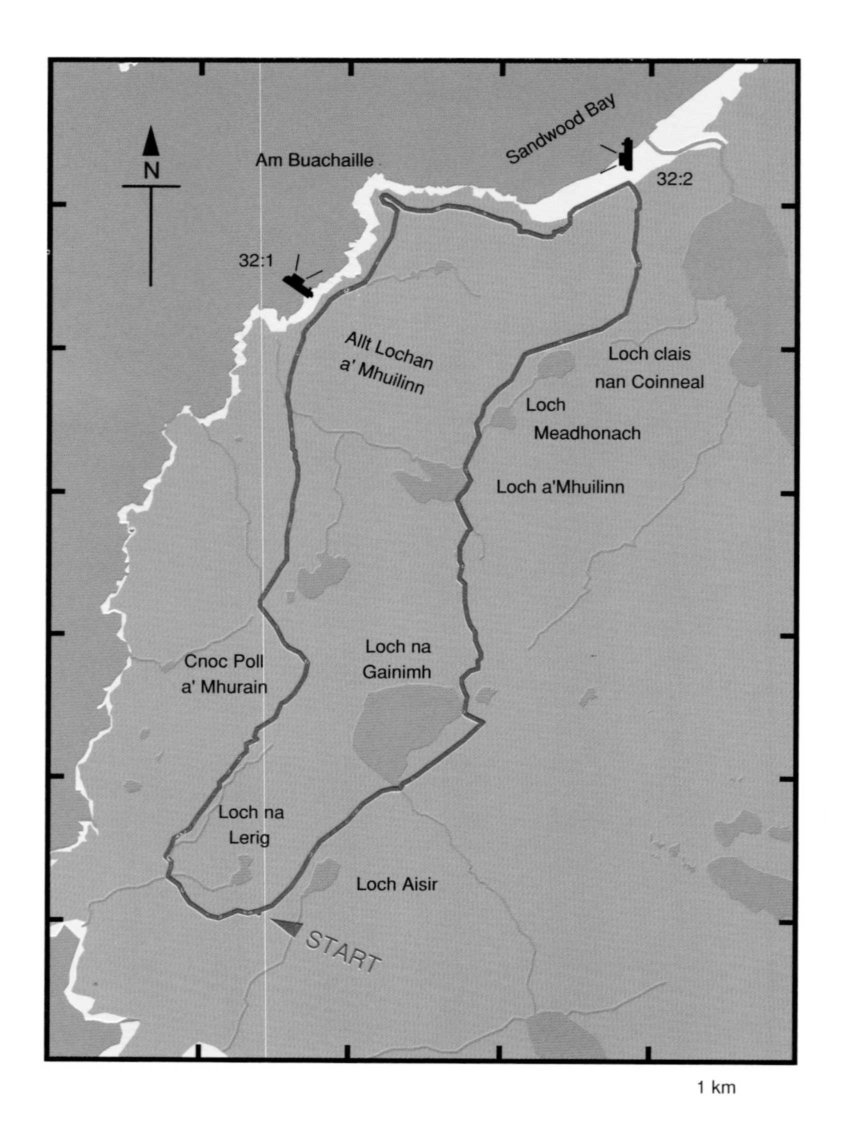

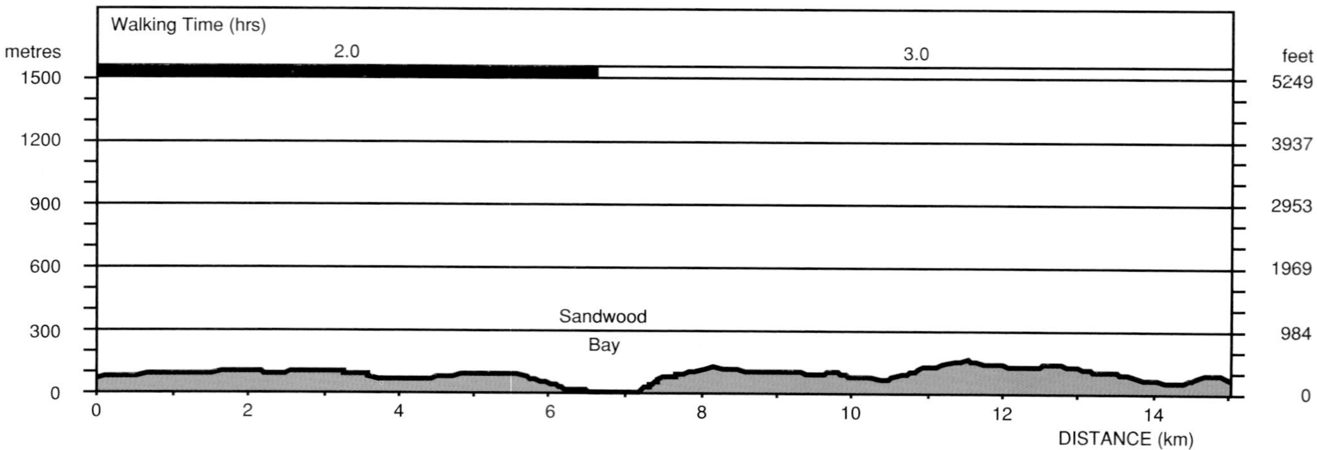

Route 32 · Sandwood Bay

STARTING LOCATION
At Blairmore, on minor road 5 km (3 miles) NW of Kinlochbervie.
OSLR 9 or OSPF 43/MR 194600.
Roadside parking on grassy verges L of Sandwood Bay track.
Accommodates approximately 12 cars.

ALTERNATIVE STARTING LOCATION
Alternative parking at Sheigra, 1 km (⅔ mile) NW of Blairmore.

PUBLIC TRANSPORT
Nearest railway station – Lairg.
Postbus, once daily, Lairg and Durness to Kinlochbervie (except Sunday).

OVERVIEW/INTEREST
Reputation as the most beautiful bay on the West Coast of Scotland.
A 2.4 km (1½ miles) crescent of clean golden sand.
Considered the most isolated beach in mainland Britain.
Reached overland only on foot.
Ancient legends abound of mermaids and ghosts.
A close encounter with the remarkable sea stack of Am Buachaille.
Sea bird breeding colonies in spring and summer.
Physically quite demanding route.

FOOTPATHS
Minimal waymarking.
Good track followed by a clear path to Sandwood Bay.
Rough clifftop path along coastline.
Some free-ranging across moorland prior to gaining approach track to Sheigra.
Final 1.5 km (1 mile) on metalled surface of a minor road.

GRADING 3
TIME ALLOWANCE
5 hours.
DISTANCE

Excluding Height	15 km	(9¼ miles)
TOTAL HEIGHT GAINED	351 m	(1150 ft)

PRINCIPAL HEIGHTS
None – highest point of route at 128 m (419 ft), MR 196625.

Blairmore to Sandwood Bay

Allow 2 hours

Leave the minor road at Blairmore by the sign at the beginning of the track: 'Sandwood Bay – 2 mile drive and 2 mile walk. No dogs allowed.' Begin between two cottages and walk NE. The surface is firm and dry and adequately level to take vehicles.

After 200 m (220 yd) pass through an iron gate in a dry-stone wall. Loch Aisir is on your R from where the track gradually and gently leads you to an incline. Look back to your rear for a view out to sea beyond the cottages of Blairmore. Prominent are the islands of Eilean an Ròin Beag and Eilean an Ròin Mór to the SW with smaller ones further S, near the entrance to Loch Inchard.

On the L of the track, a little further on, lies the S corner of the larger Loch na Gainimh. Proceed NE alongside a loch-shore of sandy banks with broad expanses of heather on your R. Near the E end of the loch, pass a rock painted with the words 'CAPE WRATH'. There is also a sketch of a lighthouse and it directs you further along the track. Where the track divides, turn L and take the one heading N. After a further 250 m (275 yd), pass between a lochan on your R and a tiny sandy beach on your L by the W-facing shore of Loch na Gainimh.

Continue N across the moorland. Looking over to the near horizon beyond Strath Shinary in the E, the modest hills of Creag Riabhach, An Grianan and Meall na Moine form a wedge-shaped skyline. Bigger mountains on a more distant horizon

include: ESE, Cranstackie; SE, Foinaven; SSE, Arkle; S, Ben Stack.

Overall, the feeling is of isolation when out on these flat moors.

At a point about 1 km (⅔ mile) beyond Loch na Gainimh, the condition of the track deteriorates significantly. Consequently, parked cars are likely here as further progress along what has become a deeply pitted surface is only possible on foot.

The track soon narrows to more of a path but the walking remains easy despite the eroded surface. On a clear day, the lighthouse at Cape Wrath is discernible NNE, seen perched on the high and distant cliffs of Britain's most north westerly point.

Walk on the R side of a tiny reedy lochan and soon after alongside Loch a' Mhuilinn by its E shore. The route of the path is marked (unnecessarily so) by cairns where the sandy surface becomes severely pitted again. Peat hags predominate for a while on approaching two small lochs on the R. Bear R, walking NE on the path to pass Loch Meadhonach and after a further 400 m (¼ mile) Loch clais nan Coinneal. Beyond them, veer ENE to gain a view of Sandwood Loch below. A ruined bothy lies close to its shore, directly E.

Proceed between fence posts, veer L and walk N down grassy slopes towards the bright sands. An idyllic and yet unfrequented haven, Sandwood Bay mesmerizes at first sight. On reaching the sand dunes, it is time to remove boots.

Sandwood Bay enjoys a reputation as the most beautiful bay on the west coast of Scotland. It is also supposedly the most isolated beach in mainland Britain. Thankfully, the bay is reached overland only by those prepared to walk. This almost ensures that it remains unspoilt. It is an undisturbed haunt, a place tainted only by legend, where mermaids brush tail fins with the ghost of a bearded sailor! Detached from the headland to the W, the remarkable sea stack, Am Buachaille, rises vertically from the sea. At the other end of the bay, a wild and rugged coastline, pitted by a succession of coves and gullies, extends NE as far as Cape Wrath.

32.1 *Am Buachaille from the lonely coast path.*

Sandwood Bay to Blairmore *Allow 3 hours*

If the sun is bright and high, it will be difficult to leave. There are tranquil rock pools to explore and sand dunes to linger on. The over-adventurous should be warned, for Sandwood Bay has a sting in its tail. The sea, inviting as it is, chills quickly to the marrow, spitting back all those who dare confront the ocean in a swimming costume! However, there is much to explore beyond the sands.

Head off across the beach to the SW corner of the bay. On reaching a wide spread of large boulders, turn L and climb a steep grassy bank away from the sands. At the top, on level ground, turn R and proceed SW to ford a burn at about the 50 m (165 ft) contour. Make for the rudimentary clifftop path by bearing WNW and walk up a little more. From above the beach, pause to look NE across the bay. The view looking down and back across the glorious 2.4 km (1½ miles) crescent of sand is unforgettable. This is the Highland Region at its loveliest and not a mountain in sight!

A little further on, look beyond the cliff edge to precarious rocky ledges below. In spring and summer, their raucous residents will have been audible for some time. The place is likely to be buzzing with nesting sea birds and species including guillemot, razorbill, herring gull and kittiwake.

Having passed outcrops of conglomerate rock, you arrive at a vantage point, adjacent to that amazing pillar of rock which first stirred the imagination when seen from the beach. From the clifftop here, you can now look down at Am Buachaille, a sea stack whose exposed rock ledges are accessible only to sea birds and the most determined of climbers. The first ascent was as recent as 1967. Beyond it, 2 km (1¼ miles) to the NW, lies the cluster of tiny rock islands of Am Balg.

Continue around the headland, gradually bearing S. Maintain a route across heathery tussocks and pursue a rough, often non-existent, path. Look out for orchids here in late spring. Rock slabs and sandstone platforms below juxtapose with clear seas in a most idyllic coastal scene. The clifftop path undulates its way SW to a wide depression where a burn flows into the sea. Bear L and walk S

32.2 *Am Buachaille from Sandwood Bay.*

along the L-hand edge of the depression. Having paid your homage to Neptune, head inland and upstream of the Allt Lochan a' Mhuilinn.

Towards the top of the depression, the path (such as it is) fades. Maintain a bearing S towards an obvious cleft in the skyline a few hundred metres ahead. Descend a little to cross a gap in some sheep fencing and ford a burn just L of where two watercourses join. Proceed upstream, on the L side of the R-hand burn, negotiating your own way across the moorland S. As you do so, gradually ascend towards the obvious cleft ahead that was noticed earlier. On reaching it, walk straight up through it between grassy banks. In places, there may be sheep tracks to help your footing. Either way, follow the course of the burn to its source at wet, mossy ground near the top. Stay drier by walking higher up on the L side.

Emerging on to higher ground, bear slightly R to a promontory a little further S. A cairn is reached at MR 196625, a point just W of Lochain nan Sac which is in sight on your L. Notice the summit

Cnoc Poll a' Mhurain to the S: the triangulation pillar is just discernible. In front of it, below and a bit to the R, the beginning of a visible track is your immediate objective. With the minimum of deviation, walk for 300 m (330 yd) SSW to pick up the N end of the track.

On gaining a more agreeable surface, turn L and press on, now making sure-footed progress SE. After about 600 m (1/3 mile), veer R as the track skirts below Cnoc Poll a' Mhurain, bearing SW. Loch na Gainimh is encountered again on your L, now as a more distant loch and from its W side.

The track then traverses relentless expanses of heather and grass as the sea reappears to your R and in the distance ahead. You are soon walking parallel to a long dry-stone wall which is 400 m (1/4 mile) away to your L. The cottages of Sheigra come into view. Descend and pass through an iron gate, followed by a wooden gate, to gain a metalled single-track road. The hamlet is a rather untidy collection of buildings. Cross a cattle grid by the red gate on the R. After a second grid, follow the road around to the L. Walk uphill, passing outcrops and a dry-stone wall prior to the road junction and houses of Balchrick. From here, proceed E, passing on your L a simple corrugated hut next to an old red phone box. The start point is roughly 300 m (330 yd) beyond this tiny post office.

32.3 *Rock pool on the beach at Sandwood Bay.*

Alternatives routes

ESCAPES

If you are feeling reckless with your vehicle's suspension system, then the first 3 km (2 miles) of the 6 km (4 miles) journey to the bay from Blairmore is just about negotiable by car. Increasingly, visitors are using it.

Obviously, like most visitors to the bay, you can simply return by the well-trodden path and track that you walked out on. Whilst this avoids the difficulties of crossing unpathed, unfamiliar and generally featureless moorland, it also denies you encounters with some impressive coastal cliff scenery, including the remarkable sea stack, Am Buachaille. The direct return option reduces total walking time by 1 hour.

EXTENSIONS

For an optional return which hugs a longer coastline and prolongs the seaward views, continue on a mainly unpathed clifftop route heading SW. From Am Buachaille, walk as far as the beach and campsite at Balchrick, 1.2 km (3/4 mile) W of your parked car. This adds difficulty in terms of confronting further natural obstacles though adds little to the total distance covered. Allow an extra 1 hour.

Strong walkers, with transport arranged at both ends, might consider following the coastline from Cape Wrath. Pursue a clifftop route S that will inevitably prove arduous, over difficult terrain and without footpaths as far as Sandwood Bay. However, the extra effort is rewarded by impressive cliffs and coves, sea birds and fine views across the North Minch to the island of Lewis in the Outer Hebrides. A satisfying day is concluded by continuing to Blairmore along the well-trodden path from Sandwood Bay as described in the main route. Allow 9 hours in total.

Appendix 1: Relevant Addresses

ASSOCIATION FOR THE PROTECTION OF RURAL SCOTLAND
Gladstone's Land (3rd Floor) (0131) 225 7012/7013
483 Lawnmarket
Edinburgh EH1 2NT

CALEDONIAN MCBRAYNE LTD.
The Ferry Terminal (01475) 33755
Gourock, Renfrewshire PA19 9QP

COACH OPERATORS (Scottish CityLink and Caledonian Express) from:
St. Andrews Square Bus Station, Edinburgh (0131) 557 5717
Buchanan Bus Station, Glasgow (0141) 332 9191/7133

FORESTRY COMMISSION
231 Corstorphine Road (0131) 334 0303
Edinburgh EH12 7AT

HISTORIC SCOTLAND
20 Brandon Street (0131) 244 3107
Edinburgh EH3 5RA

INDEPENDENT BACKPACKERS HOSTELS SCOTLAND
c/o The Loch Ness Backpackers Lodge (014562) 807
Leiskon
Drumnadrochit, Invernesshire IV3 6UT

MOUNTAINEERING COUNCIL FOR SCOTLAND
16 Grosvenor Crescent Lane (0141) 334 8336
Glasgow G12 9AB

NATIONAL TRUST FOR SCOTLAND
5 Charlotte Square (0131) 226 5922
Edinburgh EH2 4DY

ORDNANCE SURVEY (SCOTTISH REGION)
160 Causewayside (0131) 668 3281
Edinburgh EH9 1UX

RAMBLERS ASSOCIATION SCOTLAND
23 Crusader House (01592) 611177
Haig Business Park
Markinch
Fife KY7 6AQ

ROYAL SOCIETY FOR THE PROTECTION OF BIRDS
Scottish Headquarters (0131) 557 3136
17 Regent Terrace
Edinburgh EH7 5BN

SCOTRAIL INFORMATION CENTRES:
Edinburgh (0131) 555 2451
Glasgow (0141) 204 2844
Aberdeen (01224) 594222
Inverness (01463) 238924

SCOTTISH COUNTRYSIDE ACTIVITIES COUNCIL
7 Lawson Avenue (013302) 3145
Banchory, Kircardineshire AB31 3TW

SCOTTISH LANDOWNERS FEDERATION
25 Maritime Street (0131) 555 1031
Leith
Edinburgh EH6 5PW

SCOTTISH NATURAL HERITAGE
12 Hope Terrace (0131) 447 4784
Edinburgh EH9 2AS

SCOTTISH RIGHTS OF WAY SOCIETY
John Cotton Business Centre (0131) 652 2937
10/2 Sunnyside
Edinburgh EH7 5RA

SCOTTISH SPORTS COUNCIL
Caledonia House (0131) 317 7200
South Gyle
Edinburgh EH12 9DQ

SCOTTISH TOURIST BOARD
23 Ravelston Terrace (0131) 332 2433
Edinburgh EH4 3EU

SCOTTISH WILDLIFE TRUST
Crammond House (0131) 312 7765
Crammond Glebe Road
Edinburgh EH4 6NS

SCOTTISH YOUTH HOSTELS ASSOCIATION
7 Glebe Crescent (01786) 51181
Stirling FK8 2JA

Appendix 2: Statistical Summary

ROUTE	DESCRIPTION	WALKING DISTANCE Excluding Height		WALKING DISTANCE Including Height		TOTAL HEIGHT GAINED	
		km	miles	km	miles	metres	feet
1	Ben Venue	11.0	6.9	11.3	7.0	710	2329
2	Ben A'an	5.5	3.4	5.6	3.5	370	1214
3	The Cobbler (Ben Arthur)	9.8	6.1	10.1	6.3	960	3150
4	Loch Lomond and Glen Gyle	30.9	19.2	31.0	19.3	680	2231
5	Ben Vorlich	12.0	7.5	12.3	7.6	970	3182
6	Glen Finglas	23.5	14.6	23.6	14.7	720	2362
7	Ben Cruachan Horseshoe	14.6	9.1	15.1	9.4	1410	4626
8	Strath of Orchy	15.8	9.8	15.8	9.8	60	197
9	Buachaille Etive Mór	13.6	8.4	13.9	8.7	1130	3707
10	Lairig Gartain and Lairig Eilde	13.4	8.4	13.5	8.4	490	1608
11	Pap of Glencoe and Sgorr nam Fiannaidh	10.2	6.3	10.7	6.7	1110	3642
12	Loch Leven	9.2	5.7	9.3	5.8	320	1050
13	Ben Nevis and Carn Mór Dearg	20.4	12.7	20.8	12.9	1630	5348
14	Glen Nevis	13.1	8.2	13.2	8.2	340	1115
15	Lochnagar	20.0	12.4	20.2	12.6	920	3018
16	Glen Quoich and Glen Lui	15.8	9.8	15.8	9.8	230	755
17	Cairn Gorm	15.5	9.6	15.7	9.8	1040	3412
18	Loch an Eilein and Rothiemurchus	5.4	3.4	5.4	3.4	50	164
19	The Five Sisters	19.8	12.3	20.5	12.8	1770	5807
20	Falls of Glomach	16.5	10.3	16.7	10.3	690	2264
21	Bruach na Frìthe	12.8	8.0	13.1	8.2	1000	3281
22	Loch Coruisk	18.2	11.3	18.4	11.4	730	2395
23	Beinn Eighe	17.1	10.6	17.5	10.9	1150	3773
24	The Coulin Estate	9.6	6.0	9.5	6.0	10	33
25	Beinn Alligin	13.5	8.4	13.8	8.5	1120	3675
26	Upper Loch Torridon	12.3	7.6	12.3	7.7	240	787
27	An Teallach	17.7	11.0	18.2	11.3	1420	4659
28	Gruinard River	22.5	14.0	22.6	14.0	390	1280
29	Suilven	27.1	16.9	27.4	17.0	854	2803
30	Point of Stoer	7.8	4.9	7.9	4.9	240	787
31	Ben Hope	10.2	6.3	10.5	6.5	945	3100
32	Sandwood Bay	15.0	9.3	15.1	9.4	351	1150

Appendix 3: Additional Information

The Country Code

Enjoy the countryside and respect its life and work.
Guard against all risk of fire.
Fasten all gates.
Keep your dogs under close control.
Keep to public paths across farm land.
Use gates and stiles to cross fences, hedges and walls.
Leave livestock, crops and machinery alone.
Take your litter home.
Help to keep all water clean.
Protect wildlife, plants and trees.
Take special care on country roads.
Make no unnecessary noise.

Mountain distress signals

The mountain distress signals are six long whistle blasts or torch flashes, repeated at one-minute intervals. If you do not have a torch or a whistle, you should signal in the same way with repeated shouts. Continue to repeat the distress signals until your rescuers are with you. The recognized answer is three return signals.

Camasunary Bothy Code (see Route 22)

1. Never allow vandalism, including graffiti to be caused to the building or any of its contents.
2. Human waste must be buried carefully out of sight. Please use the spade provided. For health reasons, never use the vicinity of the bothy as a toilet and keep well away from the water supply.
3. Please leave no rubbish. There is no bin man that calls here so take out everything that will not burn. Never bury rubbish, this pollutes the environment.
4. Keep dogs under control, especially in the lambing season (Feb– April).
5. Fishing is strictly prohibited by the estate without permission.
6. If you do have a bonfire outside, please do it on the beach to avoid damaging the grass.
7. Finally, ensure that the fire is out and the door closed when you leave.

Bothies are used at your own risk.

INDEX

Page numbers in *italic* refer to the illustrations